D0855435

MORE PRAISE FOR DENNIS C. JETT'S
AMERICAN AMBASSADORS

"Dennis Jett, who knows whereof he speaks, has written a book that sparkles in its candid explanations of how US ambassadors are chosen, perform, and should be chosen and perform. He also provides lucid and amusing commentary on current US foreign policy and practice, citing our tendency to manifest both a desire to wage ideological jihad and a blind insistence on American exceptionalism."

—Dan Simpson, associate editor of the *Pittsburgh Post-Gazette* and former ambassador to the Central African Republic, Somalia, and the Democratic Republic of the Congo

"Ambassador Jett provides a thought-provoking, important contribution to the study of diplomacy in general, and to the role of the American ambassador specifically. He deftly weaves his own experiences into the larger narrative and addresses head-on the unique American ambassadorial system of employing both career diplomats, typically seen as competent, and political appointees, who many see as little more than hacks. Jett looks into the truth or falsity of these beliefs, demonstrating through that process why, in the age of modern communications and social media, the right ambassador in the right place can still make all the difference for the United States."

—Peter Van Buren, US Department of State, Foreign Service Officer (ret.), author of *We Meant Well: How I Helped Lose the Battle for the Hearts and Minds of the Iraqi People* and *Ghosts of Tom Joad: A Story of the #99Percent*

"*American Ambassadors* is a thorough study of the process by which we select those who would serve as the president's personal representative to foreign leaders. Ambassador Jett takes the reader step by step through the arcane labyrinth that both political appointees and career Foreign Service officers must successfully navigate to secure an appointment. Students of American diplomacy and aspirants to Ambassadorships will find it a must-read."

—Ambassador Joseph Wilson (ret. USFS), author of *The Politics of Truth*

"Dennis Jett is that rare author who knows his subject—the importance of skilled diplomatic representation—equally well in theory and practice. His book makes a compelling case that ambassadors who know little about the countries to which they are accredited, or the conduct of diplomacy, cannot represent the United States nearly as effectively as can the career professionals of the US Foreign Service."

—Steven Alan Honley, editor, *Foreign Service Journal* (2001–2014)

"If you worry that the US risks losing its footing in the world, it is due in no small part to money corrupting the ambassadorial appointment process and political gridlock in Washington. Dennis Jett tells us what ambassadors do and why sound diplomacy is key to America's leadership. This book should be a must-read for every member of Congress."

—James Bruno, author and journalist

"Known for his insightful critique and analysis of American diplomacy, Dennis Jett draws on his extensive experience as professional diplomat and scholar to explain in this volume how ambassadors are chosen, why that matters, and how the process can be improved. His book will interest anyone who cares about America's future in world affairs and enjoys an informative and provocative read."

—Kenneth L. Brown, former US ambassador to Republic of Congo, Cote d'Ivoire, and Ghana, and president of the Association for Diplomatic Studies and Training.

"A lively and informative read for anyone wondering why the United States, of all the countries that count in the world, is the only one that has a large number of ambassadors whose only job qualification is to have given money to winning presidential candidates and have little or no experience relevant to the position itself. But don't expect to be reassured. As Jett explains, it actually does matter that we have capable ambassadors abroad. At least, we don't select any of our military commanders the same way."

—Ambassador Stephen Bosworth, former ambassador to South Korea, the Philippines and Tunisia, and former dean of the Fletcher School of Law and Diplomacy, USA.

ADST-DACOR DIPLOMATS AND DIPLOMACY SERIES

Series Editor: Margery Boichel Thompson

Since 1776, extraordinary men and women have represented the United States abroad under widely varying circumstances. What they did and how and why they did it remain little known to their compatriots. In 1995, the Association for Diplomatic Studies and Training (ADST) and DACOR, an organization of foreign affairs professionals, created the Diplomats and Diplomacy book series to increase public knowledge and appreciation of the professionalism of American diplomats and their involvement in world history. Dennis Jett's study of the selection, deployment, and value of U.S. ambassadors is the 56th volume in the series.

Related Titles in the Series

For a complete list of series titles, visit <adst.org/publications>

American Ambassadors
The Past, Present, and Future of America's Diplomats

Dennis C. Jett

AMERICAN AMBASSADORS
Copyright © Dennis C. Jett, 2014.

First published in 2014 by
PALGRAVE MACMILLAN®
in the United States—a division of St. Martin's Press LLC,
175 Fifth Avenue, New York, NY 10010.

Where this book is distributed in the UK, Europe and the rest of the world,
this is by Palgrave Macmillan, a division of Macmillan Publishers Limited,
registered in England, company number 785998, of Houndmills,
Basingstoke, Hampshire RG21 6XS.

Palgrave Macmillan is the global academic imprint of the above companies
and has companies and representatives throughout the world.

Palgrave® and Macmillan® are registered trademarks in the United States,
the United Kingdom, Europe and other countries.

ISBN: 978–1–137–39566–5

Library of Congress Cataloging-in-Publication Data

Jett, Dennis C., 1945–
    American ambassadors : the past, present, and future of America's
diplomats / Dennis C. Jett.
       pages cm
    Includes bibliographical references and index.
    ISBN 978–1–137–39566–5 (hardback)
      1. Ambassadors—United States. 2. United States—Foreign
relations—2001– I. Title.

E840.J48 2014
327.2092′2—dc23
[B]   2014026294

A catalogue record of the book is available from the British Library.

Design by Newgen Knowledge Works (P) Ltd., Chennai, India.

First edition: December 2014

10 9 8 7 6 5 4 3 2 1

For Emma, Eleanor, and Sophia, who deserve better diplomatic representation and a better world than the one we are leaving them.

Contents

Figures and Tables

Figures

Tables

Acknowledgments

A great many people contributed to making this book possible. I would like to thank them and offer my apologies to any that I may have inadvertently omitted. At the School of International Affairs at Penn State, they include an extraordinary economist, Dr. Johannes Fedderke, the director of SIA, Dr. Tiya Maluwa, and the interim dean of SIA and the Law School, Admiral James Houck.

No animals were abused in the writing of this book, but over the years a number of able research assistants were. In alphabetical order, they are Jan Burnett, Matthew Ceccato, Shriya, Chadha, Ryan Crotty, Ashley Francis, Casey Hilland, Greg Kruczek, Garrett Redfield, Aridaman Shah Singh, Daniel Smith, Christine Sylvester, and Yuqi Zhao.

My former colleagues from the State Department who helped with this project are too numerous to name, but they include Adrian Basora, Eileen Malloy, Sharon Hardy, Sharon Bisdee, Harry Thomas, Robert Pearson, Skip Gnehm, Tony Motley, Genta Holmes, George Staples, and Anthony Quainton.

At the Association for Diplomatic Studies and Training, Ambassador Kenneth Brown has been very supportive and helpful. And the man who has recorded and preserved the oral histories of thousands of diplomats, Charles Stuart Kennedy, deserves special recognition. His efforts have resulted in a legacy that will be mined by scholars for many years to come. Thanks also to Chris Sibilla at ADST and to Dan Caldwell at Pepperdine University.

My thanks to Dr. Russell Riley at the Miller Center at the University of Virginia. The oral histories collected there are another tremendous resource for scholars. Another great resource is the data put together by the American Foreign Service Association. Many thanks to Kristen Fernekes and Shawn Dorman for allowing me to use that material. Another AFSA person who deserves recognition is Tex Harris, who never stops trying to make both AFSA and the State Department better organizations. Thanks also to Mike Yared for his useful suggestions for resource material.

At Palgrave Macmillan, I would like to thank Brian O'Connor, who made this book possible, as well as Nicole Hitner, and Scarlet Neath before her, whose assistance made the process much easier.

Special thanks should also go to Tim Haggerty at Carnegie Mellon University, who edited the manuscript. And also to Daniel Smith, who also read through the entire manuscript and caught many errors. Any that remain are of course my fault and not Tim's or Daniel's.

Finally, my children, Brian, Allison, and Noa, and grandchildren, Emma, Eleanor, and Sophia, provided inspiration and the incentive to try to make the world a better place. Last but certainly not least is my spouse, Lynda Schuster, my best friend and toughest editor.

Introduction

On the face of it, the first ambassador for whom I worked seemed perfect for the job. If the director of a movie called up central casting and told them to send over actors to audition for a role as an ambassador, he would have been a shoo-in for the part. He had, in fact, been an actor, costarring in movies with Marlene Dietrich and Shirley Temple. He had also been a successful politician, elected to Congress twice and as governor of Connecticut. The Connecticut Turnpike is named after him.

He came from a wealthy and illustrious lineage—his family included a senator, an admiral, and another ambassador. They could trace their roots back to the pilgrims. Tall, handsome, and silver-haired, he was fluent in several languages. According to one expert on style, he was "one of the most polished gentlemen in America" for more than half a century.[1] He was also named ambassador three times by three different presidents. In referring to him, a journalist once wrote: "If the United States could be represented around the world the way it is represented in Argentina, it would be loved by the peoples of all nations."[2]

In reality, the ambassador was a disaster—and a dangerous one at that. Although he seemed to some to be the perfect diplomat, those who knew him better considered him, in effect, a threat to national security. The reason for such a divergence of opinion is that there is more to being an ambassador than simply glitz and glamour. And when it came to John Davis Lodge, there was little else.

I did not know all of that when I was assigned to Buenos Aires as my first diplomatic posting. In early 1973, I had only been in the Foreign Service for a few weeks. All newly minted Foreign Service Officers (FSOs) are introduced to the State Department through a six-week course, a kind of boot camp for bureaucrats. There the raw recruits get basic training about the government they are to represent. Toward the end of the course, the fledgling FSOs are given a list of all the postings in the world that are available for their first tour of duty. They have to decide on their preferences and then hope that the personnel system answers their prayers.

Having grown up and been educated mainly in New Mexico, where the Hispanic and Native American cultures had an influence on even a transplanted Northeasterner like me, I decided Latin America would be my first choice. Because Argentina seemed the most exotic of the possibilities in the southern hemisphere, that country was at the top of my list. As luck would have it, none of my peers ranked it as high, so the job was mine. But first I had to take additional training, including learning Spanish.

It was then that I came across an article in the *Washington Post* about Lodge written by Lewis Diuguid, the paper's Latin American correspondent. In essence, the article said that Lodge was all style and no substance; dinners at the elegant ambassadorial residence inevitably dissolved into songfests, with Lodge belting out his favorite tunes from Broadway shows.[3] He was described as mainly being interested in getting his picture in the local newspapers. The article claimed that Lodge kept four staff members in the embassy's information section engaged full time in trying to get the local press to run photos and articles about his latest social activities.

Diuguid implied that Lodge's desire to appear in the newspapers did not extend beyond photographs and the society pages. It was an era when far more newspapers believed in having foreign bureaus, but Lodge's contacts among the dozen American correspondents based in Buenos Aires were virtually nonexistent. Diuguid wrote that he tried without success for a month to get an appointment for an interview. The article went on to quote anonymous sources, who said a serious conversation with Lodge was impossible and that if anyone had any real business to conduct with the embassy, they went to see the deputy chief of mission, the number two person in any embassy and one who is always a career diplomat.

As I read the article, I found it hard to believe it was not grossly exaggerated. I wondered how someone in such an exalted position could be such an apparent lightweight. The story was also disconcerting because it mentioned that "the ambassador's reactions to frequently perceived failings of embassy personnel have alienated him from most of his staff." I reasoned that even if this were true, I would have little contact with him. As a junior officer, there would be several layers of bureaucracy in the embassy between us. So I completed my training and departed for my first overseas tour of duty with enthusiasm.[4]

Although the job had been advertised as one where I would rotate through various sections of the embassy, when I got to post, I was informed I would be assigned to the political section just down the hall from the ambassador's office for my entire tour. That sounded great to me. Rather than spend the majority of my two years dealing with visa applicants or the embassy's maintenance problems, my time would be spent reporting on the politics of a volatile nation. Among my responsibilities was covering the rapidly expanding terrorism that was beginning to engulf Argentina.

A military junta had just allowed elections, but it had also prevented the former president, Juan Peron, from running. The Peronist candidate was nonetheless victorious and promptly resigned, paving the way for new elections, which Peron won by a comfortable margin. Peron had been a populist during his previous time in office in the early 1950s and had never hesitated to encourage and capitalize on anti-American sentiment. After 18 years in exile, however, he was an enigma. Although no one was quite sure where he stood politically, he initially had enthusiastic support across Argentina's political spectrum.

Communists on the Left, fascists on the Right, and those in between saw Peron as a potential political savior. When he first returned to Argentina from being abroad for so long, a million people went to the airport to welcome him home. As they awaited his arrival, Right-wing Peronists attacked Left-wing Peronists and scores were killed or injured.

As the internecine fighting within Peronist ranks continued, two leftist terrorist groups, the Montoneros and the People's Revolutionary Army, began attacking military bases and assassinating policemen and army officers. Right-wing death squads started to retaliate, and dead bodies in burned-out cars became an increasingly common news item. As the country seemed to be slipping into chaos, one of my chores was updating Washington on the mayhem. After a couple of attacks on embassy personnel, the official American community was cut in half to reduce the number at risk.

A few weeks after arriving in Buenos Aires, I had the opportunity to witness Lodge in action. He gave a large formal dinner at the residence for a visiting official from Washington. It was not a social occasion but rather an important opportunity to gather impressions on how the new government would conduct itself. One big question was whether Peronist officials would even come to the dinner. It was feared they might not if hostility toward the United States was going to again be one of Peron's policies. They not only came, but they also were eager to talk.

The evening unfolded, however, as if the Diuguid article had scripted the event. At the end of the sumptuous meal, as coffee and dessert were being served, Lodge called over an accordionist who had been providing soft background music. With this accompaniment, Lodge burst into song while still seated at the table and rolled off a number of tunes. We all then adjourned to the ballroom, where he continued the entertainment. Among his favorite Argentine guests was a couple whom he summoned to join him at the grand piano. While the husband played, the wife and Lodge sang duets from *Porgy and Bess* and other Broadway hits.

As the show dragged on, the Peronist officials signaled they wanted to talk to the visiting official and the deputy chief of mission privately, so they all slipped off to the library. The Peronists made it clear that the new government would be open to a constructive and productive relationship with the United States, unlike in the past. This was a significant shift in policy that would be welcomed in Washington.

Finally, after the songfest, the guests began bidding the Lodges good night and thanking them profusely for the evening. The embassy staff members were always the last to leave; it was customary to stay until dismissed by the ambassador. As we waited for this to happen, Lodge learned of the discussion that had taken place in the library while he was singing in the ballroom. He became furious at his deputy, ranting that he had been stabbed in the back before but never in his own home. Unmoved by the success of the discussions, Lodge continued to berate the poor man in front of all of us. That evening I learned an important lesson: a country is not well served by an ambassador who thinks entertaining is the most important of his duties.

Although those who inhabited the society pages with Lodge saw no faults, Washington was well aware of his shortcomings. When he had his confirmation hearing in front of the Senate Foreign Relations Committee before going to Argentina, Senator J. William Fulbright asked him what kind of government the country had. Lodge said it was democratic, even though it had been a military dictatorship for years by then.[5]

Perhaps he thought any dictator who was an anti-communist had to be embraced by the United States. He had been an unabashed supporter of Franco when he was ambassador to Spain; after leaving Argentina, one of his pastimes was mustering support for the Pinochet regime in Chile.[6] And in 1970, he wrote to President Nixon questioning whether a return to representative democracy in Argentina was in the best interest of the United States.[7]

Some in Washington thought keeping Lodge in Buenos Aires was damaging American interests even before Argentina started heading toward chaos. In November 1971, a National Security Council staff member wrote a memo to the National Security Advisor, Henry Kissinger, saying:

> We are all acquainted with Ambassador Lodge's peculiarities and accustomed to a system which requires us to make do with ambassadors (both political and career) who are sometimes less than qualified for their positions. However, the situation in Argentina has gone beyond all bounds. Ambassador Lodge and his Embassy not only fail to have any contact worthy of the name with the Argentine Government, but the Ambassador has become an object of contempt with that Government. The country is paying a very heavy foreign affairs cost by retaining Ambassador Lodge in his present position.[8]

The memo had little effect. Some months later, Peter Flanigan, an assistant to President Nixon, told Kissinger the president felt Lodge could be left in Argentina because he "was surrounded by competent people."[9] Lodge did not leave for another two years, and at that point he was already 70 years old. Ten years later, President Reagan, a friend and fellow former actor, appointed him ambassador to Switzerland.

The memo to Kissinger was marked "Secret," "Sensitive," "Eyes Only," and "Outside the System" by its author. Classified government documents, even ones marked "Secret," can be given a very wide distribution, with copies going to thousands of officials around the government. The other three captions on this particular document, however, were all designed to make sure that as few people saw it as possible. Before it was declassified, it is unlikely that more than half a dozen people had read it.

Restricting the number of people who read the memo on Lodge was essential, but not because it could damage national security, the usual justification for the government keeping something secret. It was important because personnel issues are always extremely sensitive and can have a tremendous impact on professional reputations. A memo as frank and critical as the one on Lodge would have devastated the career of a less well-connected official.

Because people's careers are at stake, personnel decisions are always tightly restricted to a small group of officials and advisors. They are therefore among the most difficult to understand. Although they are never transparent, they are always important and can determine whether an embassy functions efficiently or not.

I went on to work for and with scores of other ambassadors, both political appointees and career officers. Perhaps because Lodge was the first and the worst, his impression lasted. Twenty years later I became an ambassador, first in Mozambique and then Peru, where I had my own firsthand opportunity to experience and understand the challenges that come with the job.

Everyone is familiar with the title "ambassador," and many people think they know what the job entails. Those who had nothing but praise for Lodge certainly thought they did. Most of those impressions are wrong, however, because they do not go beyond an image of attending cocktail parties and avoiding the payment of parking tickets. Few people have any idea who gets the title or what that person really does. And in today's world of instant communication, the question is often raised as to whether ambassadors are necessary at all.

For those reasons, it seemed to me that a book that explains where ambassadors come from, where they go, what their work entails, and why they still matter would be worthwhile. There are a number of books about the Foreign Service, but they tend to be both general and generic. The treatment of this topic might be left to academics, but that would not provide much insight. Although the pursuit of grand theories to explain human interactions is a standard part of social science, they cannot explain everything. In fact, I doubt they serve to explain much at all except for the way academics talk to one another. Because success in academia is driven by the opinion of one's peers, much of what is written by academics is not intended to inform a wide audience but rather to impress a very narrow one consisting of other academics interested in the same issues.

This book therefore will not propose any single theory to predict who becomes an ambassador and why some succeed at the job and others do not. There are too many exceptions to say that there is a rule. There are certain similarities and patterns that can be described, however, even if they do not fit neatly into a theory that explains the past and predicts the future. For instance, regardless of whether a political appointee or a career officer is chosen, the process for making that decision has several common characteristics. It is always a decision by a committee where different interests are balanced and tradeoffs are required. It is also dependent on the personalities and the degree of interest, involvement, and influence of the committee members and others who are not on the committee but can influence it. Individual decisions, when viewed by someone outside of the process, may therefore make little sense because these factors come into play in ever-changing ways that often can produce a less-than-optimal choice for a specific job.

As a 28-year veteran of the State Department who observed the results of this process throughout his career and experienced it twice, I believe I can provide some insight into its operation. And having been an academic for the past 14 years, I appreciate the value of research and of gathering as many other opinions and as much information as possible.

The remainder of this book will therefore talk about the differences and similarities between career officers and political appointees in becoming ambassadors, why they get the job, and where they are likely to go. It will discuss why ambassadors are as necessary as ever despite technological and social changes. The system for choosing ambassadors is the product of history and tradition and will defy being changed even though the occasional less-than-capable ambassador will pose a threat to the nation's interests. It could be improved nonetheless and steps that would accomplish will be considered.

To do that the book will be laid out as follows: chapter 1—"A Brief History of the Title"—will begin with the founding of the country and describe how in its first century no one held the title of ambassador. That was what the envoys of kings were called, and the political leaders of the young, egalitarian republic did not want to imply that anyone held a higher station because of a government appointment. Toward the end of the nineteenth century, American interests abroad grew, as did the need for those interests to be more capably protected. There then followed 60 years of gradual professionalization of the diplomatic service until the middle of the twentieth century.

As the United States emerged from World War II as the most powerful nation on earth and began to engage in the Cold War, it realized it had worldwide interests to protect. And it had to confront communism in even the most far-flung corners of the globe. So American embassies, and ambassadors to run them, became the norm in virtually every country. It was at this time, during the Eisenhower administration, that the percentage of ambassadors who were career officers reached its peak. A ratio of roughly 30/70 for political appointees versus career ambassadors has persisted ever since.

Chapters 2–4 describe the two routes to becoming an ambassador and the steps in the clearance and confirmation process. For the career diplomat, it is not just entering the Foreign Service and working one's way to the top. There are five different specializations within the Foreign Service—political, economic, management, consular, and public diplomacy—and which one is chosen will have much to do with whether or not one becomes an ambassador.

The route for political appointees is, of course, very different, and, based on interviews with former noncareer ambassadors, oral histories, and other sources, that process will be described as well. A person taking that route has to enhance the president's political prospects in some way. That can be through making personal campaign contributions or bundling those of others, adding gender and/or ethnic diversity to the ambassadorial ranks, providing a political payoff, or simply by being a loyal staff aide or close friend. Those different types of linkages to the president are not mutually exclusive, but one is usually more predominant and more important when it comes to securing the appointment.

The two routes converge when the president makes a decision on the person to be appointed, whether it is a career officer of political appointee. At that point, the paperwork goes back to the State Department and the last steps in the process begin. The final hurdles to be cleared—obtaining a security clearance and Senate confirmation—can trip up the nominee, sometimes for reasons that have nothing to do with that person.

After this consideration of who becomes an ambassador and how that happens, chapter 5 then looks at what that person does once on the job. It also describes why the performance of ambassadors is difficult to measure. The best measure of how well an embassy is run comes from the State Department's internal auditor, the Office of the Inspector General (OIG), which is supposed to inspect each embassy once every five years. After extensive preparation in Washington, the OIG dispatches a team of about a dozen inspectors to the country in question. They talk to virtually everyone who works in the embassy during the course of their visit, which lasts several weeks. They then write up a comprehensive report that covers everything, including the performance of the ambassador. Although they were withheld from the public in the past, these reports are now public and can be found on the OIG website with only minor redactions.

These inspection reports are negotiated documents, because the inspectors discuss them extensively with those being inspected before they are put into final form. They can still be brutally candid and critical, however. The ambassadors to Malta, the Bahamas, Luxembourg, and Kenya have all resigned in recent years as a direct result of the reports done on their embassies.

After the chapter on what ambassadors do, the question of where they go will be considered in chapter 6. Different kinds of ambassadors go to different kinds of countries. There is, for instance, a clear divide between where career diplomats go and which posts are reserved for political appointees. The latter are very rarely sent to places that are dangerous or unhealthy. Even within the ranks of the political appointees, depending on the ambassador's relationship to the president, there are differences in where that person is sent. For such reasons, there are a few political appointees in Latin America, very few in the Middle East and South Asia, and there have never been any in Central Asia.

The chapter will also discuss how religion, gender, ethnicity, and sexual orientation can all play a role in determining who goes to a particular embassy and how the importance of those factors have changed over time. There is one embassy, for example, where the ambassador must not only be a Catholic but also be opposed to abortion or at least be very quietly pro-choice.

Chapter 7 will consider whether the way ambassadors are selected, what they do, and if they matter is going to change in today's increasingly globalized world. No other major country selects its highest-level diplomatic representation in the way the United States does; because it amounts to little more than selling ambassadorships, it astounds the rest of the world. It is surprising to so many because today's gravest problems can only be addressed through effective diplomatic action and cooperation. No country, not even the world's only superpower, can effectively address those challenges on its own, even though the United States often acts as if it thinks it can.

The growing cost of presidential campaigns has led to a political process driven by money where big donors are essential. To attract those donors, a certain number of them will have to be paid off with ambassadorial appointments. Although an explicit quid pro quo is illegal, this tradition continues and is a form of corruption only slightly less thinly veiled today than it was during the Nixon era when the president's personal lawyer went to jail for selling ambassadorships. The process can be improved, however, and recommendations will be made for ways to make it more transparent and thereby less likely to be abused. In a democracy, for change to occur and the defenders of the status quo to be overcome, citizens have to take the time and make the effort to understand what their government is doing and why. I hope this book makes a contribution to that process.

CHAPTER 1

A Brief History of the Title

If it were not for the charm and skill of some of the earliest American diplomats, the United States might still be a British colony. Benjamin Franklin was one of the first official envoys sent abroad as the struggle for independence got under way. His diplomatic efforts were so successful at eliciting the support of Louis XVI for the revolution that France played a vital role in determining its outcome.

Although the purpose of America's diplomats has remained essentially the same over the years—to protect and promote the interests of their country—the background, preparation, and professionalism of today's diplomats have changed significantly since the time of Franklin. In order to appreciate the importance of diplomats, and in particular ambassadors, to the country's security today, it helps to understand how their role has evolved as the United States has grown from a colony to the world's only superpower.

There were three stages in this evolution. The first period lasted a century and was characterized by the fact that virtually all American diplomats were political appointees and none bore the title "ambassador." They had varying degrees of ability, and their tenures in their positions were likely to end with the inauguration of the next president. There was no thought given to creating a cadre of career diplomats, as it was believed anyone could carry out the business of government. That belief, coupled with a degree of distrust of those exposed to foreign influences, led to the frequent replacement of the men who were appointed to diplomatic positions. The only thing they could depend on was that they had little prospect for staying in the job for long.

The second period, which lasted the next 60 years from the end of the nineteenth century until the middle of the twentieth, saw the gradual professionalization of the civil service and the creation of a corps of career diplomats who had a degree of job security. Entrance and promotion based on merit became the norm, and most diplomats could expect that their jobs would not come to an end the next time there was a new occupant of the White House. During this period, the title of ambassador began to be used and the percentage of career ambassadors gradually rose from next to nothing to about 70 percent of the total.

During the third stage, occurring over the past 60 years, the 30/70 ratio between political appointees and career officers as ambassadors has remained remarkably constant. This consistency persisted despite the fact that during this period the number of ambassadors expanded greatly, as did the number of interests they were supposed to protect. Because the Cold War was a worldwide struggle, and given the new nations that came into being as a result of decolonization, more ambassadors were needed to be dispatched to even the farthest-flung corners of the globe.

The Early Years—The Sometimes-Able Amateurs of a Third-Rate Power

In the earliest days of the republic, the focus of the founding fathers was on setting up a government and ensuring its survival. Benjamin Franklin played a key role in that effort in many ways, including by being considered America's first ambassador even though he was never given the title. He was sent to Paris in 1776 with the critically important task of ensuring French support for America's struggle for independence from Britain. Despite the fact that he did not conform to diplomatic conventions in dress or other formalities, he performed brilliantly because of his charm and intellect. Had he not been such a success, the American Revolution might well have had a different outcome.

In 1781, when American legislators created a new government under the Articles of Confederation, that new government included a Department of Foreign Affairs. A few "ministers" were dispatched to key European countries to handle the new country's official business, and a handful of "consuls" were named to help Americans do business overseas.

In the country's early years, anything that hinted at special status for a government official was considered to be against republican principles. Even though Article 2, Section 2 of the Constitution gave the president the power to appoint "ambassadors, other public ministers and consuls," for the country's first 115 years, it was represented abroad only by men with the title of minister or consul. An ambassador was considered to be the emissary of a king, and the title was believed to be inconsistent with the values of an egalitarian society.

Having fought for independence from a British king, Americans were presumably uncomfortable with lofty titles or anything that hinted at special status. This distaste for giving, or even receiving, such honors is also reflected in the Constitution. Article 1, Section 9, which mainly describes things the Congress may not do, states: "No title of nobility shall be granted by the United States. And no person holding any office of profit or trust under them, shall, without the consent of the Congress, accept of any present, emolument, office or title, of any kind whatever, from any king, prince, or foreign state."

Nonetheless, diplomatic titles mattered even to the founding fathers who were sent on the earliest diplomatic missions. John Adams, who was to become the second president, was one of those who cared about such things. As Jack Rakove notes in his book on the invention of America:

> Adams had been sorely miffed when he mistakenly thought that Congress had made him a mere commissioner while giving John Jay the higher rank of minister plenipotentiary. A similar slight had marred his previous trip, when his name appeared below that of Arthur Lee in the commission for France even though Adams held weightier credentials as lawyer and public servant.[1]

Despite the sensitivity to titles that Adams displayed, those that were given to the earliest American diplomats were modest, but so was the entire foreign policy establishment of the time. In 1789, Congress passed an act that changed the name of the Department of Foreign Affairs to the Department of State, because that department was given responsibility for maintaining certain domestic records as well as handling international relations. That same year, President Washington appointed fellow Virginian Thomas Jefferson to be the first secretary of state.

When Jefferson assumed the position in March 1790, his bureaucratic empire consisted of four clerks, a translator, a messenger, and an annual budget for domestic operations of a bit less than $8,000, including his salary. The total expenditures for the department, both in Washington and abroad, the next year totaled $56,600.[2]

Reflecting the egalitarian sentiment of the time, Jefferson made clear he had no use for the formality and intrigue that was characteristic of European diplomacy. He had enough experience as a diplomat, however, to realize that the United States had to be well represented overseas if the country was to be taken seriously. He and Washington lobbied Congress for the funds to support a small number of missions abroad headed by men with the title of minister. Each man was charged with reporting on political events in the country to which he was assigned and for handling relations with that government.

This small but growing number of American envoys brought with them a new style of diplomacy consistent with the values of their newly independent nation. This style was reflected in their dress as well as their behavior. Beginning with Franklin, American representatives abroad wore unpretentious clothing and adopted simple manners, which contrasted sharply with the formality and ostentation of European courts.[3]

The spirit of the era and the limitations of the new nation are aptly described by George Herring in *From Colony to Superpower*:

> In keeping with ideals of republican simplicity—and to save money—the administration did not appoint anyone to the rank of ambassador. That "may be the custom of the old world," Jefferson informed the emperor of Morocco, "but it is not ours." The "foreign service" consisted of a minister to France, *chargés d'affaires* in England, Spain, and Portugal, and an agent at Amsterdam. In 1790, the United States opened its first consulate in Bordeaux, a major source of arms, ammunition, and wine during the Revolution. That same year, it appointed twelve consuls and also named six foreigners as vice-consuls since there were not enough qualified Americans to fill the posts.[4]

When Jefferson became president, he continued and even extended the official disdain for the traditional trappings of diplomacy. He regarded professional diplomats as the "pest[s] of the peace of the world" and, as a result, cut back the country's extremely small representation abroad to what he considered the essential minimum.[5] He also put his personal beliefs into practice in his own office by avoiding the pomp and circumstance of his predecessors. In contrast to Washington and Adams, Jefferson made a point of dressing plainly, and he opened the presidential mansion to visitors from all level of society.

Jefferson's disdain for formality may have been motivated by his personal feelings or by an image he wished to project as president. Some presidents even today seek to deliberately downplay the aura of the office as a way to show they can connect with common people: Jimmy Carter, for instance, insisted on carrying his own bags on trips. When Bill Clinton first took office, it was decided that one way to distinguish him from his Republican predecessor was to have very few formal state dinners for visiting dignitaries.[6]

Whether Jefferson's motivation was personal or political, his approach did not sit well with some of the more traditionally minded foreign diplomats in Washington at the time. Herring notes:

> His disdain for protocol scandalized other members of the small and generally unhappy diplomatic community in Washington. Outraged when received by the president in a tattered bathrobe and slippers and forced at a presidential dinner to conform to the "pell-mell" seating arrangements respecting no rank, the British minister to Washington, Anthony Merry, bitterly protested the affront suffered at the president's table. Jefferson no doubt privately chuckled at the arrogant Englishman's discomfiture, but his subsequent codification of republican practices into established procedures betrayed a larger purpose. By adapting the new nation's forms to its principles, he hoped to establish a uniquely American style of diplomacy.[7]

Although Jefferson apparently enjoyed Merry's pique, an argument can be made for observing the strictures of diplomatic protocol. It provides a structure in which people from different countries and cultures can relate to one another with little chance of unintentional insults. For instance, if a diplomat's place at a dinner table is determined by the pecking order of protocol, then both he and his host will know where that is, and a potential insult will be avoided. In this case, Jefferson considered the insult to the British diplomat less important than the image he wanted to project.

Because of Jefferson's desire to promote that uniquely American image of simplicity, during his term of office, American envoys, even those to the most important countries, only carried the rank of minister plenipotentiary. After the War of 1812 ended, it appeared that America's survival as an independent nation was no longer in doubt, and it had, according to Herring, "surged to the level of a second-rank power."[8] That growing strength and status of the country prompted a bit of title inflation under Jefferson's successor, James Madison. The official designation for the chiefs of the most important diplomatic missions was elevated to envoy extraordinary and minister plenipotentiary.

Diplomatic titles were expanding to keep pace with the overseas influence and interests of a country that was becoming a more important player on the world stage. With its survival assured, the emphasis of American diplomacy shifted to expanding the country's commerce and avoiding entangling political alliances. To do that effectively required moving beyond Jefferson's republican principles, his disdain for diplomats, and his desire to keep their numbers to a minimum. In the decade between 1820 and 1830, the number of consuls almost doubled. They were needed to help American businessmen take advantage of commercial opportunities abroad, especially in the newly independent nations in Latin America.

The chief functions of diplomatic posts, which were embassies or legations, were the conducting of traditional diplomacy and the political work involved in the relationship between the United States and the other country. Consular posts, on the other hand, were headed by a consul or consul general and had different tasks. They dealt with commercial and consular matters, such as trade issues and the protection of American businessmen, sailors, and other citizens. Consuls were expected to be largely self-supporting and sustained themselves by the fees they charged for their services.

In contrast, the diplomats made a very meager salary and could not supplement it by selling their services. To make ends meet they were expected to draw on their personal funds, which meant in effect that such jobs were reserved for men from wealthy families. Because of the differences in functions and financial circumstances, the diplomats felt themselves superior to their consular colleagues. This feeling is not entirely absent from today's corps of diplomats.

Not only were diplomats of this era underpaid, they were also on fixed-term appointments that were often not renewed. For that reason, there may have been concern about their loyalty as well as their professionalism. President James Monroe issued an instruction that they were to respectfully but decisively decline gifts, which were "the lubricant of European diplomacy." His secretary of state, John Quincy Adams, also recommended that they return home once they had served more than six years abroad so that they might be "new tempered."[9]

This suggestion no doubt stemmed from a fear that they might develop "clientitis" or "localitis." Those are the names given when a diplomat is perceived to be arguing the position of the country to which he or she is accredited with more fervor than the country he or she represents. It is a concern that has existed as long as envoys have been sent abroad, and it is a reoccurring criticism of American diplomats that is still heard to this day.

The fear that diplomats might spend too long in another country has deep historical roots, as Warren Ilchman notes: "The members of the Continental Congress were so concerned about the possibility of

Europe corrupting the republican simplicity of its members that a resolution was passed permitting diplomats to remain abroad on their commissions for a period of only three years."[10] Clientitis is a perennial
problem because it often has some justification. Living abroad for a
few years changes the perspective of almost anyone, even those who
are representatives of their government. To press that perspective on
Washington can easily be interpreted at home as being too sympathetic
to the other side.

Although that is sometimes true, the charge often reflects the fact
that it is always easy to blame the messenger. Washington never likes to
be informed that a foreign audience has failed to embrace its latest pro-
nouncement with enthusiasm. Those in Washington who came up with
the policy are more likely to assert that the diplomats abroad did not
present it effectively rather than admit the policy might not have been
the best idea in the first place.

Even when the State Department and the White House are satis-
fied with the policy and the reaction to it, there are often others in
Washington who are not. Opponents of the president, or the president's
policies, will often blame the diplomats charged with implementing it
for the shortcomings they perceive. Critics in Congress, the media, and
think tanks find it easier to attack the bureaucrats involved, especially
when they do not want to directly criticize the president, because the
bureaucrats are rarely in a position to retaliate.

One rare occasion when a diplomat responded publicly to criticism
and did retaliate was in 2003 when former Speaker of the House Newt
Gingrich gave a speech in which he blamed the State Department for the
unpopularity around the world of the American invasion of Iraq. The
absurdity of that charge prompted Deputy Secretary of State Richard
Armitage to say: "It's clear that Mr. Gingrich is off his meds and out
of therapy."[11] Armitage was not a career diplomat, however, so he had
the luxury of being able to speak his mind without worrying about his
future employment.

In addition to cheap shots from politicians, another perennial problem, which often comes up in various forms in political debate today,
has to do with funding. Not only were American diplomats in the early
days expected to dress plainly, but they were also apparently expected to
live that way. The State Department historian describes this attitude:

> Even if the new nation's democratic ideology had not mandated repub-
> lican simplicity, the meager salaries paid to American ministers would
> have produced the same effect. In 1817, President Monroe complained

to a congressional committee about the nation's failure to provide sufficient salaries and allowances for members of the Diplomatic Service. Monroe insisted that American diplomats had to gain access to the most important circles before they could do their jobs. Congress turned a deaf ear to these arguments, and ministers at important posts such as London or Paris were forced to spend from their own private fortunes. As a result, only those with wealth could aspire to a diplomatic career. Lack of adequate funding also meant that little or no interchange took place between those serving in Washington and those overseas.[12]

Adding to the problem of meager salaries was the scarcity of representation funds, that is, the money Congress allocates to diplomats for official social functions. That is another perennial problem because Congress only hands over money for this purpose grudgingly. This reflects the reluctance of politicians to spend tax dollars for the purpose of entertaining foreigners. As a result, these funds are typically inadequate to do the job, especially in expensive capitals like London and Paris. This issue is often a part of the debate about who should go to those countries as ambassadors. One of the justifications for sending wealthy political appointees to countries where entertaining is expensive is that they can afford to pay for it out of their own pockets.

In addition to money problems, early American diplomacy often suffered from the way each president left his mark on foreign affairs in both style and substance. Some lacked interest in international affairs. With others, such as Presidents Andrew Jackson and James K. Polk, the problem was not a lack of attention, but too much of it. They dominated what little foreign policy there was during their time in office. They preferred to make decisions with a few close advisors rather than through discussions with the cabinet like those that Washington, Jefferson, and other early presidents had conducted. And they saw little need for outside advice from within Washington or beyond it.

Such factors as the president's decision-making style and the national priorities of the era have always affected the selection of who was chosen to represent the country abroad. From roughly 1815 to 1885, the country was more concerned with internal affairs than international ones. The nation's energy was largely directed at expanding its territory westward and avoiding political involvement in other countries or interference from them. These goals were greatly aided by the fact that there was a balance of power in Europe, and none of those nations wanted to upset that balance by challenging the territorial ambitions of the United States.

Besides a diminished importance being placed on foreign affairs, the American diplomatic corps also suffered from the fact that a "spoils system" was the prevailing method for filling government jobs as a reward for political supporters. This applied to diplomatic and consular positions, and both the quality of American diplomats and their image suffered as a result. Jackson's attitude was that "the duties of public officers are so plain and simple that men of intelligence may readily qualify themselves for their performance." When Polk took office, he followed suit, and as a result "U.S. policymakers and diplomats, once an experienced and cosmopolitan lot, were increasingly parochial, sometimes amateurish—and often proud of it."[13]

The State Department historian describes how the system worked and its effect on the quality of those chosen as chiefs of diplomatic missions:

> Attitudes like those of Jackson perpetuated both amateurism in government and a disdain for public service. The egalitarian celebration of the common man worked against efforts to improve the quality and status of those who conducted foreign relations. Some ministers still gained appointment because of their experience and talent. More often than not, however, personal wealth, political services, or social position, were the only requirements. Many lacked qualifications—even the most elementary knowledge of diplomatic etiquette.[14]

Some of the diplomats of this period had problems other than a lack of etiquette. The youngest person ever to be chief of a US diplomatic mission was Edward Rumsey Wing, who was appointed minister to Ecuador in 1869 at the age of 24. He drank himself to death at his post five years later.[15]

Although the ability of American diplomats may have been low in the middle of the nineteenth century, the importance of international trade to the American economy continued to grow and that required the size of the foreign affairs bureaucracy to expand as well. The staff of the Department of State increased to 43 in Washington and to 27 diplomats and 88 consuls abroad. By 1860, 45 people held appointments in the diplomatic service, and they were responsible for 33 different embassies and legations. The budget to support these missions rose to $1.1 million. As the State Department and the number of overseas missions grew, modest attempts at reform and reorganization took place in order to improve the way those missions were organized and operated. For the first time, US citizenship was required to receive a consular appointment.

Congress also had a hand in reforming the State Department, like it has from time to time throughout the country's history. In 1856, legislation was passed that, among other things, set the salaries for ministers at $10,000 for most posts and a maximum of $17,500 for the most expensive postings, such as those in London and Paris. This salary cap was not raised for more than a century until after World War II.

Although Congress periodically mandates changes in the foreign affairs bureaucracy, it is easier to legislate reform than to appropriate the resources to pay for it. This reflects the traditional ambivalence toward foreign affairs in general and diplomats in particular, and it is a reoccurring theme among some politicians. When Republicans made large gains in the number of congressional seats they won in the 1994 elections, many of the new representatives came to Washington bragging about the fact that they did not own passports.[16]

The 1856 effort did make modest improvements in the diplomatic and consular corps but did not make appointment to either of them merit based. Those who filled these jobs still largely depended on their political connections rather than their professional qualifications. Although a few positions were given to men of ability and experience, they were the exceptions.

Nonetheless, in the latter part of the nineteenth century, there was a growing tension between the need to have more effective representation abroad and the simultaneous need to limit the level of engagement with the rest of the world. Immigration, urbanization, and industrialization were reshaping the American economy and increasing the importance of foreign trade more than ever before. Although this was an argument for expanding the foreign affairs bureaucracy handling commercial affairs, a desire to avoid political involvement overseas pushed against expanding the number of diplomats, for it was feared they might engage in political intrigue.

In 1877, President Rutherford B. Hayes declared himself firmly in favor of America's "traditional rule on noninterference in the affairs of foreign nations." Some saw this as a good reason to have no diplomatic corps or at least a smaller one. The number of consular and diplomatic posts declined slightly in the 1870s, which was the first time that had happened in the country's history. It was only a brief setback as the number of posts continued to increase in number after 1880. By the 1890s, the State Department staff had grown to more than 80, in part because of the inefficiency of its methods of operation, which had changed little since the days of John Quincy Adams.

As with the charge of "clientitis," there is a tendency among politicians and pundits to blame the failings of diplomats for anything abroad that they fear, dislike, or simply wish to use to their political advantage. Because the public often has little understanding of international issues and what diplomats really do in the service of their country, it is a common tactic that has occurred over and over again throughout American history. The State Department historian describes an extreme example from this era:

> Xenophobic Americans regularly condemned their representatives abroad as subversive, and some cast doubt upon the need for any contact whatsoever with the Old World and its representatives. In 1885, for example, Senator William E. Robinson of New York insisted "... this diplomatic service is working our ruin by creating a desire for foreign customs and foreign follies. The disease is imported by our returning diplomats and by the foreign ambassadors sent here by monarchs and despots to corrupt and destroy our American ideals." The Senator's solution was to quarantine entering diplomats "as we quarantine foreign rags through fear of cholera."[17]

All of the diplomats that the senator wished to quarantine were political appointees, as patronage was still the order of the day for diplomatic and consular jobs, even though it had begun to change for other federal employees. The State Department positions, whether diplomatic or consular, were handed out as rewards for political loyalty to the president. Because the title of ambassador was still considered too pretentious for a republic, none of them carried that rank.

The lack of such a rank meant that envoys from much smaller countries that were represented by ambassadors often received more deference than American envoys did. Titles mattered and the protocol that mandated a clearly defined pecking order had more impact than simply who sat where at formal dinners. It could also affect who gained access to the "most important circles" that President Monroe described.

The lack of diplomatic rank was not the only problem faced by American envoys abroad. Some historians have described the three decades that followed the Civil War as the least active era in American foreign relations. There were several rationales behind this isolationism. Many in Congress believed diplomatic relations would inevitably drag the United States into foreign wars. Others felt that foreign relations were largely unnecessary because there was more potential for harm than good.

Another rationale for the isolationism of this era is one that also has echoes today in the never-ending debate about the role of diplomats. Some interpreted the laying of the first telegraph cable across the Atlantic in 1866 as meaning that two foreign ministers could communicate as easily as if they were sitting across from each other at a table.[18] It would not be the last time that technological advancement was offered as a reason why diplomats are less useful than they were in the past and perhaps unnecessary.

Despite the reservations of the isolationists, the lack of engagement with the world came to an end with the Spanish-American War of 1898, and ever since, America has been engaged with the rest of the world to a much greater extent than it was during its first century. As the nineteenth century drew to a close, the territorial and political ambitions of the United States took it to places such as Cuba, Hawaii, the Philippines, and elsewhere. The drive to expand across the continent to the Pacific had run its course. In 1893, which as it turned out was the year the first American diplomat was given the title of ambassador, a young professor gave a talk at the annual meeting of the American Historical Association. In it, Frederick Jackson Turner spoke about "The Frontier in American History," and he pointed out that in 1891 the US Census Bureau had put out a pamphlet that asserted that frontier was now "closed," seeing as there was no more land to conquer and settle.[19]

Any new pretensions of empire would therefore have to find their expression overseas. As Americans adjusted to that new reality and began to believe and act as the citizens of a country that had become a world power, the quality of its diplomats became a question that could not be ignored. The prevailing view for much of the nineteenth century, particularly during the presidency of Andrew Jackson, had been that the business of government was not all that complicated. As a result, the United States was the only Western nation that rejected the idea of permanent diplomatic missions and held fast to the notion that career diplomats were unnecessary.[20]

As the United States entered its second century with growing economic and political interests abroad, American diplomats were not up to the task of protecting those interests. Ilchman describes how unready the country was:

> In 1888, America's changing world relations found the diplomatic service unprepared. The service was tied down by an antiquated system of appointments and a menacing inflexibility. No adequate salary scale existed. Members were not selected for their qualifications for diplomacy, and they, in turn, entered the service for reasons quite apart from desiring to serve the nation. The service was spoils-ridden and could offer no prospect of permanent tenure or promotion by merit.[21]

The State Department was not only unprepared to protect America, but it was also lagging behind the rest of the government in terms of reform. In 1883, Congress passed the Pendleton Act, which required that federal government jobs be given on the basis of merit through competitive examinations. It also created the Civil Service Commission to ensure the provisions of the act were followed.[22]

This legislation came about because of one particular case of a job seeker. Once elected, a new president was immediately hounded by scores of people wanting employment. In 1881, Charles Guiteau was one of those who believed the spoils system should have provided him a government job. He wanted to be minister in Vienna, and when that did not happen, he said he would accept being consul in Paris. Lacking any argument for the appointment other than his ambition, Guiteau's request was brusquely rejected by Secretary of State James Blaine. To express his disappointment, Guiteau assassinated President Garfield.

Garfield's murder spurred his successor, Chester A. Arthur, to become a reformer and to support passage of the Pendleton Act, which transformed the civil service. America's government had grown sufficiently large and complex that it could not be left only to patronage appointments that turned over with every new president. Oddly enough, the act did not bring about similar changes in the State Department. Apparently the diplomatic corps was not ready for reform yet, but that would soon change.[23]

The Middle Years—A Player on the World Stage Recognizes the Need for Better Diplomats

In 1892, European countries implicitly recognized the increased importance of the United States by raising their diplomatic representation in Washington from the level of minister to that of ambassador. The following year, Congress finally overcame its long-standing aversion to the title and responded by creating that rank in the American diplomatic corps.[24] It was bestowed for the first time in 1893 when Thomas Bayard was appointed ambassador to Great Britain. A month later, an ambassador was named to France. That same year, ambassadors were appointed to Germany and Italy, because all four countries had already elevated their representatives in Washington to the rank of ambassador.[25]

Although the rank was finally established, an ambassador was not placed in charge of every American diplomatic mission. Embassies in less important countries were still headed by a diplomat with the rank of minister. It was not until the late 1960s that it became the practice that any chief of mission would bear the title of ambassador if the country had normal diplomatic relations with the United States.[26]

Not everyone has always welcomed the expansion of the ambassadorial ranks. Ellis Briggs, a career officer who had seven postings as ambassador, wrote in his memoir in the early 1960s that he thought increasing the number of ambassadors and elevating legations to embassies diminished the power and prestige of an ambassador. He lamented the passing of the days when the Chief Usher at the White House knew not only every ambassador by name but also the country in which each ambassador served, as well.[27]

Although some at the time may have had similar misgivings, as the professionalization of the diplomatic and consular corps began in earnest early in the twentieth century, growth in the number of ambassadors was part of the process. One of the biggest boosters of professionalization was President William Howard Taft. In each of his four State of the Union speeches from 1909 to 1912, Taft spoke about what he had done to improve the State Department and urged Congress to help institutionalize reform. In his last such address, he explained the need for change by saying: "The Department of State was an archaic and inadequate machine lacking most of the attributes of the foreign office of any great modern power." He also made a pitch for a bipartisan foreign policy: "The fundamental foreign policies of the United States should be raised high above the conflict of partisanship and wholly dissociated from differences as to domestic policy. In its foreign affairs the United States should present to the world a united front."[28]

Taft accompanied this pitch to end politics at the water's edge with a recounting of his accomplishments in making the diplomatic and consular officers more professional and ensuring that their selection and advancement was based on merit rather than partisan political considerations:

> Expert knowledge and professional training must evidently be the essence of this reorganization. Without a trained foreign service there would not be men available for the work in the reorganized Department of State. President Cleveland had taken the first step toward introducing the merit system in the Foreign Service. That had been followed by the application of the merit principle, with excellent results, to the entire consular branch. Almost nothing, however, had been done in this direction with regard to the Diplomatic Service. In this age of commercial diplomacy it was evidently of the first importance to train adequate personnel in that branch of the service. Therefore, on November 26, 1909,

by an Executive order I placed the Diplomatic Service up to the grade of secretary of embassy, inclusive, upon exactly the same strict nonpartisan basis of the merit system, rigid examination for appointment and promotion only for efficiency, as had been maintained without exception in the Consular Service.

How faithful to the merit system and how nonpartisan has been the conduct of the Diplomatic and Consular Services in the last four years may be judged from the following: Three ambassadors now serving held their present rank at the beginning of my administration. Of the ten ambassadors whom I have appointed, five were by promotion from the rank of minister. Nine ministers now serving held their present rank at the beginning of my administration. Of the thirty ministers whom I have appointed, eleven were promoted from the lower grades of the foreign service or from the Department of State. Of the nineteen missions in Latin America, where our relations are close and our interest is great, fifteen chiefs of mission are service men, three having entered the service during this administration. Thirty-seven secretaries of embassy or legation who have received their initial appointments after passing successfully the required examination were chosen for ascertained fitness, without regard to political affiliations.[29]

Although President Taft and his predecessor, Theodore Roosevelt, had pushed professionalization, there was ironically some backsliding under Woodrow Wilson, a president best remembered for his involvement in international affairs. That backsliding demonstrated that if the changes designed to bring about a more professional corps of diplomats were not to be left to the whim of the president, Congress had to make them into law. This it did with the passage of the Rogers Act in 1924. The act created a unified Foreign Service by merging the diplomatic and consular officers together, established a personnel system for assignments, mandated that entry into the service and promotion within it be on the basis of merit, and set a retirement age of 65.

Table 1.1 demonstrates the effects of the reforms, inspired by Roosevelt and Taft and aided by the enactment of the Rogers Act, during the first half of the twentieth century. In essence, what it says is:

- The number of embassies headed by an ambassador grew significantly, but the percentage of those embassies headed by career diplomats grew much faster.
- At the same time, the number of embassies where the chief of mission had a title other than ambassador declined significantly and the percentage of noncareer chiefs of mission heading those embassies went from nearly all to nearly none.

Table 1.1 Changes in Chiefs of Mission, 1915–1950

Year	Number of missions	Number of missions headed by an ambassador	Career ambassadors (%)	Number headed by a COM with a different title	COMs who were career officers (%)
1915	42	12	17	30	3
1920	44	10	10	34	41
1925	50	13	23	37	49
1930	55	16	33	39	56
1935	56	17	41	39	54
1940	51	20	55	31	58
1945	53	35	60	18	72
1950	73	56	68	17	94

An ambassador to a particular country is always the chief of mission, but a chief of mission did not always bear the title of ambassador. Prior to 1893, none did. During the course of the twentieth century, a growing percentage of chiefs of mission were given the title of ambassador. Today, it is the rare exception where the title inflation that Ambassador Briggs feared does not apply.

In the first half of the twentieth century, therefore, there was tremendous growth in the number of embassies and the number of ambassadors. And the percentage of those ambassadors who were career officers grew even more rapidly until it reached its peak—a place where it has been stuck ever since.

The Past 60 Years—Professionalization Hits Its Limit

Shortly after the end of World War II, the percentage of career ambassadors reached about two-thirds of the total number of ambassadors appointed by the president. The ratio of 30 political appointees to 70 career ambassadors has roughly remained the same ever since, regardless of the party in power. Table 1.2 is the breakdown by administration.

Although the ratio between political versus career appointees has remained at around the same level since the Eisenhower administration, there have been further attempts to professionalize the ranks of ambassadors. Partly in reaction to the criminality of the Nixon administration, under President Carter, the Foreign Service Act of 1980 was

Table 1.2 Career vs. Political Ambassadorial Appointments, 1953–2008

Administration	Total	Career (%)	Political (%)
Eisenhower	214	146 (68%)	68 (32%)
Kennedy	120	73 (61%)	47 (39%)
Johnson	148	89 (60%)	59 (40%)
Nixon	233	159 (68%)	74 (32%)
Ford	97	60 (62%)	37 (38%)
Carter	202	148 (73%)	54 (27%)
Reagan	420	261 (62%)	159 (38%)
George H. W. Bush	214	147 (69%)	67 (31%)
Clinton	417	301 (72%)	116 (28%)
George W. Bush	453	317 (70%)	136 (30%)
Total	2,518	1,701 (68%)	817 (32%)

Source: American Foreign Service Association and Library of Congress.

passed. Among its provisions is a description of what should be the qualifications for someone nominated as ambassador:

> An individual appointed or assigned to be a chief of mission should possess clearly demonstrated competence to perform the duties of a chief of mission, including, to the maximum extent practicable, a useful knowledge of the principal language or dialect of the country in which the individual is to serve, and knowledge and understanding of the history, the culture, the economic and political institutions, and the interests of that country and its people.
>
> Given the qualifications specified in [the proceeding] paragraph, positions as chief of mission should normally be accorded to career members of the Service, though circumstance will warrant appointments from time to time of qualified individuals who are not career members of the Service.
>
> Contributions to political campaigns should not be a factor in the appointment of an individual as a chief of mission.

Whether it was the impact of the 1980 act or not, there was a change in terms of the percentage of ambassadors who were political appointees. For the five presidents who were in office immediately before the passage of the act, 35 percent of the ambassadors were political appointees. For the five presidents who have been in office since its enactment, it has been 30 percent. Since 1980, it has been slightly higher for Republican presidents (31 percent) and less for Democrats (27 percent).

It is too early to tell what the percentage will be under the current administration, but at least for President Obama's first term in office, the 30/70 ratio held.

As a candidate, Obama talked frequently talked about the need to change the way Washington does business. He even explicitly criticized the practice of giving ambassadorships to big campaign contributors. After he was elected, however, it became clear he was not going to be very different from his predecessors.

His rhetoric quickly changed once the election was over, reflecting perhaps the need to reward those who had supported him. In a press conference in early January 2009, the president-elect had this exchange with a reporter:

> Q: Throughout the campaign, you talked a lot about changing the way things work in Washington. But I want to go outside of Washington a little bit to some of those foreign embassies and plush ambassadorial residences. Will you be appointing big donors in the time-honored tradition to foreign embassies to serve as ambassadorships? Or will you draw solely from the ranks of career foreign service?
>
> THE PRESIDENT-ELECT: My general inclination is to have civil service, wherever possible, serve in these posts. I want to recruit young people into the State Department to feel that this is a career track that they can be on for the long term. And so, you know, my expectation is that high quality civil servants are going to be rewarded.
>
> You know, are there going to be political appointees to ambassadorships? There probably will be some. I don't—you know, I think it would be—it would be—it would be disingenuous for me to suggest that there are not going to be some excellent public servants but who haven't come through—through the ranks of the civil service. But, you know, as we roll out our ambassadors, you'll be able to make an assessment in terms of the professionalism and high quality of the people that we appoint.[30]

There are two personnel systems in the State Department—one for the Foreign Service and one for the Civil Service. Employees under the latter largely hold jobs in Washington and go overseas for short periods, if at all. The career ambassadors are, with very few exceptions, drawn from the ranks of the Foreign Service and almost never from the Civil Service. Foreign Service officers can be assigned to any of the 275 diplomatic missions in the world and generally spend the majority of their careers abroad. It is not clear whether the president-elect knew the difference between the two systems at that point or whether he did not think it a distinction worth making. One thing is for sure: he did learn rapidly that the way Washington works has its advantages, and he quickly began to name big donors to ambassadorial posts, often provoking criticism from the media.

The percentage of political appointees always runs higher early in a four-year term; when there is a change of administration, all ambassadors submit their resignation to the new president. Those of the political appointees are usually accepted in short order, especially when a different political party occupies the White House. Those of the career officers are rarely accepted, and instead they are almost always allowed to serve out the remainder of what is usually a three-year term. That gives the new president a higher number of political ambassadorships to fill in the early months in office than there will be during the remainder of the term.

In May 2009, after four months in office and the rollout of a number of big donors for various ambassadorial posts, the White House press spokesman, Robert Gibbs, was reduced to trying to deflect criticism of these appointments with humor. This exchange took place on May 28:

Q: Robert, at least four of the ambassadorial nominees the President announced yesterday were big-money raisers for his campaign. Is that changing the way Washington works when he makes appointments like that?

MR.GIBBS: Mark, I think you may know that the President was asked in the transition and said there will be some—let me quote him— "political appointees serving abroad. It would be disingenuous for me to suggest that there are not going to be some excellent public servants, but who haven't come through the ranks of civil service." I think yesterday we rolled out a number of both career and non-career ambassadorial appointments. I think you see a group of committed individuals and proven professionals that are eager to serve their country. Some of those individuals were fundraisers; some of those were career ambassadors; some of those were people that left either teaching or some other thing like that—like Miguel Diaz to become our ambassadorial appointment to the Vatican, somebody who has a distinguished record—or a Congressman like Tim Roemer, who has served on the 9/11 Commission and with some distinction in Congress, to be our ambassador to India. So I think the President was exceedingly forthcoming in that in January.

Q: Back on ambassadorships. Traditionally, the post[s] in Paris and London do go to personal friends of the President, as opposed to career diplomats. What are Mr. Rifkin's qualifications to be ambassador to France? Does he speak French? Is he a close personal friend of the President?

MR.GIBBS: He does, and is a friend of the President. I think the
President saw him in the last few days. Again, as I said—and I'll be
happy to give you a bio for—

Q: We've got the bio you put out, but it doesn't address that.

MR.GIBBS: Doesn't address?

Q: His specific qualifications.

MR.GIBBS: Well, again, I think there are—as I said a minute ago, there
are both career and non-career people that are appointed—

Q: Understand.

MR.GIBBS: I think that Mr. Rifkin is somebody obviously who has a
strong professional background, desires to serve this country, and the
President believes he'll be good as the next ambassador to France.

Q: And Mr. Susman for Great Britain or for the United Kingdom is-
what his—

MR.GIBBS: He speaks English. (Laughter.)

According to his official biography, Louis B. Susman is a lawyer and
banker with extensive corporate experience, but there is no indication
that he has any significant international or government experience. Aside
from his ability to speak English, he has another attribute that made him
an attractive candidate for an ambassadorship—his willingness to donate
his own money to election campaigns and to "bundle" the contributions of
others. He was so good at it that his nickname was "the vacuum cleaner."
According to press reports, he and his wife gave more than half a million
dollars to various Democratic candidates and bundled between $200,000
and $500,000 from other donors for Mr. Obama's campaign.[31]

So although the Pendleton Act and the Rogers Act have cut back on
the spoils system and patronage, campaign contributions still matter in
determining who gets certain jobs. When President Nixon was in office,
he once told his closest staff members that "anybody who wants to be an
ambassador must at least give $250,000."[32] But at least he was fair about
selling the office: he gave back one man's contribution when it became
clear he would not get Senate confirmation. Although such explicit
linkage between campaign donations and jobs is illegal, today there
is no shortage of people who might think they are entitled to special
consideration because of what they did to get their candidate elected.
In 2012, the Obama campaign listed 41 people who bundled between
$200,000 and $500,000 and 27 people who gathered up half a million
dollars or more. Such disclosures are not required by law and not every
recent Republican presidential candidate has been interested in transparency. Senator McCain made a list of his bundlers public in 2008. In
2012, Governor Romney flatly refused to disclose who his were.

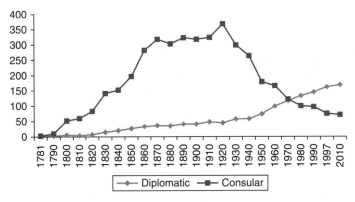

Figure 1.1 Number of Diplomatic and Consular Posts

The three periods through which the United States passed are demonstrated in figure 1.1, which shows the number of diplomatic and consular posts from the beginning of the republic to the present day.

The graph illustrates the features of all three eras. For the first century, commercial interests grew far more quickly than the traditional diplomatic ones did. Congress and the presidents of the nineteenth century could see the need for consular posts, but they still resisted a more rapid expansion of the diplomatic missions. Fewer diplomatic missions meant fewer opportunities for political problems. The opportunity for greater commerce with other nations caused the number of consular posts to grow rapidly until it peaked around 1920. Diplomatic posts also increased in number but at a very slow and steady pace.

The year 1920 was the high-water mark for consular posts, because once the professionalization brought about by the passage of the Rogers Act kicked in, the number of consular posts declined precipitously. They could no longer be established wherever patronage and a sufficient flow of revenue from selling consular services would permit them.

In the mid-twentieth century, the United States emerged from World War II as the most powerful country in the world and almost immediately entered into the Cold War with the Soviet Union. When the struggle to ensure that capitalism would triumph over communism heated up, America had interests everywhere and embassies were established to protect them. In addition, the postwar unraveling of the European empires in the third world caused dozens of new countries to come into being. The United Nations was founded in 1945 with 51 original member states. It had double that number by 1961 and more than three times that many by 1978.[33] It got another big boost in membership with the demise of the Soviet Union, and now it has 193 nations. The United States has embassies in nearly all of them, and who gets to represent the United States in all of those countries and how they are chosen will be explained in chapter 2.

CHAPTER 2

Who Gets to Be an Ambassador— The Traditional Route

On the website of an organization called the Council of American Ambassadors, there used to be a Frequently Asked Questions page, which included the question "How can I become an Ambassador?" The answer was "The traditional path that one follows to become an Ambassador is to join the United States Foreign Service."[1]

There is a bit of irony in that response, which may be why it was removed from the council's website. As the name implies, the council is made up of former ambassadors, but none of its members took that "traditional path." The council only accepts noncareer ambassadors into its ranks and all of them took another path, which is not described or even mentioned.

This chapter and chapters 3–4 will discuss both paths in detail, their differences and similarities, and the steps along the way to becoming an ambassador. Chapter 5 will then consider where these two paths lead in terms of the country to which an ambassador might be assigned. The differences between the two paths will make clear why the two routes lead to different sets of possible embassies.

The traditional path requires not just joining the Foreign Service but pursuing a full career in it. To get into its senior ranks and be considered for an ambassadorship rarely takes less than 20 years. The nontraditional path does not involve decades of government service, but instead it requires a person to have a political, economic, or personal relationship with the president. Those three types of relationships are not mutually exclusive, and often two or all three can come into play, but there is usually one that seems the most prominent. Whatever the combination, the relationship has to be strong enough that the president feels the person should be rewarded with an ambassadorship.

Whether it is the traditional or nontraditional route, the process of becoming an ambassador can be reduced to three steps: selection, clearance, and confirmation. The selection process is different for the two paths, but both lead to the White House, where the president decides on whom to nominate to the Senate for an ambassadorship.

The president has about 3,000 jobs to fill by appointment throughout the government.[2] Because of the workload, there is always a committee that is responsible for making recommendations on such decisions. The president will ultimately sign off on the appointments, but the committee does the work and presents the names of those recommended to the president for approval. A committee not only eases the president's workload but also offers the president some insulation from job seekers. As will be explained later in the chapter, it allows the president to say no without saying no and avoid saying yes to the wrong person by mistake. If President Garfield had such a committee, he might have lived to serve out his term of office.

In the case of the traditional path trod by career diplomats, the committee is made up of high-level State Department officials; for the nontraditional path taken by political appointees, it is composed of White House officials and the occasional informal advisor. In both, the committee members often represent different interests, and therefore there is always some balancing of those interests involved when arriving at a decision on whom to recommend to the president for an embassy.

One particular interest cannot always prevail, and there has to be a certain distribution of appointments among the different interests. If an interest were not important enough to ever win, it would not be important enough to have a seat at the table. Because of that, a decision on a particular individual may seem curious, but the horse trading inherent in a committee process may have required picking a candidate who may not seem the best person for the job in question.

There is also bargaining that takes place between representatives of the two committees, because the White House must come to an agreement with the State Department on which posts will be held by political appointees and which will go to career diplomats. The process is a complete mystery to those on the outside, and the bargaining within and between the two committees will often make the resulting decision even harder to understand. Personnel decisions always affect the professional reputations of those who are chosen and those who are not, and therefore such decisions are extremely sensitive and the process is never transparent.

There are other imponderables that make the process opaque and unpredictable. The bureaucratic skill, force of personality, interest level, attention span, connections—especially to the president—and commitment to the process of a committee member all determine how effective that person will be in representing the interests of his or her group.

Despite the potential for clashing egos among the high-level officials that make up these groups, a degree of consensus is required for these committees to do their work properly. If there is not agreement, a higher authority has to be consulted for a decision. For the traditional route, that can be the secretary of state, and for the nontraditional route, it can go all the way to the president. But committee members are usually loathe to admit they cannot agree, and there are only so many times the committee can fail to reach a decision before a secretary of state or president will begin to wonder whether the committee has the right membership or leadership.

The threat to "take it to the president" or the secretary may be used by a committee member in an attempt to veto an appointment, but it is an option that can only be used sparingly. And it cannot be used at all if the head of the committee is empowered to arrive at a recommendation even in the absence of consensus. Although this sounds abstract, it will become clearer when the selection phase of the two routes is explained and compared in the subsequent sections.

The Traditional Route

To understand the route for career diplomats, it helps to know a bit about how the State Department is organized and how it hires people. There are more than 70,000 people working for the State Department.[3] Only about 8,000 of them have any real chance of becoming ambassadors, and even for them, it is an extremely small chance.

Here's why: the 70,000 plus employees are divided into three groups—those in the Foreign Service, those in the Civil Service, and locally employed staff. The last group is the largest, with about 46,000 people. They are hired locally for jobs at the 275 embassies, consulates, and other diplomatic posts around the world and are usually citizens of the country where the diplomatic post is located. They do not have security clearances and therefore do not work with classified material. They range from drivers and mechanics to senior advisors on press, cultural, and commercial affairs and any number of other topics. No embassy could function without them, and employing them is much less expensive than sending Americans to do the job. Many of them spend their careers working for the US government, and at times their lives can be at risk because they become targets for terrorists.

The Civil Service employees number about 11,000 and work mainly in Washington. They again do a wide range of jobs and include lawyers, intelligence analysts, environmental specialists, and administrative and clerical staff, to name a few of those jobs. They only rarely work overseas for any length of time. Because their job and work conditions are similar to those of other Washington bureaucrats, their pensions and compensation structure are the same as those in the Civil Service in other agencies. They tend to stay in the same job, and their promotion largely depends on higher-level positions opening up and their moving into them.

The remaining 14,000 State Department employees are in the Foreign Service and therefore are considered available for assignment anywhere in the world that the United States has a diplomatic presence. Because of that and because of the inherent hazards, their personnel system is different from that of the Civil Service and the provisions for their pensions are more generous. They usually spend the bulk of their careers abroad, although they periodically return to Washington for assignments in the State Department and for training.

The 14,000 Foreign Service employees are either generalists (about 8,000) or specialists (about 6,000). The specialists are communications technicians, information systems managers, secretaries, security officers, and others whose work is largely technical.

The First Steps for Career Diplomats

The 8,000 generalists are also referred to as Foreign Service Officers (FSOs). Career ambassadors are almost entirely drawn from the senior ranks of the Foreign Service. Becoming an FSO and being able to start the long climb to those senior ranks is an ordeal in itself. It is a multistep process that begins with the Foreign Service Officer Test (or FSOT, for those who speak acronym). The FSOT is the written entrance exam to the Foreign Service, and it is offered several times a year.

The only requirements to take the FSOT is that a person be an American citizen who is more than 20 years old, but younger than 60 years old. On that basis, there are about 200 million Americans who are eligible to take the exam. Woody Allen once said that "showing up is 80 percent of life," however. In the case of the FSOT, it is more than that, given that only around 20,000 people out of the 200 million show up to take the exam each year.

The number of applicants can vary greatly in response to the economy and the general public perception of national service and the State Department. When unemployment rises, so will the number of the people who take the exam. When there is a prominent figure who inspires people to consider a career as a diplomat, the numbers also rise. Secretaries of state like Colin Powell and Condoleezza Rice have undoubtedly inspired more minorities to take the exam. And female secretaries of state like Madeleine Albright and Hillary Clinton have no doubt done the same for their gender.

There is no requirement for education level, major in college, language proficiency, or anything other than age limits and citizenship to take the exam. The likelihood of passing the FSOT without a college education is extremely low, however. It would be like trying to score highly on a standardized test for graduate or professional school, such as the GRE or the LSAT, without the benefit of an undergraduate education.

Based on budget projections and the needs of the Foreign Service, the State Department decides far in advance how many people it will hire in a given year. It then adjusts the passing score on the FSOT to reflect that number. In a normal year, about 350 people are hired as new FSOs to replace those who have retired, quit, been fired, or left the Foreign Service in some other way. When the State Department's budget is expanding and more FSOs are being added, as was the case after 9/11 and again when Iraq and Afghanistan required a large number of officers, the hiring level went up to more than 500 annually. With the budget battles that have come to characterize Washington policy debates in more recent years, the prospects for any growth in the number of FSOs seems limited and the State Department will be fortunate if it can avoid having to reduce the number from the current level of about 8,000 generalists.

Anyone contemplating taking the FSOT should not be discouraged by the odds and should remember that many of those who do get into the Foreign Service have taken the test more than once. And following Woody Allen's dictum, just showing up for it reduces the competition from 200 million to 20,000. Because the test is open to anyone under the age of 60, and over the age of 20, everyone has multiple opportunities to take the exam. The average age for new FSOs is about 30 and many of those who pass the FSOT have taken it several times.

Those who are thinking about taking it should first consider what the job entails. The best book to provide a sense of what the people working in an embassy do on a day-to-day basis is one put out by the

American Foreign Service Association entitled *Inside a U.S. Embassy*. It describes the kinds of jobs that are common to most embassies and takes the reader through a typical day in the life of that person from one hour to the next. It also discusses some of the challenges a career in the Foreign Service poses for families.

These challenges are considerable. The following list outlines some aspects of diplomatic life that indicate how different the career is from the one someone in the private sector or a civil servant in Washington might experience. Anyone who has a serious problem with any of these should reconsider whether he or she wants to take the FSOT.[4]

- It is the "Foreign" Service. The majority of the career is spent living abroad. Although assignments to Washington are also part of the job, there is a limit of five years at any one stretch of time working in Washington. That is because there is a tendency for some officers to try to prolong their time there by taking a series of jobs in the department. Once a person takes up residence in Washington, his or her spouse gets a job, and their kids enroll in schools, it is difficult to pull up roots and go overseas again. Exceptions to the five-year limit are hard to justify, however. Dealing with aging parents is also made more difficult if it has to be done from overseas.

- The flip side of having to live abroad is that one also has to live at least part of the time in the Washington area. Few people can escape being assigned there several times during their career. It is an expensive city, with well-paid lobbyists bidding up the prices of housing to the point where mere civil servants usually have to live in the distant suburbs. Another reason for families with children living a long way from Foggy Bottom is that public schools within the District of Columbia are not great and the private school options are very costly. Living in the suburbs means braving some of the worst traffic in the country to get to work, but at least the Metro subway system provides a good public transportation alternative.

- Assignments abroad are usually three years in a normal country, but they can be two years when conditions are difficult. In places like Iraq and Afghanistan, where the threats to diplomats are extremely high, a tour of duty can be as short as one year. An assignment to a high-threat post is unaccompanied, which means leaving one's family behind. Although an unaccompanied tour is not required, many FSOs will have at least one during their careers. Conditions change from one day to the next, but one news article in mid-2013 noted that 14 percent of FSOs were currently on an unaccompanied tour, which represented a five-fold increase in the last decade.[5] That percentage will decrease when the number of diplomats in Kabul and Baghdad return to something closer to their prewar levels, but separation from one's family is going to be a continuing and common feature of diplomatic life.

- Moving an average of every three years is hard not only on spouses and other family members but also on one's personal property. There is an informal rule of thumb that the damage done in three overseas moves equals that of one fire. Therefore, things that one really does not want to lose should go into storage, which also means they will be inaccessible for years at a time.

- The pay is good but not great. So if the accumulation of wealth is an important goal, it would pay to look to the private sector.

- Officers must learn at least one language to a reasonable level of fluency. On the State Department's scale of one to five, a minimum of a three is required in both speaking and reading in one language for promotion from the junior ranks to the middle grades. Most officers will attain that in more than one language.

- Officers must deal with other cultures. There will be exposure to many different ones, and although that makes for a career where one is constantly learning something new, it is not without its challenges and frustrations.

- Officers must spend time in more than one country. It is unusual to have even a second tour of duty in the same country, unless speaking a particularly difficult language is involved, so specialization in just one country is impossible. Specialization in one region is fairly common, however, especially for political and economic officers.

- Officers must be prepared to be a target. There will never be a final victory in what has been called the global war on terrorism. Terrorism is a tactic that will be around as long there are people who want to make a political point by killing innocent people. Some will try to express their displeasure with the policies of the US government by assassinating one of its representatives, and diplomats will always remain potential targets because of their symbolic value and their vulnerability in overseas locations.

- Officers must live with health threats. Although American health care is expensive and statistically lags behind that of most other economically developed countries, in the vast majority of countries in the world where the United States has a diplomatic presence, the quality of health care is far worse. Diseases like malaria and inferior medical facilities will be threats that, like terrorism, are always going to be there.

- Officers live in a goldfish bowl. The standards of conduct and accountability are higher in government than they are in the private sector, and the attention any questionable conduct receives from the public and the media will also be greater. This is all the more true for diplomats overseas, and especially true for ambassadors.

One other challenge of being in the Foreign Service is that one must follow the president's foreign policy, given that the president was the one who was elected and gets to decide what that policy will be. It is therefore the job of a diplomat to implement that policy and argue on behalf of the regime in power in Washington regardless of how he or she feels about it personally. Those who disagree with a policy have several options, including

- *acceptance*: a person can simply accept the policy and do his or her best to faithfully implement it despite any personal misgivings;
- *protest within the system*: there are ways to protest the policy and make an argument to Washington for changing it through official channels. One way to do so is through the "dissent channel," which provides a means to send a message through the official communications system making those arguments. Such messages are handled in a special fashion, are given very limited distribution, and usually receive a formal reply. Their recommendations are also usually ignored;[6]
- *protest outside the system*: a leak to the press or to an organization like WikiLeaks is another, albeit riskier, alternative. The prosecution of leakers is something that Washington seems to be serious about at the moment. Even when one goes through the proper procedures for getting something published, official retaliation is possible. If someone goes public in a way that shows the flaws in a policy to which Washington is still clinging, retribution is more likely than a review of the policy. Anyone interested in a case study of this should read Peter Van Buren's *We Meant Well*;[7]
- *resignation*: one can resign in protest. A few FSOs resigned over the failure of the Clinton administration to act more promptly in Bosnia. A few more did so over the invasion of Iraq by the Bush administration. Unless a person has at least the minimum

of 20 years of service required for a pension or a trust fund provided by wealthy relatives, there are serious financial implications to worry about with this course of action; and

- *transfer*: another possibility is to request a transfer to a part of the world where the policy is less objectionable. If someone does not like the policy with regard to the Middle East for instance, a transfer to Latin America may be a solution.

If a person is not discouraged by the realities of Foreign Service life, he or she can sign up for the FSOT. When signing up for the exam, the applicant must choose one of the five career tracks in which to compete—political, economic, consular, management, or public diplomacy.

Those who pass the written exam are invited to submit a personal narrative to the Qualifications Evaluation Panel (QEP). The panel consists of three FSOs who read the narratives and, based on those narratives, the person's test scores, and other factors, ranks the candidate among the others in that career track. At that point, if a person ranks high enough, he or she can proceed to the oral exam.

The oral exam is an all-day ordeal starting at 7:00 a.m. It can end as late as 6:00 p.m. and consists of a group activity, an individual interview with two examiners, and a case management exercise. These activities are described in detail on the State Department's website.[8]

The department points out that in this selection process, it is looking for the following 13 dimensions, which it wants in all FSOs:

- *composure*: to stay calm, poised, and effective in stressful or difficult situations; to think on one's feet, adjusting quickly to changing situations; to maintain self-control
- *cultural adaptability*: to work and communicate effectively and harmoniously with persons of other cultures, value systems, political beliefs, and economic circumstances; to recognize and respect differences in new and different cultural environments
- *experience and motivation*: to demonstrate knowledge, skills, or other attributes gained from previous experience of relevance to the Foreign Service; to articulate appropriate motivation for joining the Foreign Service
- *information integration and analysis*: to absorb and retain complex information drawn from a variety of sources; to draw reasoned conclusions from analysis and synthesis of available information; to evaluate the importance, reliability, and usefulness of information;

and to remember the details of a meeting or event without the benefit of notes

- *initiative and leadership*: to recognize and assume responsibility for work that needs to be done; to persist in the completion of a task; to influence significantly a group's activity, direction, or opinion; and to motivate others to participate in the activity one is leading
- *judgment*: to discern what is appropriate, practical, and realistic in a given situation and to weigh the relative merits of competing demands
- *objectivity and integrity*: to be fair and honest; to avoid deceit, favoritism, and discrimination; to present issues frankly and fully, without injecting subjective bias and to work without letting personal bias prejudice actions
- *oral communication*: to speak fluently in a concise, grammatically correct, organized, precise, and persuasive manner; to convey nuances of meaning accurately and to use appropriate styles of communication to fit the audience and purpose
- *planning and organizing*: to prioritize and order tasks effectively, to employ a systematic approach to achieving objectives, to make appropriate use of limited resources
- *quantitative analysis*: to identify, compile, analyze, and draw correct conclusions from pertinent data; to recognize patterns or trends in numerical data; to perform simple mathematical operations
- *resourcefulness*: to formulate creative alternatives or solutions to resolve problems and to show flexibility in response to unanticipated circumstances
- *working with others*: to interact in a constructive, cooperative, and harmonious manner; to work effectively as a team player; to establish positive relationships and gain the confidence of others and to use humor as appropriate
- *written communication*: to write concise, well organized, grammatically correct, effective, and persuasive English in a limited amount of time

At each of the three steps—the written exam, QEP, and oral exam—roughly two-thirds of candidates are eliminated or drop out. For those who survive all three, the final steps are a background investigation, a medical exam, and being placed in rank order on the register from which people are hired.

The background investigation is necessary for a high-level security clearance, and it is as thorough as it is time consuming. The medical exam is to ensure the candidate has no medical conditions that cannot be managed in remote parts of the world where transportation, communication, and health care may be primitive. Because an FSO is available for worldwide assignment, the exam makes sure that travel is possible from a medical standpoint.

Once placed on the register, a person can remain there for 18 months or until he or she is given an offer of employment. When the offer comes depends on one's ranking on the register, when training classes begin, and how many people the budget will allow to be hired. This whole process will usually take a year, and although there have often been suggestions that good candidates are lost because of its length, it is doubtful that the process can or will ever be accelerated very much.

So, who survives this process and who does the department hire? The first thing a new FSO does is report to Washington to take the A-100 course (which is where I first learned about Ambassador Lodge.) It is a six-week boot camp for bureaucrats that is designed to educate the new officers about the government they are about to go overseas and represent.

Statistics from ten A-100 classes in 2012 and 2013, which included about 730 new FSOs, show that nearly half (44 percent) were women, a little more than half were single, and a quarter were hired in the political track. The other four tracks each had approximately 18 to 19 percent of the new officers. A quarter had previous State Department experience as an intern, civil servant, or Foreign Service specialist. Three-quarters had a post-graduate degree, and more than 80 percent had worked, volunteered, or studied abroad. About 12 percent had been Peace Corps volunteers. Besides the Peace Corps the most common previous types of work experience were in the military, finance, and information technology and as lawyers, journalists, and teachers or professors.

Any A-100 class is an eclectic group, and the backgrounds indicated by these figures do not cover the whole range of who is hired. In age, the range is from the early 20s to the mid-50s, with an average of about 30 years old. Based on these demographics, it is safe to say that an advanced degree, time spent abroad, and significant work experience, especially in the government, will all improve one's chances of getting into the Foreign Service.

Could a person with only an undergraduate degree and no real work experience or time spent abroad get hired as an FSO? It is possible, but that someone who fit that description would have to have some pretty amazing other qualities to compensate for lacking much of the background the State Department desires in its new FSOs.

Given the pattern of hiring from the five career tracks, could candidates improve their chances by opting to take the test in a particular track even if it was not what they wanted to do in the Foreign Service? There are several reasons why this might be a bad idea. Of the nearly 21,000 people who took the FSOT in the fiscal year ending in 2012, 30 percent opted to compete for the consular track, 16 percent for the economic track, 16 percent for public diplomacy, 14 percent for management, and 24 percent for a career as political officer.

It is unclear why the consular track would be the most popular. It is certainly true that many who sign up for the FSOT could find consular work attractive. Some of it is not, however. Most new officers, regardless of their career track, spend their first overseas tour in consular jobs, and those tours can be very taxing. They can easily involve interviewing a couple hundred applicants each day who are seeking tourist visas to visit the United States. In some countries, the vast majority of these applicants are lying about their intentions to return to their home country and the consular officer must decide in the space of two or three minutes whether it is likely that they will.

Another reason for the popularity of the consular track could be that many people think it will be the easiest of the five tracks in which to be hired. If that is the case, enough people have thought that to make just the opposite true. Because so many people have signed up recently to test in the consular track, the chances of any one of them succeeding is actually much lower than they are in the other tracks.

The other reason why testing in an undesired track is a bad idea is that candidates have to justify their choice, and a weak justification might ring untrue or at least cost the applicant points. Finally, if a person is successful at getting hired for a career track they do not really want, it might prove difficult to switch once the career begins. And being stuck in a career path that does not really interest someone is not the secret of a happy or successful life.

Getting to the Top

Whether a career in the Foreign Service is successful or not, it begins at the bottom of the rank structure. There are six grades below the Senior Foreign Service (SFS), starting with class 6 and going up to class 1. These correspond roughly to the Army's officer structure of six ranks below general, starting with second lieutenant and going up to colonel. Depending on education and experience, however, a new FSO enters at class 6 with a bachelor's degree, class 5 with a master's degree, and class 4 with a doctorate. In other words, one can enter as the equivalent of a second lieutenant, a first lieutenant, or a captain.[9]

No one wears their rank on their collar, shoulder, or sleeve in the Foreign Service, unlike in the military. The entry level will therefore affect only the size of the paycheck each month, the possibilities for second assignments, and eventually the number of steps on the long road to the top. Whether an officer enters at class 6, 5, or 4, the first tour for that officer is generally spent doing consular work for two years during his or her first overseas tour.

Doing that kind of work and being available in theory for assignment to anywhere in the world is what distinguishes the Foreign Service from the Civil Service. Another difference is that in the Foreign Service, the rank of an officer is not necessarily congruent with the rank of the job that he or she holds: each job will have a rank associated with it, but in practice the person holding that job can be one or two ranks below that level (called a stretch assignment), at that level, or above that level.

Promotion depends on annual evaluations, which go into an officer's file. The file gets reviewed each year by a promotion panel, which analyzes the files of all the officers in a class and ranks them from top to bottom. Then, depending on the budget, the needs of the State Department, and other mitigating factors, a line is drawn and those above it are promoted and those below it wait and hope to make it next year.

For example, if the head of the economic section in a small embassy were a class 2 position, the person being assigned to that job would normally have a rank of class 2 (but might also be class 3 or 4 or class 1). If the person were promoted while holding that job, it would have no effect on his or her current position, but it would come into play in the competition for his or her next assignment. Holding a job that is one or two grades above a person's rank is obviously very helpful for promotion purposes, because it demonstrates to the review board that a person can handle a higher level of responsibility, which is what the review board cares about most.

To become an ambassador requires being promoted into the Senior Foreign Service (SFS) after ascending through the lower ranks of class 6 to 1. With a very small number of exceptions, career ambassadors are drawn from the SFS, which has four ranks: counselor, minister counselor, career minister, and career ambassador. They correspond to generals with one, two, three, or four stars in the military, although the rank of career ambassador is rarely awarded.

As with promotion at the lower levels, the chances of getting into the SFS vary greatly from one year to the next for reasons other than an officer's performance. Again, other factors, such as the needs of the Foreign Service, the State Department's budget, and the rate of retirement of senior officers, also create or limit opportunities for promotion into the SFS.

At present, those who succeed in making it into the SFS have usually spent about 22 years getting there. The State Department publishes promotion statistics each year in *State Magazine* (which also can be found online), and the figures for 2012 promotions show that 402 class 1 officers competed for entry into the SFS and the 104 who succeeded had an average of 21.5 years in the Foreign Service.[10]

Besides the budget, the needs of the Foreign Service, the time spent in it, and the rate at which senior officers are retiring, the career track a person chooses also affects his or her chances for getting into the SFS. Table 2.1 indicates how each track fared in being promoted from class 1 to counselor, which is the lowest of the senior ranks. Although these numbers represent only a snapshot, and they change from one day to the next, they are not likely to vary that much over time.

The table indicates that management and political officers had the best chances of getting into the SFS, with 12.6 and 11.5 percent of the FSOs in those tracks being promoted into the SFS. Economic and public diplomacy officers were not far behind, with 10.5 and 10 percent respectively. Only 7.3 percent of consular officers are in the SFS, however. So although it may be the most popular choice for those taking the FSOT, consular officers have a relatively slimmer chance than do their colleagues in the four other tracks to make it into the SFS.

Table 2.1 Senior Foreign Service by Career Track

Career track	Number of FSOs	Number in SFS	SFS (%)	Track in SFS (%)
Management	1,202	151	18.3	12.6
Consular	1,531	112	13.6	7.3
Economic	1,611	169	20.4	10.5
Political	2,124	244	29.6	11.5
Public diplomacy	1,465	148	18.0	10.0
Total	7,933	824		

Source: State Department Human Resources Bureau; data is current as of March 31, 2013.

And Getting to the Top Is Not Enough

Getting into the senior ranks is a necessary, but not necessarily sufficient, condition for becoming an ambassador. There are about 120 ambassadorial slots that are traditionally filled by career officers. Of those positions, about half are held by political officers, a little less than 20 percent come from the economic track, and about 10 percent each come from the other three tracks.[11]

The reason why the total for the five tracks actually add up to a little less than 100 percent is because there are a few exceptions to the tradition of career ambassadors coming from the senior ranks of the Foreign Service. A very small number of members of the State Department's Civil Service employees are given ambassadorships each year. In addition, career ambassadors can be appointed from three other agencies that have their own cadres of overseas specialists—the Foreign Commercial Service of the Commerce Department, the Foreign Agricultural Service of the Agriculture Department, and the United States Agency for International Development (USAID). These three agencies would not generally have more than one person from their ranks holding an ambassadorial position at a time, however.

Why are political officers seemingly overrepresented, whereas management, consular, and public diplomacy officers are underrepresented in the ranks of career ambassadors? The *Foreign Affairs Manual* (FAM) lays out the guidelines and procedures for virtually everything the State Department does. The FAM spells out, in very general terms, what it considers essential for promotion into and within the SFS.[12] It stresses that the qualities or precepts that a promotion board should consider "shall emphasize performance which demonstrates strong policy formulation capabilities, executive leadership qualities, and highly developed functional and area expertise."[13] The essence of diplomacy is dealing with foreign governments, and it is therefore not surprising that the first quality listed in the FAM is policy formulation. That is easier for political and economic officers who work more directly with policy issues to demonstrate than it is for consular, management, or public diplomacy officers.

The State Department also has a tradition of placing more importance on political work than on any of its other functions. The Rogers Act of 1924 may have unified the Foreign Service by bringing officers from all of the career tracks together in the same agency, but it did not end that institutional bias. In addition, those officers doing political work are more likely to interact with senior officials who mainly concern themselves with policy issues. That no doubt works to the advantage of political officers in securing deputy chief of mission (DCM) and chief of mission (COM) positions.

That is not to say that the officers in the other three tracks do not have strengths. In fact, they will often manage larger and more diverse organizational units than those of political and economic officers. The lack of managerial experience often makes it more difficult for political and economic officers to make the transition to being deputy chief of mission, which requires the supervision of a much larger and much more diverse group of people.

Grabbing the Brass Ring

The selection phase for becoming an ambassador is a process that is as long and complicated for senior officers as the hiring process is for junior officers, and it is a lot less transparent. All ambassadors, like all other presidential appointees, serve at "the pleasure of the president," and there is no fixed term of office. But because of the time, paperwork, and effort involved in getting an ambassador selected and to post, an ambassador's tour of duty is almost always three years. Occasionally, conditions in a country might be so difficult and dangerous, such as those in present-day Iraq and Afghanistan, that the tour of duty is reduced to two years, but those exceptions are rare.

There also might be a bit more variation in the length of a political ambassador's time at post because the timing of presidential elections could have more of an effect on obtaining confirmation from the Senate for a political appointee than it would for a career ambassador. Rather than make an appointment late in a presidential term, an incumbent political appointee is more likely to stay in place until the next term commences.

A three-year tour of duty is normally the case because the process of selecting a new ambassador and getting that person confirmed takes so long. Knowing which posts will be vacant well in advance is therefore essential. Most personnel changes in the Foreign Service, including for ambassadors, take place in the summer. In March of the preceding year, the director general, who is the most senior personnel officer in the State Department and always a senior FSO, sends out a message to the other senior officers in the department and overseas asking for nominations for candidates to replace the ambassadors who will complete their tours in 15 to 18 months' time.

The nominations can come from a large number of officials in the department. The State Department's organization chart or wiring diagram provides an idea of how many there are (figure 2.1). Each box represents an official who can attempt to have some influence on the process by proposing and pushing for his or her favorite candidates.[14]

Below the secretary of state there are 2 deputy secretaries of state, 6 under secretaries of state, 6 assistant secretaries for regional bureaus, 18 assistant secretaries for functional bureaus, and 25 other assorted offices headed by directors, ambassadors-at-large, special representatives, and other functionaries. Each assistant secretary has a principal deputy assistant secretary and three or so other deputy assistant secretaries. They can all suggest names for potential ambassadors, as can ambassadors abroad and even people who wish to put their own names forward as candidates.

All of these various officials can participate in the process to the extent that they want to be active in it. Some will vigorously push their candidates forward, whereas others will contribute little or nothing. One of the problems is that most of these officials are political appointees. They often have had limited contact with career officers and therefore have little notion of who the best candidates for ambassadorships might be. Unlike the 30/70 ratio between political appointees and career officers who are ambassadors, the vast majority of senior officials in the department are not FSOs, and the trend in recent years has gotten worse from the point of view of the Foreign Service. In fact, the number of FSOs in those jobs has declined to the extent that the president of the American Foreign Service Association and the president and chairman of the board of the American Academy of Diplomacy wrote an article for the *Washington Post* about what they called the marginalization of the Foreign Service in which they suggested that it had reached the point of being a diplomatic crisis.[15] They described the situation as follows:

> The most visible factor is the overwhelming—and growing—presence of political appointees in mid-level and top leadership positions at the State Department. For all their merit, political appointees are short-term officials, subject to partisan, personality-specific pressures. They do not notably contribute to the institution's longer-term vitality, and their ascension creates a system inherently incapable of providing expert, nonpartisan foreign policy advice. When transient appointees hold the bulk of its leadership positions, the Foreign Service is undermined. This situation spawns opportunism and political correctness, weakens esprit de corps within the service and emaciates institutional memory.

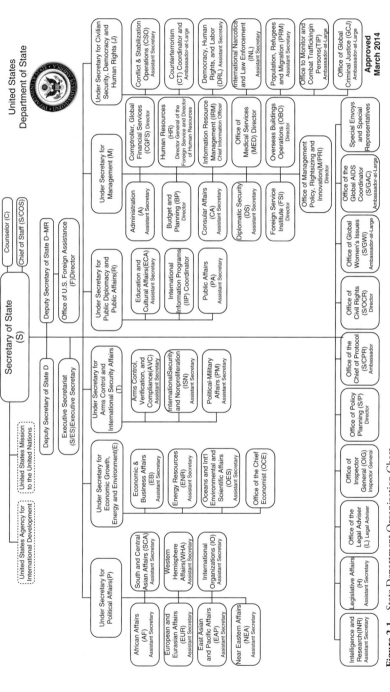

Figure 2.1 State Department Organization Chart

Source: http://www.state.gov/r/pa/ei/pa/ei/rls/dos/99494.htm.

Since 1975, the number of top leadership positions at the State Department, defined as deputy secretaries, undersecretaries and assistant secretaries, has increased from 18 to 33. The share filled by career Foreign Service officers has fallen from 61 percent in 1975 to 24 percent in 2012. Only five of the 35 special envoys, representatives, advisers and coordinators appointed during President Obama's first term were Foreign Service officers.

Regardless of whether the increasing number of "transient appointees" in high-level positions in the department is a diplomatic crisis or not, it does have an effect on who becomes an ambassador. Some of these appointees decide they want the job themselves. Despite lacking any experience in an embassy, they can sometimes influence the system enough to be placed in charge of one. More importantly, they are generally unfamiliar with the department and the members of the Senior Foreign Service, yet they can play key roles in the selection process if they want to do so by pushing for "their" candidates.

In this system, those who are not serving in Washington are at a disadvantage, because it is harder for them to become known to officials in the department. The more ambitious officers mix their overseas assignments with tours in Washington and are particularly attracted to staff jobs for senior officers.

The focal point for the process is the director general's office, where all of the nominations from all of these potential nominators are collected. The Human Resources Bureau vets the names and checks them with the Bureau of Diplomatic Security, the Inspector General, and the Equal Opportunity Office to ensure that none of the candidates has problems that would call into question his or her suitability for being nominated as an ambassador.

If a candidate was successful in the selection process and it was then shown that he or she had a record of sexual harassment, discrimination, or security violations, it would be highly embarrassing. Recommending such a person to the president and then having that record come out once the nomination is made public is a nightmare the system works hard to avoid. Even an accusation of impropriety or an illegal act can prevent a person from further consideration, because such charges have to be resolved before the name can move forward. That can mean proving the negative or, in other words, demonstrating one's innocence, and that can take years.

After the vetting of the names, the director general, in consultation with the regional assistant secretaries, will draw up a short list for each embassy. The short list usually consists of three to five candidates, and all of them are usually highly qualified for the post. The regional assistant secretaries are consulted because although an ambassador is the president's representative in a country, he or she reports not directly to the president, but to the secretary of state through the assistant secretary for the region. That assistant secretary also writes the fitness report of the ambassador and so some degree of compatibility between the two is essential.

The short list is then presented to the Deputy Secretaries Committee, or D Committee for short, so named because the two deputy secretaries of state chair it. This committee is responsible for making a recommendation to the secretary of state on who should fill each career ambassadorship. (Acronyms are an important part of the bureaucratic shorthand of the State Department, and the more letters there are in the acronym of an office, the further down the food chain it is. The office of the secretary, the two deputy secretaries, and the six under secretaries all have single-letter designations.)

In addition to the two deputy secretaries, the D Committee can include the under secretaries and other officials from the seventh floor of the department. The director general of the Foreign Service, who is always a career officer, helps guide the committee through its deliberations. Its composition is fixed by tradition, however, rather than any regulation, and its membership can therefore vary. Under secretaries who have little State Department experience or interest in the process can opt out or be left out.

The D Committee meets repeatedly over the summer and into the early fall. It reaches agreement on a single candidate for each embassy and forwards it to the secretary. The secretary can reject a recommendation but will almost always accept the candidate selected by the committee and forward it to the White House. If the secretary had strong feelings about a particular candidate, they would have already been expressed by one of his or her senior staff members, who can participate informally in D Committee deliberations.

The D Committee has an interesting challenge. It must weigh the respective merits of a pool of highly qualified candidates and select a person who has the skills required for a particular embassy. In doing so, the committee will look at the candidates' experience in the region and in policy formulation, language ability, and managerial skills. The committee also has to consider gender and ethnic diversity, as well.

So what does it take to emerge from the pack as the person chosen to be the next ambassador to a particular country? The most significant factors that work in a candidate's favor are

- *performance and corridor reputation*: the opinion of one's peers matters greatly, and the assessment of a person's competence depends on formal as well as informal measurements. If an officer has risen quickly through the ranks, it will be reflected by good annual evaluations and rapid promotion. Besides the contents of one's personnel folder, a person will also have a reputation among other officers that either confirms that formal assessment or marks an officer as someone with problems that are not reflected by it;
- *connections*: a high-level official pushing the person's candidacy can help a great deal. The higher up the better, but the bureaucratic skills, time, and enthusiasm devoted to the task by the endorsing official can matter much more than rank;
- *no one with veto power in opposition*: the support, or at a minimum the acceptance, of the regional bureau and its assistant secretary is essential;
- *experience*: service at least once as a deputy chief of mission is generally considered a requirement. Experience in the region is also usually essential;
- *language ability*: a 4/4 in reading and speaking the language in question helps and a score below a 3/3 will likely disqualify a candidate regardless of other favorable factors; and
- *luck and timing*: being available for a new assignment when an opportunity comes up and having the right language skills and experience for that position are important.

Conversely, things that will work against a candidate include

- a lack of recent regional experience, because a regional bureau will always ask what a candidate has done for it lately before it agrees to accept someone for consideration;
- a lack of assignments in Washington, because creating a network of contacts that can speak to the qualities of the candidate cannot be done as effectively from overseas. Corridor reputations are built much more quickly in Washington, where one comes in contact with far more FSOs, than they are overseas;

- a nomination that comes only from the candidate, which will be accepted but will go to the bottom of the pile and get little serious consideration; and
- an under secretary for the candidate's career track who is ineffective at promoting the ambassadorial prospects of officers in that track.

Although merit matters most, it would be a mistake for an FSO to assume that his or her talents and hard work will be recognized simply because he or she is talented and hard working. It happens, and the personnel system tries to ensure that it does, but it is rare. Given the competition to get to the top, those who engage in some degree of self-promotion and making the right contacts are usually going to succeed at the expense of those who do not engage in such practices.

That does not imply that officers spend the bulk of the workday reminding people how wonderful they are. It can mean seeking jobs that are not only challenging but that also put one in a position to get some recognition for his or her efforts. Given the limited number of other FSOs with whom one comes into contact overseas as opposed to working in the Department of State, that means taking jobs in Washington. It also means recognizing that everyone has what has often been referred to as an "old boys' network," whether they want one or not. This network includes the officer's corridor reputation and contacts, and it can be used to one's advantage or, if not used, it can become a disadvantage.

Does all of this mean that officers who have not specialized in one regional bureau and are not from the political or economic track are out of the running? No; they can certainly be competitive, but they need to overcome any deficits they have by drawing on other strengths, such as having high-level endorsement and support.

As noted earlier in the chapter, public diplomacy officers have the lowest representation in the ambassadorial ranks even though they develop some obvious skills during their careers that would prepare them well to be ambassadors. One reason they have been less successful is their relatively recent integration into the State Department. Prior to 1999 they belonged to the US Information Agency (USIA) and, like the officers in the Foreign Commercial Service, the Foreign Agricultural Service, and USAID, they had little prospect of becoming ambassadors, with rarely more than one or two serving at any point in time.

When USIA was absorbed into the State Department, the position of under secretary for public diplomacy and public affairs was created.

There have been eight people (six of them women) who have held the position in just 13 years, and the job became vacant again in mid-2013. Although all eight had experience in public relations or journalism, none had any State Department experience or spent a significant amount of time in government. A career officer held the job as acting under secretary, but that was for only two months.[16] As one blogger noted, the average tenure of those who have held the job was about 500 days.[17]

Despite calls to put a career professional in the job,[18] in September 2013 the Obama administration nominated Richard Stengel, a former managing editor of *TIME* magazine for the position. The only male who had held the job previously was James K. Glassman. Glassman is best known for having written a book predicting that the Dow Jones Industrial Average would hit 36,000 by 2005. The Dow barely broke 11,000 that year, and the book was described by Paul Krugman, a Nobel prize–winning economist, as silly and riddled with basic errors in math.[19]

Glassman was also known for his success at combining journalism and public relations. In one opinion article, he argued against an increase in the federal excise tax on cigarettes, saying that smokers saved the government money by dying at a younger age.[20] If only they would go more quietly without all that coughing. Glassman's predecessor as under secretary was Karen Hughes, whose most notable characteristic was the fierceness of her loyalty to President George W. Bush.[21]

The relatively small numbers of public diplomacy officers who become ambassadors is no doubt at least to some degree due to the ability and length of time in office of those who have held the position of under secretary for public diplomacy. The person who could be their most important advocate has never stayed in the job long and probably had little interest in effectively promoting their fortunes. That message gets translated within a bureaucracy as meaning that the ambitious should find another career track if they want to become ambassadors. With the highest-level public diplomacy official changing every other year and not knowing the department and its people in the first place, public diplomacy officers are not likely to have a high-level advocate working on their behalf when the D Committee makes its decisions.

The other career tracks all have a potential advocate at a senior level who is usually more active and adept at the personnel game. Political officers have a natural supporter in the under secretary for political affairs, who is the fourth ranking official in the department and usually the highest-ranking career officer. Economic officers have the under secretary for economic affairs, the fifth ranking official in the department.

The interests of management officers are in the hands of the under secretary for management. There is only an assistant secretary for consular affairs, but often the director general will work to ensure that consular officers get the consideration they deserve for ambassadorships.

Once all of the advocates who are willing to weigh in have done so and the regional assistant secretaries have let their wishes be known, the D Committee meets behind closed doors and makes its decisions. The results are not always what one might hope. In the words of one former director general who had to oversee the process: "Often, I regret to say, decisions were not made on the basis of qualifications, but on whether the secretary wanted it, or the National Security Advisor wanted it, or the deputy secretary wanted it, etc."[22]

Although the results may not be pretty from everyone's standpoint, once the D Committee makes its decisions, a list with a recommendation for each ambassadorship is passed to the secretary. Once the secretary approves the list, it goes to the White House. This happens several times a year, because the D Committee handles a limited number of embassies in each of its meetings and the names are forwarded as the decisions are made.

Usually there will be prior agreement between the White House personnel office and the State Department as to which embassies will be reserved for political appointees and which will be given to career ambassadors. At other times, a new round of negotiations and horse trading will take place between the department and the White House over some of the embassies.

Even at this level, the interest and effectiveness of the officials involved will have a great effect on the outcome. If a secretary of state does not have the time and the will to go to bat for career ambassadors or lacks clout with the president, the White House chief of staff and presidential personnel office are likely to attempt to increase the number of political appointees. Such factors are dictated by the personalities involved and vary greatly from one administration to the next. They are particularly dependent on a president's management style, views about Washington in general and the State Department and the Foreign Service in particular, as well as on whom the president chooses as secretary of state.

None of this is spelled out in the *Foreign Affairs Manual* or by any law or regulation. It is driven mainly by tradition and modified in many different ways by each successive generation of senior leadership in the State Department and the White House. How it plays out from one administration to the next can therefore change in ways that are imperceptible to outsiders and even to most of those within the institutions as well.

Once the White House receives the list and works out any differences with the department, it will go to the president for approval. When the president signs off, it goes back to the State Department to begin the next two steps—clearance and confirmation. It is usually well into October or November before that happens. Even though it is now fall and the process has been under way since spring, the process will not be completed until the following summer. That is because although the selection phase for career officers has been completed, the last two phases—clearance and confirmation—still remain. Before considering what they involve in chapter 4, the selection process for political appointees will be described in chapter 3.

CHAPTER 3

The Nontraditional Route

For those not wishing to enter the Foreign Service and spend 20 years working their way up through the ranks to become a senior FSO, only to have a slim chance of becoming an ambassador even then, there is a second route to obtaining the title. They can attempt to join the roughly 30 percent of ambassadors who are political appointees and not career civil servants.

Although the traditional route has all of the built-in problems and imperfections of any personnel system devised and run by human beings, merit plays an important role in who gets to be an ambassador. Luck, timing, and connections matter, but first and foremost one has to perform well to rise up through the ranks before getting the nod from the D Committee. Annual evaluations, on which promotions in the Foreign Service are based, are the principal indicators of ability, and over the course of a couple decades, an FSO will have many different rating and reviewing officers writing those assessments.

The nontraditional route is shorter and less complicated, and although merit is a factor, it is just one of several. Because political appointees come from such a wide variety of backgrounds, merit, like beauty, is in the eye of the beholder. There have been some attempts to describe what does count, however.

One writer, who has conducted hundreds of oral history interviews of former diplomats, put it this way: "Today, as has been the rule since the first days of the Republic, appointments of nonprofessionals to ambassadorial positions have largely been awarded for success in other fields."[1] Success in a field other than diplomacy is certain true for some political appointees, but that would not seem to be a sufficient description, because there are many successful people in any field. To rise to the level of being considered for a presidential appointment really depends on having a personal, political, or economic relationship with the president or, at a minimum, that kind of relationship with someone who has considerable influence with the president.

Those who defend the nontraditional path will argue that success in another field is sufficient proof of merit and potential for being an ambassador. But is success as a real estate developer sufficient preparation to run an embassy? Likewise, are those who simply inherited a large fortune and gave a portion of it to the right candidate fully prepared?

Chapter 5 will consider the qualifications question as well as the relative merits of career officers versus political appointees. The current chapter will be confined to describing the process for selecting political appointees and explaining how it is different from the process for Foreign Service Officers (FSOs).

The selection of career ambassadors is an annual exercise that has a well-defined bureaucratic process and has to produce approximately the same number of candidates each year. It is subject to change in the sense that the cast of bureaucratic characters constantly changes, creating turnover in the composition of the D Committee and among those who try to influence that committee. Nevertheless, the process follows a known route because its structure and procedures are fixed by tradition.

The process for political appointees, on the other hand, can change radically, because it depends primarily on how the occupant of the White House wants it organized and to whom that president turns for advice. Those decisions are entirely up to the president. In recent decades, all administrations have shared two trends—a more professional and systematic approach to filling the jobs requiring presidential appointments and the initiation of the process increasingly earlier in the electoral calendar.

With thousands of government jobs to fill, deciding who will fill them cannot wait until Inauguration Day. With the ratification of the Twentieth Amendment in 1933, the inauguration was moved from March 4 to January 20, reducing the transition time and making planning all the more important. Today the process begins not only before the election takes place but also before the major party candidates have secured their party's nomination. When it starts is up to the candidate, but any presidential campaign gives some thought to it even before the first primaries take place.

Although it is clear that a great deal of planning is necessary to avoid beginning a presidency unprepared to assume the responsibilities of the office, planning efforts in the past had to be conducted almost clandestinely. According to the man tasked with organizing the staff for Ronald Reagan when he was the president-elect, "presidential personnel cannot wait for the election because presidential personnel has to be functional on the first day, the first minute of the first hour. But it has to be behind-the-scenes, not part of the campaign and certainly not known to the public."[2] The reason for the secrecy was to avoid the charge from other candidates or the media that the candidate doing the planning was already measuring for new drapes in the Oval Office before the people had spoken. Despite this potential accusation, there has been such widespread recognition of the need for advance planning that there has been bipartisan support for legislation designed to deal with the issue.

That was not always the case, and the attitude toward presidential transitions has evolved as the business of government has grown and become more complex. For most of the country's history, the transitions from one presidency to another were haphazard, informal, and funded by the winning candidate.[3] Prior to 1963, there were no formal arrangements for the handoff of power from one administration to the next and no federal funds to support such efforts.

That ended with the passage of the 1963 Presidential Transition Act (PTA), which provided government funding for transition efforts following the election. The act was prompted in part by the fact that the incumbent president, John F. Kennedy, had spent $300,000 of his own money on his transition.[4] Congress realized that continuing with such a system would mean the readiness of a new president to undertake the responsibilities of his office would depend on that president's personal wealth.

Although the PTA provided government support for a president's transition, it was not without its limits. It set a ceiling of $900,000 for such expenses, which would be equivalent to around $6.7 million today. President Obama spent twice that amount on his transition in 2008.

The 1963 act was amended and expanded in 2000.[5] It authorized additional support to the transition to be provided by the General Services Administration (GSA) and authorized the GSA to begin discussions with the presidential candidates before the election in order to develop plans for computer and communications systems to support the transition.

Even with the government underwriting some of the transition costs and providing other support thanks to the expanded PTA, there was further acknowledgment that there are still only two and a half months between a president's election and the inauguration. After another bipartisan effort, Congress passed the Pre-Election Presidential Transition Act, which was signed into law by President Obama in October 2010. It instructed the GSA to offer each candidate, upon nomination, a range of services that includes fully equipped office space, communications equipment, briefings, training, and the initiation of security clearances for prospective personnel.[6] This assistance is not provided just to the two major party candidates but also to any other candidates determined to be eligible on the basis of criteria similar to those used to establish who can participate in the presidential election debates.[7] To meet those requirements a candidate has to be constitutionally eligible to be president, appear on the ballots of enough states to have at least a mathematical chance of winning the election, and have the support of at least 15 percent of the electorate in public opinion polls.[8]

One reason for the need for more time and planning has been the growing number of people who are seeking jobs from the president. Technology has brought many innovations, and one of the consequences is that, thanks to the Internet, anyone can easily put his or her name forward for a presidential appointment.

President George H. W. Bush received 16,000 résumés before his inauguration. By the end of the Clinton administration, the White House had 190,000 of them in its computer files. The Obama transition team collected and reviewed more than 300,000 résumés in a short time at the start of his administration.[9] Now anyone seeking a noncareer job in the federal government can go to a page on the White House website and apply online.[10]

There is never a shortage of applicants for such positions. Chase Untermeyer was in charge of transition planning for President George H. W. Bush. When an article appeared in the *Washington Post* mentioning that fact, he was inundated with résumés from job seekers. In an oral history interview at the Miller Center at the University of Virginia, Untermeyer described how he dealt with the flood:

> Soon, there got to be quite a pile. I needed a place to keep these résumés, so I went into the closet of my apartment and there was a very good-sized cardboard box, which had contained a Texas hill country smoked turkey, which some friends had sent me the previous Christmas. It was a good box with handles and it just seemed to be exactly what I needed for this purpose.
>
> So that from that point forward, when people called and said, "I'd like to send you my résumé," I would tell them, "Well, you can do that if you want but I can't do anything with it but I will promise that I will put it in the turkey box." And the turkey box became a famous metaphor for that particular part of the transition planning process.
>
> I will say that not everybody fit in that category, that out of those who contacted me before the election, there were a couple of people who actually did get appointments and served with great distinction, so we

can't be so cavalier. There are some people who are not politically sophisticated enough to know that sending in your résumé is not the way you do things. But they proved to be able people, just not politically sophisticated, and therefore the turkey box had its function.[11]

Untermeyer went on to be head of Bush's Office of Presidential Personnel (OPP). He points out that although some of those who put their résumés into such a system did obtain jobs requiring a presidential appointment, they were the rare exception. There are hundreds of thousands of applicants for a few thousand jobs, and the kinds of qualifications reflected in a résumé are a small part of what is required to win this lottery. Unwittingly perhaps, the name "turkey box" is therefore an appropriate term for the place where the applications of the politically unsophisticated are placed.

For those who lack an understanding of the ways of Washington, there is no shortage of advice on how to advance one's prospects for a position in government. The National Academy of Public Administration puts out "A Survivor's Guide for Presidential Nominees," which has lots of useful tips, such as the need to work aggressively through the transition team, the White House Office of Presidential Personnel, and the cabinet secretary to secure a job. This requires tapping any connection, no matter how indirect, and looking for a powerful promoter. A member of congress who is close to an incoming cabinet secretary, a Washington lobbyist who raised money for the president's campaign, and others can be enlisted to make phone calls on behalf of the job seeker. In other words, according to one former assistant secretary of the Treasury, job seekers must "be absolutely shameless about it."[12]

All of the shamelessness creates a flood of résumés from aspiring presidential appointees and today it takes a lot more than Untermeyer's turkey box to deal with them. A newly elected president has to have an administrative structure to manage job seekers long before taking office. That structure also protects the president from the well connected, who require more special handling than just tossing their résumés into the turkey box.

In his oral history interview at the Miller Center, E. Pendleton (Pen) James, who was the head of the OPP during the Reagan administration, described one incident following Reagan's election but before his he had taken office:

Ronald Reagan is out in Palm Springs, California at Walter Annenberg's estate. The New Year's Eve party that he always gives for the beautiful people. I'm in Washington working. I'm not home for Christmas, so I get the call late one afternoon from Ronald Reagan, the President-elect. He says, "Pen, I've decided"—I'll use names because I will edit these names out—"for the Ambassador to St. James I want to put John So-and-So in that ambassador's job." That's a plum ambassador. There are three plums—England, France and Italy. "Fine, Mr. President," and I wrote down the decision.

Ed Meese called me later and I said, "Oh, I talked to the Governor today and he wants to go with Bill and Mary and Jane, and on St. James he wants to go with John whatever." Ed almost dropped the phone. He said, "He can't do that." Now, I never heard anybody say, "He can't do that." He said, "That guy opposed us. He wasn't on our team. He didn't raise money. He can't do that." Then I get a call from Deaver. Ed had just called Mike. Mike called me. "He can't do that." I said, "Well—" I felt like I did something wrong. And he said, "Don't do anything on that until we get back."[13]

Despite the misgivings of his closest advisors, Reagan believed he had made a commitment that he could not go back on, and he felt he had to go ahead with the appointment. But after that experience,, he knew that when approached directly by a close friend, a senator, or anyone else seeking a presidential appointment for someone, he could simply respond that he was going to "put it in the process" without making a commitment.

James was too discrete to name the ambassador, but it was John J. Louis, Jr., Reagan's first ambassador to the Court of St. James. His maternal grandfather founded the Johnson Wax Company, and Louis's personal wealth was estimated at $300 million. He contributed one-tenth of 1 percent of that fortune to Richard Nixon in 1972, and his reward was getting to represent the United States at the twentieth anniversary of the independence of Gabon. That plus serving as the international marketing director for three years for the S. C. Johnson Company, the corporation into which Johnson Wax had evolved appears to have been the sum total of his international experience.[14]

Louis not only lacked any significant background in international affairs, but he was also viewed as shy and unenthusiastic about public speaking and the kind of socializing that goes with being an ambassador in a major European country.[15] He was also perceived, no doubt correctly given the origin of his appointment, as lacking any influence with the White House. He was generally judged somewhere between invisible and ineffective.[16] As one British newspaper tactfully put it in his obituary in 1995, Louis was "well liked but not well known."[17]

That he got the job through the influence of Reagan's close friends the Annenbergs is clear. Why he wanted the job, given that he had neither the relevant experience nor any interest in public speaking or socializing, is not clear. The ambassador's residence on the edge of Regent Park in London is beautiful, and the job title does enhance any résumé, however. It also gives those who inherit hundreds of millions of dollars and high-level corporate positions an opportunity to be recognized for something more than the unearned wealth and privilege that come from choosing the right parents.

If that was Louis's motivation, it apparently did not include working particularly hard. He was best remembered for taking a vacation in Florida after having been on the job for less than a year and deciding not to let the outbreak of the Falklands War interrupt his time off. While Secretary of State Alexander Haig tried unsuccessfully to broker a ceasefire between Great Britain and Argentina, the ambassador continued his holiday and did not return to the embassy until a week and a half after the crisis had started.[18]

In September 1983, after only a little more than two years on the job, Louis submitted his resignation to Reagan, citing a desire to return to "the business affairs and civic, educational and charitable work which had been my life until your honored me with this appointment in 1981."[19] Whenever a high government official says he or she is resigning prematurely because of a desire to spend more time doing something else, it almost always means he or she was fired. There was, of course, no hint of that in Reagan's letter back to Louis accepting his resignation. It was full of praise, expressions of gratitude, and regret that Louis was leaving.

The Reagan administration was the first to impose a strict three-year rule on ambassadorial appointments. Before that, ambassadors—both career and political appointees—would often try to stay on as long as possible in comfortable posts, whereas those in difficult ones occasionally attempted to get out earlier. Because the whole process from the selection of an ambassador to his or her swearing in normally takes a full year, it was clear that for these rotations to go smoothly, there had to be a predictable timetable to follow. And so it was established that all ambassadors would serve a term of three years. That continues to be the case today, with a few exceptions usually made for political appointees because it is difficult to get a replacement confirmed when a presidential term is nearing its end.

The departure of Louis after two years was a clear sign that he was pushed overboard rather than him deciding to jump ship. He served with little distinction at a difficult time, and relations between the two countries suffered because of it. But according to James, the appointment of Lewis was the only time that Reagan was blindsided, and all subsequent ambassadorial candidates had to go through the OPP first.

Because presidents can avoid the problem of being pressured to commit to making an appointment before it can be properly vetted by his staff, it is important to get the personnel machinery up and running as soon as possible in the electoral process. Thanks to the government support provided by the various presidential transition acts, it is now possible to do so earlier, to be more open about it, and to have more federal funding to support it than in the past.

In 2012, Mitt Romney became the first candidate to take advantage of such support before the election. He assembled a team to conduct the planning for the desired transition that never happened. Although the transition team's candidate lost the election, their work was not entirely for naught, because it was published as a 138-page report detailing how they prepared for a Romney administration.[20]

The report, entitled the "Romney Readiness Project 2012," included a detailed plan for the first 200 days of a Romney presidency. Under the heading of "Personnel" in the plan was a PowerPoint slide that described the different ways to organize the filling of jobs in the new administration:

> Presidential appointments are of intense interest to the White House and to departments and agencies. The appointment of ambassadors is a classic example of a frequent conflict of these interests.
>
> - Some administrations have allowed cabinet secretaries great latitude in assembling their departmental "teams." (Carter administration)
> - Other administrations have sought tight White House control in sub-cabinet appointments.
> - A third approach involves establishing a working partnership in which the White House Office of Presidential Personnel and the respective department have a mutual veto. In practice, this generally works well.[21]

As the slide notes, conflict between competing interests is part of the process of selecting people for presidential appointments, especially when it is for the title of ambassador. This conflict occurs not only between the White House and the State Department but also within both organizations.

Conflict within the State Department arises for several reasons. There are always many contenders for every ambassadorship, there are competing bureaucratic interests among the various bureaus and career tracks that want their share of the ambassadorial pie, and there are numerous high-level officials at the assistant secretary level and above who are seeking to reward their favorite officers. Those competing interests result in a process that is characterized by inevitable horse trading and bargaining as those various interests are taken into account.

Conflict within the White House arises from a different, but somewhat similar, calculus, and it always results in a process where opposing interests have to be taken into account. In his oral history interview, Pen James described the characteristics that he sought in potential presidential appointments. James had worked in an executive search firm and in the Nixon administration's presidential personnel office before taking charge of the OPP for President Reagan. He was from California, a conservative, and a long-time supporter of Reagan, but he was a professional headhunter and not a political operative.

As mentioned earlier in the chapter, he had to operate behind the scenes during the transition and had no contact with the campaign staff while he was making plans for the personnel decisions that had to be instituted after Inauguration Day. As a result, when his appointment as head of presidential personnel was announced, the political operatives, many of whom were hoping for a job in the new administration, immediately asked, "Who is Pen James?" and began to question his qualifications for the job.

The biographic description of James in the archives at the University of Texas addresses that questioning when it states in part:

> When Reagan assumed the Presidency in January 1981, James became head of the Office of Presidential Personnel. James continued to oversee the recruiting of people with proven commitment to Reagan's ideas and high competency, as he had during the campaign and transition periods. He deflected criticism from those who thought he was wrongly downplaying longtime loyalty to Reagan, including past work on Reagan political campaigns, as a factor in filling positions.[22]

The example of James demonstrates what is perhaps the fundamental conflict within the White House when it comes to awarding jobs—the importance placed on loyalty and ideology as opposed to the importance of ability and experience.

In his oral history at the Miller Center, James described the qualities he sought when finding people to fill these jobs:

> We came up with five criteria. I'm sure you've read these in history. We said we would appoint—there would be five screens we'd do on every appointment.
>
> Number one: We'd appoint men and women who are philosophically committed to Ronald Reagan—what Reagan was programming, what he

was running for, what he campaigned for, what initiatives he wanted. We wanted to make sure we bring in men and women who are committed to that philosophy of government.

Second: We would appoint men and women who had integrity to do the job, whose background and ability were above reproach—we all have scars—but who were people of integrity.

Third: We used toughness. Toughness was a very important one, because if you take this job you are going to be buffeted daily by special interest groups, by lobbyists, by political campaign hangers-on to influence your decision on that area of government that you have responsibility for. By toughness we meant the ability to withstand that pressure, to shade your decisions and hang in there with what Reagan wants you to accomplish.

Fourth was competence. We wanted to make sure that the men and women we brought in for whatever job had some competence to do the job. I mean, if you're in agriculture, or you're in health or in engineering, or you're in science, [or] you're in technology, if you're in finance, that your background has some capabilities to know how to do that job.

The fifth criterion would be team player. By team player, we didn't mean sycophants or hangers-on, but [those] who were really taking these jobs—because whoever takes these jobs—their career is going to be enhanced to a certain extent by the very nature of that. We recognize that, but we don't want that to be their primary motive for taking the government job—so that I can use this to get a bigger law firm, or whatever it would be.

We came back and we said we will use this screen on all the people we talk to—philosophy, integrity, toughness, competence, and team players. That was one thing we did. We tried to do that.

The other thing we tried to do was make sure—you need a balance in the administration. We can't end up with everybody from California, which would have been easy. We were all Californians, but we wanted to make sure that there was a geographic distribution from the Midwest, the East Coast, to the South, to the West Coast, the Northeast, Southeast, and all that. You need a geographical balance. We looked at the racial balance—white[s], Hispanics, women, male.[23]

When James was asked if all of these qualities were of equal importance, he responded: "They're all equal. Well, I'd have to put philosophy first, yes." In this case, philosophy can be translated as loyalty to the president and the president's ideology. Because he was a former professional in the executive search business, James put an emphasis on ability, although even he readily acknowledged that "philosophy" was the primus inter pares of attributes.

That brought him into conflict with those who made no bones about insisting that ideology and loyalty to Reagan were far more important than experience and competence were. Lyn Nofziger, who had served for years as Reagan's press secretary and political strategist, was made assistant to the president for political affairs when Reagan took office. Nofziger noted when he got to the Reagan White House:

> I found very quickly that the people who were running the personnel operation had no concept of the political part of government. They were looking for competent people. I tried to explain to them that the first thing you do is get loyal people, and competence is a bonus. We spent a lot of time making sure that Reagan people were getting into government, and that non-Reagan people were being kept out of government.[24]

Rewarding the right people for the right reasons seems to have been a consistent feature of Nofziger's approach to government. After he left the Reagan administration, he was convicted, fined, and jailed for multiple violations of the Federal Ethics in Government Act because of illegal lobbying activities.[25]

Another person who agreed with Nofziger's priorities, even though she worked for James and eventually went on to replace him as head of the OPP, was Helene Von Damm. She was an immigrant from Austria with a high school education, but she had worked her way up in Reagan's election campaigns and when he was governor of California. She was Reagan's personal secretary in the White House prior to moving to the OPP to become James's deputy.

In her memoir—which she used in the best Washington tradition to settle a few scores with her old adversaries in the administration—she explained how she viewed her job: "The Office of Presidential Personnel is key to the ideological tone of an administration. We had the responsibility for seeing to it that the Reagan Revolution was waged by true Reaganites. I looked for qualified, competent, intelligent people who shared our philosophy."[26] Although she did not list it first, it was clear that "sharing the philosophy" was an essential element of a job seeker's qualifications. It was also the Reagan philosophy as she defined it, and there were many people whom she did not consider conservative enough, including the first lady.

Although there was conflict between the advocates of competence and those who put ideology first, there are always other actors who push their own candidates for their own reasons, which may not have much to do with either quality. The vice president, cabinet officers, senior

White House staff, senators, congressmen, governors, and others can all put names forward and do their best to ensure their names are selected. In the end, it comes down to whose advice the president wants to follow, and that is entirely up to the president. But unless the president is personally acquainted with a candidate, much will depend on the personnel process that is established.

This process has been professionalized significantly, starting with the appointment of Fred Malek as the director of the Office of White House Personnel in 1970, during the Nixon administration. He created a group of 30 people that included experts in executive search business, such as Pen James. James described the problems the Nixon administration faced when making staffing decisions in his oral history:[27]

> What we recognized was that there were a lot of weaknesses in the administration, in the staffing. So we set up a group under Malek at this time. Say Fred's up here. Down here was me, and over here was a fellow by the name of Dan Kingsley. Every time there was a vacancy it was given to me and given to Dan. Dan was a political guy. He went out and saw who, politically, should be rewarded for this job. I was not a political guy. I went out and said, "Who can we find that can fill this job and do a good job, and recruit him or her in here?" That's how we separated and tried to make sure that when the President made the decision he had an option between the political guy who got him elected, or a substantive person.
>
> I have to say, to my amazement, Nixon always went to the substantive person. The reason he could do that was because there's a lot of jobs the President fills, so patronage—give them an ambassadorship, put them on a board or commission—you've got two thousand of them. But he really recognized that he made a mistake by staffing his administration in the old BOGSAT system and just bringing in cronies or politicians.

BOGSAT was the acronym James used to describe the White House personnel system before the OPP was enlarged and professionalized under Malek. It stands for "bunch of guys sitting around a table," with the "guys" being the president's closest advisors. Although the OPP provides the necessary administrative structure to handle the appointments process, before a decision goes to the president, the last stop is still those guys sitting around a table bargaining over whom to recommend to the president. How they handle that task and the inevitable conflicts that arise from it depend on the people the president puts into such positions and how much influence each of them have with that president.

There are other ways to be valuable to the winning candidate's campaign, which will be discussed shortly. First, consideration needs to be given to the question of how many ambassadorships the White House will have to fill. Despite the long tradition of a 30/70 ratio between political appointments and career officers, that number is always a result of negotiations between the White House and the State Department, and negotiations over specific posts can often be a source of conflict between the two organizations.

The degree of conflict is largely determined by the president's attitude and management style. When describing Reagan's foreign policy in *From Colony to Superpower*, Herring describes why there were so many conflicts during his presidency:

> Reagan was grandly indifferent to detail. He was the sloppiest administrator since Franklin Roosevelt. His White House staff was totally inexperienced in foreign policy, and amateur night was a regular occurrence.
>
> Conflict within the administration made the Vance-Brzezinski [the secretary of state and national security advisor respectively under President Carter] feud look like a love feast in comparison. Paraphrasing Air Force General Curtis LeMay, hard-line NSC staffer Richard Pipes observed that while the Soviets were the adversary, "the enemy was State." For its part, Haig's State Department refused to share important documents with the NSC. Reagan was isolated from the NSC by White House advisers and his wife, Nancy, who feared the ideologues who staffed it would reinforce his hardline tendencies. The policy process suffered from an excess of democracy, James Baker later recalled, "a witches' brew of intrigue, elbows, egos, and separate agendas." The most detached chief executive since Calvin Coolidge, Reagan refused to adjudicate the nasty disputes among his subordinates.[28]

A president who has a less strident ideology, a measure of respect for the Foreign Service, and a less chaotic management style would have an administration with far less conflict in the ambassadorial selection process. Presidents Carter and George H. W. Bush, the latter of whom was himself an ambassador, would fall into that category. The briefing materials prepared for Governor Romney encouraged him to take a collaborative rather than confrontational approach toward negotiating with the department about ambassadorships.

If the president believes career officers cannot be trusted to implement foreign policy, then the White House will push harder to put more men and women who share that president's philosophy in such positions than there were in the past. That is exactly what happened in the case of the Reagan administration. The State Department, Office of the Historian, in its *Short History of the Department of State*, described the Reagan era in uncharacteristically blunt language:

> The process of appointment of principal officers in the Department of State and ambassadors became increasingly politicized during the Reagan Administration, with some appointments causing controversy. Reagan was forced to withdraw the nomination of Ernest Lefever as assistant secretary of state for human rights and humanitarian affairs when a majority on the Senate Foreign Relations Committee concluded that he was not an advocate for human rights and rejected his nomination. The Foreign Service Act of 1980 stipulated that the President should "normally" appoint Foreign Service officers, not political supporters, as ambassadors. Nonetheless, during his first term Reagan proposed nearly as many political as Foreign Service ambassadors. The American Foreign Service Association charged in 1981 that this record made "a mockery of the careful selection and long and varied experience which professional career officers bring to senior assignments within the service." Although Shultz reversed the trend, the number of non-career ambassadors was higher under Reagan than under any President since Herbert Hoover. Although Reagan made some distinguished appointments from outside the Foreign Service—such as Arthur Burns in Bonn—his critics pointed to ambassadors of lesser distinction. [Under Secretary for Management Ron] Spiers publicly complained in 1987 that such appointments demonstrated "a lack of respect" that would "have a corrosive effect on the career service."[29]

Nowhere was that lack of respect more clearly demonstrated than in the people who followed Pen James as the head of Reagan's Office of Presidential Personnel. Helene Von Damm made her dislike and distrust of the State Department plain in her memoir with sentences such as:

- "The State Department is the most hidebound, stubborn, supercilious agency in Washington."
- "I regarded their claims to expertise skeptically. Sure, they knew languages and histories of the countries we deal with every day, but when it comes to the actual making of policy they are in no better position than anyone else to make decisions."
- "The State Department continued to be my bête noire for the length of my stay in personnel. I suppose if there was one area where I would say I and the Reagan administration failed, that was it."[30]

Von Damm saw enemies everywhere and not just at the State Department. She believed that many of Reagan's top advisors as well as Mrs. Reagan "were slowly diminishing the influence of all the conservatives in the administration" because they were not real conservatives in her estimation. She also apparently thought that being Reagan's secretary had given her more insight into the real Reagan than his wife possessed.[31]

In his oral history, Under Secretary Spiers discussed his relationship with some of Von Damm's successors and how negotiations with the White House about ambassador positions were complicated by the relationships between those who sat on the committee that made such decisions:

> Initially, I tried to develop a good working relationship with John Herrington, President Reagan's personnel chief, and that worked out well. I can remember very vividly the first time I went to his office. Herrington was very rough on me and the Foreign Service. He was almost rude. It became quite clear to me within minutes that he regarded my position as one to be occupied by a political appointee. He thought that [Secretary of State] Shultz had made a great mistake by not going outside the system to fill the Under Secretary's position.
>
> I was the first Under Secretary for Management who was not a political appointee. But after this rough start, we worked well together; although I was not his man in the Department, we spoke the same language. I liked him a lot. I found that he was someone with whom you could do business. He would tell me quite candidly whom they had to find jobs for and I would tell him whom we had that had to be placed. We worked out these problems in a cooperative way.
>
> I was able to discuss with him the concept of a career service and what my preoccupations were, such as my concerns for attracting and keeping first-rate people, if they felt that as they reached the zenith of their careers, they would be preempted for the most desirable assignments by less capable or experienced people. I told him that I had worked in London for political ambassadors, such as David Bruce, Elliot Richardson and Ann Armstrong, all of whom I found very good, but they were, unfortunately, not representative of the political appointees.
>
> Political appointees to ambassadorial positions present both a qualitative and quantitative problem. I firmly believe that a modicum of good political appointees is good for the Foreign Service. Herrington, in the final analysis, admitted that the White House had made a number of marginal appointments to Ambassadorial positions because they did not consider them to be very important. In essence, if the party owed someone a political debt, that could be paid off with an ambassadorial appointment because ambassadors "didn't do anything."

We had long dialogues about what an Ambassador really does and why he or she was important to the conduct of U.S. foreign policy as well as the President's success. It was a role that required quality people. Several times, I was able to tell Herrington that the person he wanted to place was not going to measure up and meet the requirements of the job. In those instances, he looked around the rest of the federal bureaucracies and found other assignments for those people. In summary, I think Herrington and I had a very good and productive relationship, but unfortunately it only lasted for a brief time because he was soon promoted to be Secretary of Energy.

Harrington was replaced by Bob Tuttle, with whom I could not have the same relationship. It was a very difficult time. Don Regan replaced Jim Baker as White House Chief of Staff beginning in 1985. He was also very difficult and was very angry with me at one point because I had made a speech to the National Association for Public Administration, parts of which had been quoted in an article. The speech was supposed to be off-the-record, but Bernie Gwertzman, I believe, had obtained a copy and wrote an article from it. That so incited Regan that he forbid me to attend White House meetings on Ambassadorial appointments.

These were periodic meetings in which the State Department was represented by the Deputy Secretary—first Ken Damm and later John Whitehead—and myself. The meetings were intended to be negotiating sessions for the allocation of Ambassadorial appointments between political appointees and career officers. That storm blew over after a brief time and after Howard Baker succeeded Regan, there was no further problem.

Tuttle was the son of a California car dealer who was a member of the Reagan "Kitchen Cabinet." He was [a] complete political animal and had no comprehension of the operations of the Department that Herrington had shown. He took a very mechanical approach to the placement of political appointees. In one instance, for example, I had succeeded in obtaining approval of a career officer as our Ambassador to Canada. Tuttle had wanted to send a political appointee. At the meeting with Regan, I said that Tuttle's man just was not appropriate and suggested a career officer—Tom Niles. The White House said OK, but wanted in exchange another Ambassadorial post. I suggested Equatorial Guinea, which they readily accepted. So we "traded" Canada for Equatorial Guinea, which is a commentary on the White House's approach to [the] placement of political appointees.[32]

Spiers notes that the White House believed they could name "marginal" candidates for ambassadorial appointments to pay off political debts because ambassadors do not do anything. As chapter 4 will discuss with regard to the nominations of three major fundraisers to be ambassadors in Hungary, Argentina, and Norway, that attitude appears to be alive and well in the Obama White House.

The Tuttle that Spiers referred to was Robert Tuttle. Tuttle's father, Holmes Tuttle, was a self-made man who had become wealthy by establishing a chain of auto dealerships. He was also part of Reagan's kitchen cabinet, the group of long-time friends and wealthy businessmen who served as Reagan's informal advisors. Robert Tuttle followed his father into the auto business and also parlayed his father's relationship with Reagan into a job in the White House. He was named director of the OPP in 1985 and held the position until the end of the Reagan administration.[33] Tuttle's description of how he handled these duties in his oral history interview made clear his attitude toward those with whom he had to work:

> As time went on, and I got the respect of Don Regan, I really did a lot of studying about Ambassadors. The Constitution is quite clear that the President has the absolute right to appoint the Ambassadors, but in the last 50 years Foreign Service Officers have garnered almost 70 percent of the ambassadorial appointments.
>
> What's happened, also, is the world has really changed. It's much more economic. Maybe they had a point after World War II at the height of the Cold War—and there are some places where there should be a Foreign Service Officer—but, if you think about it, almost everybody today has a lot of foreign experience. They've worked in other countries.
>
> The Associate Director I had working for me on foreign appointments was really good. State would send us—she would get a list of Ambassadors that were coming up. I said, "Let's get aggressive." Typically, what State wanted us to do—they would say, "Just have the President decide who he wants as non-career Ambassadors, and send us over a few names. They most likely will be golfing buddies of the President, or contributors, and we'll take care of them." I said, "You know what? We're going to put up a candidate for every post." But we've got to be serious about it. We would look at every country. We'd know three or four months in advance, and we'd start to go out and find people. Here again, the computer served us well.
>
> Now, I'm gaining the respect of Don Regan, so we have these ambassadorial meetings, which were attended by Don, John Whitehead, the National Security Advisor, and me. We present a candidate for every post, and as a result of that, and with the support of Don and the President, we got the percentage up to the highest it's been in a long time. It was over 40 percent. Of course, [Secretary of State] Shultz didn't like that at all.
>
> Remember when Shultz wanted to send Jack Matlock to Moscow? I didn't protest. But on the other countries, I think it's important to

propose a non-career candidate for each post. A lot of countries, not all of them, but Morocco, for example, has always wanted a non-career Ambassador. They perceive that that person has access to the President. I believe very strongly in non-career Ambassadors. I don't believe that because you've given money or your best friend is the President—ultimately, it's the President's decision, but I think it's the job of the Personnel Office to do the same thing in Ambassadors that we try to do in the other appointments—to find people who were both committed to the President's agenda and competent to serve in that country.

I would probably not be good for a lot of countries, but you might be. We didn't do it willy-nilly. We were very aggressive in that area, very aggressive, to the point where Shultz got real upset. I remember we had a meeting over at State. We had breakfast. My Associate Director who handled State had prepared a memo on Ambassadors, and it was really good. She was a lawyer. It was great. I gave it to Don [Regan]; I remember sitting there, and he starts in. He said, "George, I've been doing a lot of studies about Ambassadors," and out comes this memo. He was really good.[34]

Tuttle's description of the dynamics of these negotiations shows some of the important factors at work. Having no previous government experience, he was trying to gain respect as a bureaucrat and prove himself as a Reagan loyalist. He believed one way to accomplish that, and to implement the Reagan revolution at the same time, was by contesting every ambassadorial appointment and putting up a potential political appointee for each embassy, even though there was no precedent for such a practice in the twentieth century. If he shared Von Damm's belief that Shultz was not a true conservative, then angering the secretary of state in the process was just a bonus.

Although Shultz was willing to engage on behalf of the Foreign Service, Tuttle had a significant advantage. He reported to Donald Regan, the White House Chief of Staff, a powerful and aggressive boss who gave him license to act in the way he did. As Regan's obituary in *The New York Times* put it, "because of President Reagan's style of delegating authority, Mr. Regan was widely regarded as one of the most influential White House chiefs of staff. The post enabled him to determine much of what the president heard and saw day to day."[35]

Reagan's style of delegating authority, his lack of interest in the details of governing, and his reliance on long-time friends and advisers more than foreign-policy heavyweights and Washington experts did not only affect personnel decisions. He was the only president in modern times to not issue formal rules in his first days in office designed to govern how national security decisions were to be made.[36] The resulting chaos, which was described by Herring, also played a part in later events, including the Iran-Contra scandal.

The lack of bureaucratic structure and the ability to control access to the president was a source of great power for Regan, but they ultimately led to his disgrace. With people like Oliver North running operations designed to please the president and respond to his vague guidance in spite of being illegal, scandal was inevitable. When it happened, Regan became a convenient scapegoat and was fired in February 1987.

According to the independent counsel that investigated the Iran-Contra affair, Regan "was forced to resign because he was unable to contain the continuing political damage being done to President Reagan by public exposure of the Iran-Contra matters."[37] The story of his dismissal appeared in the media before Regan was informed of it. Tuttle called Frank Carlucci, another White House official, and insisted that Carlucci give Regan the news. Characteristically, Reagan had avoided an unpleasant conversation by not even informing his chief of staff that he was fired. Carlucci, after checking with Reagan and urging him to tell Regan personally, had to then rush to Regan's office to tell him that the news was true and insist that he had to take the call from the president.[38]

In such an environment, lower-level officials, have as much authority as they want to assume and can get away with, as Oliver North showed in his contribution to the Iran-Contra scandal. Lower-level functionaries like Tuttle and Von Damm were therefore able to affect the personnel process much more than they could in a White House with more bureaucratic structure and with a chief of staff who had less power.

Ironically, although both Tuttle and Von Damm made no secret of their contempt for the State Department, both pulled the necessary strings to become ambassadors themselves. Von Damm left the OPP to return to her native Austria as ambassador. As she describes in her memoir, while in Vienna, she dumped her husband of many years and married for the fourth time. The lucky man was an Austrian whom she thought was handsome, sophisticated, charming, and wealthy.[39]

She was then surprised when there was such a negative reaction in Washington toward her marriage to a national of the country to which she was accredited that she was asked to step down. She found this all the more unjustified because, by her account, there was not a newspaper in Austria that did not editorialize about what a great job she had done.[40] After she lost her title of ambassador, the charming Austrian husband did not hang around long. Within six months, he declared the marriage over "without warning, emotion, or a trace of guilt" according to Von Damm.[41]

Tuttle did not go directly from his White House position to an ambassadorship. He returned to California but stayed active in politics and put his considerable inheritance to good use maintaining political contacts and making contributions to political campaigns.[42] He became ambassador in London in 2005 under George W. Bush and did his best to use public diplomacy to shore up waning British support for the war in Iraq, even though he was often out of step with official pronouncements from Washington.[43]

The conflict and chaos that were the hallmarks of the Reagan administration changed dramatically when George H. W. Bush succeeded him. Bush wanted to continue with Reagan's conservative philosophy regarding policy, but he could not have been more different from his predecessor in his attitude toward the Foreign Service. Untermeyer described this approach and the White House's relationship with the State Department as follows:

> The special view that George Bush took toward ambassadorships was that he certainly was going to name people who were not career Foreign Service. At the same token he honored and admired the Foreign Service. He had actually, after all, worked with the Foreign Service in many posts along the way. He had great confidence in their skills and ability, and he didn't view the situation as a sort of battle in which the appointees of the President had to fight an entrenched Foreign Service in order to try to carry out the foreign policy of the President.
>
> He was determined, in fact, to increase the percentage of ambassadorships held by career Foreign Service officers. At the end of the Reagan administration, the proportion was approximately 65 percent career, 35 percent non-career, and sometimes it had slipped if you will or the number of Foreign Service officers had slipped somewhere down toward 60 percent. Bush very much wanted to get it as quickly as possible to a 2/3, 1/3 split; that is 67 percent Foreign Service and eventually up to 70 percent, which was the goal, and I believe he attained it, although that was after I left Presidential Personnel. This was also a very conscious area to avoid what happened in the Reagan administration.
>
> The Reagan administration, or at least people in it if not Ronald Reagan, did have a great deal of suspicion and hostility toward the Foreign Service and felt that the President's wishes could only be protected by a much larger number of non-career Foreign Service officers. There therefore was a constant battle, literally fought out in the Roosevelt Room of the West Wing in which delegates, you might say, of the State Department would arrive to face people from Presidential Personnel and

they would wrangle over every ambassadorship, even those posts that had always gone to Foreign Service officers in dusty tropical places that you wouldn't think a Beverly Hills resident would ever want to go. But usually the White House would have a candidate and they would fight it out and out of this would come the deal. The deal would be, you get some and we get some.

This was a case in which, to many people in the conservative movement, and I say specifically in the Reagan White House, that they did not view George Shultz as an ally of the President. George Shultz was certainly emphatically conservative on foreign policy issues, but perhaps as his way of making peace within the State Department family, he fought the Foreign Service's battle in the White House over ambassadorships. So there was a great deal of feeling that the Secretary of State was not a friend when it came to these matters. I needn't go into too many details of what I heard happened in the Reagan White House, since I wasn't there, but needless to say, George Bush wanted to avoid this.

The relationship between the White House and the State Department was different because Bush's management style, opinion of career diplomats, and relationship with his secretary of state were all very different from those of Reagan. Given James Baker's relationship with President Bush, Untermeyer just took Baker's suggestions for ambassadors and positions within the State Department, as well, and processed them.

Untermeyer notes that not all cabinet secretaries were created equal when it came to the appointments within their departments, however:

There were certain Cabinet officers, namely Jim Baker and Nick Brady and to some extent Bob Mosbacher, who would, of course, get what they wanted just because of who they were. The more troublesome cases came with, you might say, the second tier of Cabinet officers who were politically astute, not part of the Bush first circle, who nevertheless knew the ways of Washington and were clearly out to get their appointees.

And then there was a third tier of Cabinet Secretaries who were less insistent on "their appointments." I found that that phrase was one that I wished that I had a Presidential bar of soap that could scrub out the mouths of any Cabinet Secretary who referred to assistant secretarial level jobs as "my appointments." Because, of course, they are the President's appointments.[44]

A secretary of state and other cabinet members will have varying degrees of control over the presidential appointments within their departments. The degree of control will depend on the extent to which the president, and by extension the senior White House staff, are willing to delegate that authority. The influence of a cabinet secretary also increases if he or she has three things—a personal relationship with the president that allows the secretary's opinions to be given weight, the bureaucratic ability to see those opinions get expressed at the right time and place in the process, and the interest to invest the time and effort required to have an impact on the process.

But there are other factors that determine who gets a presidential appointment besides the relative power of a cabinet secretary and the ideology and ability of the job seeker. This is where the economic, political, or personal relationship with the president or someone who has influence on the president comes into play. An economic relationship simply means the person contributes generously to the president's election campaign or to those of other influential politicians. There is no shortage of examples of this kind or relationship.

Pen James noted that President Nixon consistently put substantive candidates ahead of ones who got him elected. Jerry Jones, who also worked with Malek in the OPP, also observed that Nixon put ability ahead of ideology. He quoted Nixon as saying, "I want excellent people. We are not going to put dumb-o's in these jobs. I don't care what they did for us in the campaign."[45]

Either Nixon's priorities changed after a few years in office or he was more honest about his priorities with his closest advisors and simply putting on an act for those who worked in the White House personnel office. A White House tape recording made public in 1997 revealed that in mid-1971 Nixon told his chief of staff, H. R. Haldeman, "my point is that anybody who wants to be an ambassador must at least give $250,000."[46]

In 2011, the transcript of Nixon's testimony to a grand jury investigating the Watergate scandal was made public. On that occasion, Nixon was colorful but not as candid as he was with his chief of staff. At one point, he explains to the grand jury why it was not vitally important to have an ambassador to Luxembourg who does not have "extraordinary" qualifications for the position. As will be discussed in chapter 5, this was not the last time the ambassador to that country was less than extraordinary.

In making this point, Nixon cited the example of a wealthy socialite named to that post by President Truman, saying that "Pearl Mesta wasn't sent to Luxembourg because she had big bosoms. Pearl Mesta went to Luxembourg because she made a good contribution." Presumably Nixon was not referring to a cash contribution, although he added, "but may I say she was a very good ambassador in Luxembourg. And when you talk about selling ambassadorships, I don't want the record of this grand jury even to indicate that people of wealth, because they do make contributions, therefore should be barred from being ambassadors."[47]

Nixon was at least true to his word when he said contributions should not preclude appointment as ambassador to Luxembourg. Nixon's personal lawyer, Herbert Kalmbach, went to jail for illegal campaign fund solicitations and helping raise money to buy the silence of the seven men involved in the Watergate burglary. One of the people with whom he discussed contributions and ambassadorial appointments was Ruth Farkas, the wife of the founder of a chain of department stores.

Kalmbach testified that Peter Flanigan, a senior White House aide, told him that Farkas was interested in giving $250,000 in exchange for being named ambassador to Costa Rica. But when they met to discuss it, Kalmbach discovered she had a different opinion. In what has become a classic line cited ever since in articles about the selling of ambassadorships, she reportedly said to Kalmbach, "isn't $250,000 an awful lot of money for Costa Rica?"[48]

She and her husband had never previously contributed to Nixon's campaign, but they had supported other Republican politicians, including Congressman John Wyman of New Hampshire. Wyman, who went on to lose a Senate race by the narrowest of margins, had been calling White House and State Department officials since 1969 on behalf of Mrs. Farkas in an effort to get her an ambassadorship.[49] His efforts finally paid off when on September 20, 1972, Flanigan telephoned Wyman to inform him that Farkas had been approved for Luxembourg.

On September 28, she met with Maurice Stans, the finance chairman of Nixon's reelection campaign. Less than a week later, the first installment was made of what eventually totaled $300,000 in contributions to the campaign. Six days after the final payment was received on February 21, 1973, the White House sent her nomination to be ambassador to Luxembourg to the Senate.[50] Even though Senator J. William Fulbright, the chairman of the Senate Foreign Relations Committee, voted against her and denounced the appointment, Farkas was approved and presented her credentials in Luxembourg in May 1973.

When asked about his role in the affair, Wyman insisted that it was not a specific exchange of an ambassadorship for the contributions, but he claimed the money merely established her "eligibility" for the job.[51] The reaction of Senator Gale McGee, a Democrat from Wyoming, also saw no impropriety in what was clearly a pay-to-play arrangement. McGee, a member of the Foreign Relations Committee, even laughed about the custom of giving ambassadorships to big campaign contributors, saying "the money—that's par for the course. It used to be a cheaper price, but that's Nixon's inflation."[52]

Farkas did have other qualifications that helped establish her eligibility besides the size of her bank account, and these no doubt helped her win confirmation. She had an MA from Columbia and a PhD from New York University, spoke French and Spanish, had worked for years as a professor at New York University, and was an authority in educational sociology.

She was quickly confirmed by the Senate and went to post. She was considered to have done a good job as ambassador, but ironically she was not happy. Her deputy, James Phillips, went into her office one day and found her in tears. She was distraught because her husband spent little time in Luxembourg and she had tired of being separated from him and wanted to leave. She said the White House insisted she stay, however, because Wyman was then running for the Senate and her departure might set off some unwanted newspaper coverage. As soon as the election was over, she left.[53]

Farkas was not the only one in her family to question the cost of her appointment. Her husband complained that $300,000 was too high a price to pay for such a small country like Luxembourg. He did have a point. That amount in 1972, once adjusted for inflation, would exceed $1.5 million today, which the research of my colleague Johannes Fedderke and I find would be more in line with what it would take to buy London.[54]

In her oral history, Farkas said she got angry at the suggestion that she bought her ambassadorship for what she said was a $175,000 contribution before the election and an equal amount after Nixon was reelected.[55] Although she had other qualifications that could be used to argue that the appointment was based on merit and not just on money, there are other instances where that kind of argument is impossible to make with a straight face.

One such case is Joy Silverman, who was nominated to be ambassador to Barbados by President George H. W. Bush in 1989. The appointment was strongly opposed by Senator Paul Sarbanes, a Democrat on the Foreign Relations Committee who pointed out that Silverman had "no foreign policy experience, no job history and no college degree."[56] The best that President Bush could do in his statement announcing her nomination was to note that she had been active in his election campaign and to point out that she had attended the University of Maryland, sat on a couple of boards, and had done some charity work.[57]

Although she had apparently never worked for a living, she did not have to, because she was born into a wealthy family and married well. She and her husband gave generously to Republican causes and supplemented those contributions by holding fundraising events for Republican candidates. Charles Untermeyer, the director of the OPP at the time, criticized Sarbanes for blocking the nomination and asserted: "This isn't over yet. She is the person the President has the fullest trust in to go to Barbados and we're eager to see her get there."[58]

In his oral history interview, Untermeyer gave a somewhat different spin on the nomination. He recalled that there was "a very delightful woman named Joy Silverman from New York who had been a major fundraiser, who was named to the highly crucial post of Barbados, who actually had to have her name withdrawn because of Sarbanes's objecting to her not being prepared for that post."[59] According to this view, being a socialite is sufficient preparation to be an ambassador to an island nation in the Caribbean.

Given her lack of any meaningful qualifications or experience, it is reasonable to assume that Silverman earned the president's trust by buying it. Despite Untermeyer's defiant stance, the nomination was sent back to the White House, and Silverman asked that it not be resubmitted to the Senate. Even given the resistance from Sarbanes and the publicity generated by the confrontation, it is not clear that President Bush would not have tried again otherwise.

The abuses of the Nixon administration that made the name of a condominium complex on the Potomac synonymous with government scandal prompted the passage of the Federal Election Campaign Act in 1974 and the Ethics in Government Act in 1978.[60] As the Silverman case indicates, those laws did not eliminate the practice of nominating people for ambassadorships in exchange for campaign cash.

Money is an increasingly vital concern of any politician aspiring to be the next occupant of the White House. The modern presidential campaign has become a hugely expensive operation. In the 2008 election, spending for the campaigns of Senator McCain and Senator Obama reached a combined total of one billion dollars. In 2012, the amount spent on the campaigns of Governor Romney and President Obama each surpassed the billion-dollar mark.[61]

Despite the fact that the Federal Elections Commission has been rendered largely ineffective by partisan politics, lax enforcement, loopholes, and unclear laws and regulations,[62] there are limits to what a person can contribute to a presidential candidate.[63] The limit is adjusted in odd-numbered years for inflation, but currently the amount an individual can give to each candidate is only $2,600. When the possible donations to political action committees, the national committee of a party, and other candidates are included, the maximum rises to a biennial limit of $123,200. In April 2014, the conservative majority of the Supreme Court struck down that overall limit in *McCutcheon v. the Federal Election Commission*. This decision followed on the same path as the *Citizens United* case, where the court held that corporations should be granted the same freedom of speech as individuals are and should be able to spend unlimited amounts of money on attack ads. Justice Stephen Breyer, writing for the four justices who dissented, noted that the decision would allow "a single individual to contribute millions of dollars to a political party or to a candidate's campaign."[64]

The limitation that existed prior to these decisions seemed largely meaningless, however, seeing as there were other ways for an individual to funnel money into elections with no limits. Sheldon Adelson, a billionaire casino owner, became the largest contributor to an election in American history in 2012. He and his wife gave at least $100 million and probably closer to $155 million according to one study done by ProPublica, an investigative journalism foundation.[65] If it is the higher figure, it would be six times the previous record for campaign contributions by an individual.[66]

There will not be an Ambassador Adelson any time soon, however, given that the money went to Mitt Romney and a host of other losing Republican candidates. It may not have been such a bad bet by the casino owner, though. Had Romney been elected and implemented his proposals on taxes, Adelson would have enjoyed a $2 billion tax cut according to one estimate.[67] And criminal investigations by the Justice Department of Adelson's operations might have also quietly gone away.

Besides direct contributions, another way to help a candidate is to bundle the money given by others. Those types of contributions do not have to be reported. Although McCain and Obama did so voluntarily in 2008, in 2012 Romney refused to disclose who his bundlers were. The Obama campaign, on the other hand, listed more than 700 "volunteer fundraisers" who had bundled more than $50,000 in 2012.[68] Furthermore, donations to the presidential inauguration have no limits, so that is another way to show one's support for the president and to ingratiate oneself. There is therefore no shortage of people who will have a substantial economic relationship with a new president.

Because there are so many people with that kind of relationship to the president, campaign contributions are not enough to seal the deal if that is all the person has in his or her favor. They need a patron. Clearly Congressman Wyman labored long and hard to ensure that Ruth Farkas's eligibility for the job was recognized and rewarded.

Some politicians are not shy about pushing the White House staff about their favorite candidates. When Robert Tuttle was asked what aspect of being Reagan's personnel director was the most onerous, he said: "The worst experience I had was with Senator [Alfonse] D'Amato. Again our legislative director asked me to meet with D'Amato because of someone D'Amato wanted to be an Ambassador and we hadn't delivered. I never had anyone talk to me like that, including my own drill sergeant in basic training."[69]

D'Amato did not fail to get all of the appointments he sought for his friends. Chase Untermeyer described how in the transition from President Reagan to his successor, all of the noncareer ambassadors were immediately replaced, with one exception: "I recall retaining only one Ronald Reagan Ambassador as of 1989, a fellow named Charlie Gargano, who was a political ally of Senator D'Amato of New York, and it was a way of doing a nice thing for Senator D'Amato. So Charlie Gargano stayed in Trinidad, but everybody else was subject to being replaced."[70]

Gargano began his career in public service in 1981 when President Reagan named him deputy administrator of the Federal Urban Mass Transportation Administration.[71] His ability to make friends in high places, like D'Amato, and to use his positions for personal gain led to his ambassadorship. But as will be discussed in chapter 4, it prevented him from getting a second one.

Presidents also have personal friends, and those relationships can be used as springboards to ambassadorships. One example is Vinai K. Thummalapally, who was named to Belize by President Obama in 2009. Thummalapally had the good fortune to have Barry Obama as a roommate in the summer of 1980 at Occidental College. (Barry is the name the president used at that point in his life.) The two spent some of their time together debating foreign policy, watching Lakers basketball games, and partying.[72]

It no doubt helped that Thummalapally financially assisted his former roommate's election campaign. He reportedly bundled contributions in the $100,000 to $200,000 range. Thummalapally's predecessor in Belize was also the college roommate of the president who nominated him—George W. Bush.

Sharing a dorm room with a future president is extremely useful for one's career. Going to college together or with someone close to a future president can also be helpful. Crystal Nix-Hines, who was nominated by Obama in 2013 to be ambassador to UNESCO, the United Nations Educational, Scientific, and Cultural Organization, headquartered in

Paris, did both. She attended Princeton with Michelle Obama as an undergraduate and then went to Harvard Law School with the president.[73] Nix-Hines was also a top fundraiser for the president, bundling more than $1.2 million for him since 2007.[74]

Sometimes going to college together is enough. George W. Bush appointed Roy Austin as ambassador to Trinidad and Tobago. Austin had given no money to Bush or the Republican Party and had not been active in politics.[75] He had, however, gone to Yale with Bush, and both belonged to Skull and Bones, a secret society that also counts Secretary of State John Kerry, Bush's opponent in 2004, among its members. Bush appointed at least ten Bonesmen to government positions according to one article.[76]

Born in the Caribbean, Austin was a Penn State professor and an expert in the region, but he claimed in one interview that he made no effort to get the job.[77] Besides his friendship with Bush, Austin had one other thing going for him, however. He is African American. Elections are won not only with huge amounts of money but also by energizing a party's core constituencies and getting them to go vote. It should be obvious even to a casual observer of politics that the Republican and Democratic parties do not have the same constituencies and therefore make their appeals to motivate different groups of voters. Rewarding representatives of those constituencies will be part of the calculation in determining who becomes an ambassador.

Even though 90 percent or more of African Americans typically vote for the Democratic candidate for president, it is not a group that the Republicans can afford to ignore. To appoint no ambassadors of color would be to invite charges of racism, and therefore it is mandatory for Republican presidents to recruit candidates like Professor Austin to avoid that accusation.

There are other kinds of political factors that result in ambassadorships even for unlikely candidates. Obama nominated Jon Huntsman, the former Republican governor of Utah, as ambassador to China in 2009. Huntsman was one of the cochairmen for the campaign of Obama's opponent, Senator John McCain, but he had extensive Asian experience and was fluent in Mandarin Chinese.

In his remarks announcing the appointment, President Obama noted Huntsman's Republican roots, but he justified the appointment by saying that a man of Huntsman's experience and knowledge could bring about a new relationship with China.[78] Others read a more political motive into the move, with some claiming it was designed to ensure that Huntsman would not oppose the president in the 2012 election.[79]

If that was the intention, it did not work, given that Huntsman resigned in January 2011 and returned to the United States to campaign for the Republican nomination. He never gained any significant support from Republican primary voters, however, and was never a serious contender for the nomination. He was apparently too moderate and was criticized by some conservatives for associating himself with the Obama administration.

If Huntsman's nomination to be ambassador to China was motivated by political factors, it may not have been the last time it was used for that purpose. In December 2014, President Obama announced he was naming Max Baucus to the post. An article in the *Washington Post* listed three reasons why Obama might want to send Baucus, a Democratic senator from Montana who had announced he was not running for reelection, to Beijing.[80] First, it would allow the Democratic governor in Montana to appoint a replacement until the next election and thereby help the Democrats maintain their majority in the Senate by giving that person a leg up on any Republican challenger. Second, it would remove a credible critic of the president's health care initiative. And third, Baucus is familiar with China because he has worked on trade issues and visited the country on several occasions. Like most things in Washington, the relative importance of each of these reasons, if indeed they do reflect the motivation of the White House, is impossible to determine. But knowing something about China came in third on the *Washington Post*'s list.

Ambassadorial appointments can also be used politically in other ways, such as to compensate for real or imagined weaknesses in the president's résumé or to fill particularly sensitive posts. Military officers are occasionally called upon to play such a role.

Neither President Obama nor President Clinton had any military experience and were criticized by commentators, who implied that this lack would cause them to be weak on matters of national defense. They both appointed former military officers as ambassadors. Clinton sent William Crowe, a former admiral and chairman of the Joint Chiefs of Staff, to London. According to his obituary in *The New York Times*, Crowe was one of the few retired senior officers who endorsed Clinton during the election campaign, "undercutting Republican criticism that Mr. Clinton's objections to the Vietnam War would make him unacceptable to the military."[81]

Clinton also named Pete Peterson as the first post-war ambassador to Vietnam. Renewing diplomatic relations with Vietnam was controversial at the time and some wanted a fuller account of missing American servicemen before taking such a step. The fact that Peterson was not only a former military officer but also a prisoner of war during the conflict helped overcome such resistance.

On President Obama's part, he named several former generals as ambassadors. For example, Karl Eikenberry was sent to Afghanistan, which was an important mission, seeing as Obama had balanced his policy of getting out of Iraq with a troop surge in Afghanistan. Having a former general as ambassador would show that the military relationship was the most important part of our interest in that county. Ironically, Eikenberry strongly opposed the surge, telling Washington that it would only deepen the dependence of an unreliable ally on American armed forces.[82] He was ignored, and the surge went ahead anyhow.

President George W. Bush had military experience and was apparently immune from charges that he would be weak on national defense because of a lack of experience in uniform. He appointed no career military men as ambassadors. His military service, however, consisted only of pulling strings to jump to the head of a two-year waiting list to get into the Texas Air National Guard. Serving in the reserves at that time, unlike today, was a guaranteed way to avoid seeing combat.

Bush was not the only one to use such tactics to dodge the draft. Dan Quayle, the vice president of Mr. Bush's father, and John Bolton, the ultra-hawkish conservative, used the same means of serving in that part of the military in order to eliminate any chance of being sent to Vietnam.[83] Bolton was appointed by Bush to be ambassador to the United Nations, yet he was never confirmed, even though the Republicans had a majority in the Senate at the time. He is now a regular commentator on Fox News and invariably pushes an aggressive approach to every issue especially when it comes to sending troops abroad to fight.

Ambassadorial posts can also be used to reward campaign workers, loyal staffers, and long-time political allies. President Clinton's ambassadors to Japan were former Senator and Vice President Walter Mondale and former Speaker of the House Tom Foley. The current ambassador in Tokyo is Caroline Kennedy. She has had no significant experience that would qualify her for the job and contributed only a few hundred dollars to President Obama's campaign, but she did give him an early and enthusiastic endorsement in 2008 by comparing Obama to her father.[84]

Sometimes ambassadorships are considered consolation prizes for politicians who are voted out of office. In his oral history interview at the Miller Center, former President Carter talked about the possibility of giving them to members of congress who had taken an unpopular stand on an issue and been defeated for reelection.[85]

On other occasions, ambassadorial posts can be used to solve difficult personnel problems in Washington. Chase Untermayer gave the following description of how he dealt with the fact that Bruce Gelb, the director of the US Information Agency, could not get along with Richard Carlson, who was the director of Voice of America and nominally his subordinate:

> Dick Carlson is a very able, polished man from California who had been in broadcasting out there and became director of Voice of America in the Reagan administration. He was one of those whom we retained in a particular position. He was an old face who stayed in an old place you might say, because he was so very good. Bruce Gelb was a personal friend of President [George H. W.] Bush, not necessarily one of his closest friends, but he was somebody he'd known going back as far as Andover days and was from New York. His brother Richard Gelb was the CEO of Bristol-Myers, and Bruce had been involved in the company business and certainly been a big Bush supporter. He very much wanted to be head of the USIA and that was an early decision to put him there. He was not a successful choice unfortunately, because he was not well suited to government life. He was not able to get along well with people in other departments and agencies or within his own, and it was just a very uncomfortable fit.
>
> One of those with whom he sparred was Dick Carlson. Now, Dick Carlson was more sinned against than sinning in this entire operation, but he liked to give back as much as he got from Bruce Gelb. So Dick got a certain degree of blame for keeping this feud going, which broke into the open and required some active mediation in the West Wing of the White House by David Bates and me, David Bates being the Secretary to the Cabinet, which is the function in any White House for liaison from the White House or the President out to departments and agencies.
>
> So it fell to David and me to try and mediate this dispute. We brought the two parties together as I recall in 1990, and we sat them down and had about an hour's harangue in which they talked the issue out, and just like in marriage counseling we got them to agree to try another time and to work together and to try to move on so as to serve the administration. Well, our success was brief and Bruce Gelb and Dick Carlson got at it again, which led to a decision, about a year later, that they both had to go. As I said, Dick Carlson was the more aggrieved party in all of this, but it was clear that we couldn't leave Dick Carlson in his spot and only get rid of Bruce Gelb, since Bruce

Gelb was the old friend of the President and he would have felt particularly hurt and betrayed.

So, in the classic way that things happen in government, ambassadorships were found for both of these individuals.[86]

In other words, when Untermeyer's best efforts to get the two to reconcile their differences failed, embassies were found to which to they could each be sent. To solve the personnel problem without looking like anyone was being fired, Gelb was made ambassador to Belgium and Carlson was sent as ambassador to the Seychelles.

Untermeyer referred to the Seychelles as the "country club islands" because of their scenic beauty. During the Clinton administration, the embassy in the Seychelles was closed as a cost-cutting move, so that particular country club is no longer a full-time option. The ambassador in Mauritius is accredited to the Seychelles and visits the islands only occasionally.

Whether it is to county-club islands or the most important capitals in the world, presidents do not appoint noncareer ambassadors solely because of merit or because of the belief that they are the very best person for the job. They appoint those who are most successful at self-promotion. But it is not simply a question of singing one's own praises. *The New York Times* reporter Nicholas Confessore had this advice on how to play the game:

> Interviews with more than a dozen donors, Democratic officials and advisers involved in the discussions revealed some unspoken rules: Volunteer for more than one country. Be prepared to serve for only two years, so that a second round of envoys can be appointed before Mr. Obama leaves office. Don't mention how much money you raised for the campaign (but don't expect much if you didn't raise at least a million dollars). Let it be known where you want to go, but don't publicly campaign for the job.[87]

This advice applies mostly to campaign contributors. Successful aspiring ambassadors can also have personal or political relationships with the president and not just economic ones. In analyzing the backgrounds of political appointees in recent administrations, it is nearly impossible to find a case in which there is no evidence of at least one if not more of these three kinds of relationships coming into play.

Regardless of the type of relationship with the president and the initial route to the nomination being markedly different from the one that career officers take, the remaining steps on the road to an embassy are the same. Once they get the president's approval, the budding ambassadors have to go through the clearance process and be confirmed by the Senate. Although those steps should be routine and automatic, they rarely are. They can take longer than the initial phases, and they can end the hopes of an aspiring ambassador for the most unlikely reasons. That is what will be described in chapter 4.

CHAPTER 4

The Last Steps—Clearance and Confirmation

Although career officers and political appointees take different routes to the president's desk, once the president approves their names, they all undergo the same final two steps of the process—clearance and confirmation. A great deal of initial screening takes place before a person's name is put before the president for approval, but it is not nearly as detailed as what takes place during the clearance phase.

The State Department will have reviewed the records of career officers and checked with the offices that handle discrimination and sexual harassment complaints, security violations, and other kinds of infractions that might be reported officially. Political appointees will have been reviewed as well, with calls to references and no doubt a quick run through an Internet search engine.

These cursory examinations reveal only the most obvious obstacles, however. There are a large and growing number of issues that can derail an appointment, and the small mountain of paperwork that is required from those being considered is intended to bring these problems to light before the president publicly announces the appointment and sends it to the Senate.

Each administration makes up its own questionnaire reflecting its own concerns and the latest problems that may have cropped up in the process, and all appointees—career and political alike—have to begin the clearance phase by responding to it. In 2008, the Obama administration used a form with 63 questions to determine the suitability of its ambassadorial candidates and nominees for other presidential appointments. The full questionnaire can be found in appendix A. Here are the eight sections it contains and a few of the questions from each section to give an indication of the breadth of the search for problems:

1. *Professional background*: Briefly describe the most controversial matters you have been involved with during the course of your career.

2. *Publications, writings and speeches*: If you have ever sent an electronic communication, including but not limited to an email, text message or instant message, that could suggest a conflict of interest or be a possible source of embarrassment to you, your family, or the President-Elect if it were made public, please describe... If you keep or have ever kept a diary that contains anything that could suggest a conflict of interest or be a possible source of embarrassment to you, your family, or the President-Elect if it were made public, please describe.

3. *Relationships and affiliations*: Please specifically describe any affiliation you, or your spouse or any member of your immediate family have, or have had, with any financial, banking, mortgage or insurance institution that is currently the subject of federal government intervention as part of the ongoing economic crisis. This question includes, but is not limited to, the following: Fannie Mae, Freddie Mac, AIG, and Washington Mutual.

4. *Financial information*: Are there any categories of personal financial records (e.g., individual, partnership or sole proprietorship tax returns, mortgage documents, loan agreements) that you (or your spouse) will not release publicly if necessary? If so, please identify these records and state the reasons for withholding them.

5. *Tax information*: Please furnish a copy of each federal and state (and, if applicable, municipal or foreign) tax return, including any amended return, for 2005 and all subsequent years. If filed separately, furnish the same documents for your spouse.

6. *Legal and administrative proceedings*: If you have ever been investigated by any law enforcement agency (whether federal, state, military, local, Indian, or foreign), arrested for, charged with, or convicted of violating any law, regulation or ordinance (whether federal, state, military, local, Indian, or foreign), please identify each such instance and supply details, including: date, place; law enforcement agency; and court. Provide the same information for your spouse and for each child over 21, and for any business with which you have been affiliated (e.g., as a director, officer, partner, trustee, or holder of any significant ownership interest), and

furnish all pertinent records. You may exclude traffic offenses for which the fine was less than $50.

7. *Domestic help*: Do you presently have or have you in the past had occasional (to be sure, a monthly housekeeper is covered) or regular domestic help (e.g., a housekeeper, babysitter, nanny, or gardener)? If yes, please indicate the name and years of service for each individual and also provide a brief description of the services rendered. Have you complied with all federal, state and local laws and regulations related to the employment of individuals listed?

8. *Miscellaneous*: If applicable, please list the names, addresses and phone number of cohabitants within the last ten years. A cohabitant is a person with whom you share bonds of affection, obligation, or other commitment, as opposed to a person with whom you live for reasons of convenience (roommate) ... Please provide the URL address of any websites that feature you in either a personal or professional capacity (e.g., Facebook, My Space, etc.) ... Do you or any members of your immediate family own a gun? If so, provide complete ownership and registration information. Has the registration ever lapsed? Please also describe how and by whom it is used and whether it has been the cause of any personal injuries or property damage ... Have you had a complete physical within the past year? Please describe your overall health and any medical treatment you are currently receiving ... Do you know anyone or any organization, either in the private sector or government service, that might take steps, overtly or covertly, fairly or unfairly, to criticize your nomination, including any news organization? If so, please identify and explain the potential basis for criticism.

The last of the 63 questions sums up the purpose of this enormous and time-consuming effort:

Please provide any other information, including information about other members of your family, that could suggest a conflict of interest or be a possible source of embarrassment to you, your family, or the President-Elect.[1]

Once a presidential appointment is announced and sent to the Senate for confirmation, the cost of it going down in flames because of some previously unpublicized problem is more than just embarrassment to the nominee. It can damage the president's reputation and give the impression that the administration is so poorly run that it cannot even select capable and competent people for senior positions.

The problem is that the list of potential pitfalls is long and keeps on growing. Prior to the Clinton administration, not much attention was paid to the domestic help that a nominee employed. That ended when Clinton nominated Zoë Baird to be attorney general. She had admitted to the White House staff and Senator Joe Biden, the then chairman of the Judiciary Committee, weeks before her confirmation hearing that she had hired two illegal immigrants to work as a nanny and driver and had not paid their Social Security taxes. Neither the White House nor Biden thought at the time that was enough of a problem to disqualify her.

Once her hiring practices became public, the criticism from the media and Republicans poured forth. *The New York Times* editorialized that the president, his advisers and Senator Biden seemed "separated by some invisible shield from the feelings of everyday Americans" and were unprepared for the public to be angry about the revelation that the nominee for the most senior law enforcement position in the government had knowingly violated the law. This, the *Times* pointed out, was not fulfilling Clinton's "promise to hold his appointees to the highest standards."[2] As a result of this incident, all subsequent nominees have had another set of disclosures to make and another standard that they were required to uphold. The list of these standards continues to grow as new problems arise and new forms of potential embarrassment are discovered. In the Obama administration's questionnaire, concern about any relationship to the economic recession brought on in part by mortgage lending abuses is evident.

Technology and social media are also providing new opportunities for aspiring presidential appointees to inflict mortal wounds on their chances for the job. The possibility that emails, texts, instant messages, and Facebook posts might contain revelations that would make someone unable to be confirmed must now be addressed.

And even seemingly innocent leisure activities can lead to disqualification. Take the case of Marc Lasry, a billionaire hedge fund manager who bundled $856,606 for President Obama's election campaign.[3] Lasry also had a close relationship with Bill and Hillary Clinton and employed their daughter, Chelsea, for a number of years.[4] The relationship was so close, in fact, that the former president announced at two fundraising events in New York City that Lasry was about to be named as Obama's next ambassador to France. The events were raising funds for Terry McAuliffe, who was running for the governor of Virginia.

They were also described by people close to McAuliffe as "a test run for the Clinton network of donors and supporters" in advance of a run for president by Mrs. Clinton in 2016.[5]

Unfortunately, in addition to being a major donor, Mr. Lasry also had the habit of playing high stakes poker in games arranged by people who ran a nationwide criminal enterprise. In April 2013, federal prosecutors in New York indicted 34 people, including Lasry's pokers friends, on charges that they were part of two Russian American organized crime enterprises that engaged in racketeering, money laundering, extortion, and various gambling offenses. Within 18 months, more than half of the 34 had pled guilty to the charges.[6]

Lasry withdrew his name from consideration a week after the indictments were announced, citing "business reasons" as his motivation. There was no indication that he was involved in any of the criminal activities, and a source close to him claimed it was a complete surprise to him that his poker partners were accused of violating the law.[7]

In truth, business reasons may have prompted Lasry's withdrawal, seeing as two such potential problems were reported when he removed his name from consideration. Because he is considered a "key man" in his hedge fund, the investors in it would have had to grant him permission to leave the position, and it was supposedly not clear that all of them would have gone along. The other potential problem was that $3.7 billion of the $11.5 billion that the fund manages are invested in Europe, which would seem to some a built-in conflict of interest.[8]

Yet it seems hard to believe that those problems could not have been anticipated sooner and that Lasry's decision coming a week after the indictments were issued was just a coincidence. Although it is unclear whether it was coincidence or not, one thing is certain: the next set of potential appointees will have to answer questions about their card-playing habits.

Another thing about the Lasry case that is likely not a mere coincidence is that the former president chose to announce the impending nomination at a gathering of major campaign contributors. These were people like the ones whom Lasry once invited to his home in Manhattan for a $40,000-a-plate dinner in support of the Obama reelection effort.

Normally one of the most closely held secrets in Washington is the name of someone being considered for appointment as ambassador. If, as in the Lasry case, something comes up that prevents the nomination from going forward to the Senate, embarrassment to the president and the failed nominee can be avoided if the possible appointment has not been made public. Private disappointment is far preferable to public spectacle, and the latter is much more likely to lead to checkbooks being closed the next time an expensive fundraising dinner is held.

It is therefore highly unusual for anyone, especially a former president, to announce to a crowded room the name of a person the current president is going to nominate for an ambassadorship. But although Bill Clinton cannot run for president again, someone in his family is thinking about doing so in 2016, as the people close to Terry McAuliffe intimated. It would not take an overly cynical mind to see the announcement as Bill Clinton's way of telling a gathering of potential major donors that the store for selling ambassadorships will be open for business as usual should his wife succeed Mr. Obama.

The names of people being considered as nominees are closely guarded secrets, but there are occasions when they are deliberately leaked. All big donors are going to get their phone calls returned from the White House, and if they express interest in an ambassadorship, they are going to be considered regardless of their qualifications. The bigger the donors, the more prestigious the posts to which they aspire and the more carefully they have to be handled if they are not going to see their wishes fulfilled.

In a list of Obama's top fundraisers published by *The New York Times* in September 2012, the fourth name on the list was Anna Wintour.[9] At the time, she was editor-in-chief of *Vogue*, the fashion magazine, and she had attained that position on the list by bundling nearly $2.7 million to support the president's reelection.

Shortly after the election, rumors began to circulate that Wintour was being considered as the next ambassador in London. One London newspaper called it a "thank you gift" for her fundraising efforts.[10] Others in the British press were more explicit in their criticism, calling it ludicrous and a step too far.

The American press was not much kinder. This exchange took place at the December 5, 2012, White House press briefing with Jay Carney, the press secretary:

> Q: Just to change the subject for a second, what qualities does the President look for when he's going to pick an ambassador? Especially to an important ally like France—France or the U.K.
> Q: Someone very well dressed. (Laughter.)
> MR. CARNEY: I anticipated the question you're asking, and I can tell you in advance—I will answer the question, but that I have no personnel announcements. I'm not going to engage in speculation about

possible personnel announcements. I think that the President, in all of his personnel appointments, looks for talent, wisdom and character in his appointees, and he would do that regardless of the position.

Q: Is it important for a diplomat to be diplomatic?

MR.CARNEY: One of the—(laughter)—I mean, another way of addressing that is to answer the question that there have been enormously effective diplomats in this country's history who have not necessarily risen through the diplomatic corps. Now, we have enormously talented—

Q: I mean, just even in their personal lives, or pop culture, you are—

MR.CARNEY: I don't know—I understand that that's a rhetorical question, and diplomacy is effectively performed by diplomats. But we had one of the greatest diplomats of his generation pass away not long ago—Richard Holbrooke—and I think everyone who knew him or who sat across the table from him would agree that he was not by anyone's traditional definition particularly diplomatic.

Q: No, but he was also a brilliant negotiator and—

MR.CARNEY: So they come in all types and sizes and approaches.

Q: Has the President seen *The Devil Wears Prada*? (Laughter.)

Q: Before we go to—question, you don't deny that Anna Wintour can become ambassador from the United States—

MR.CARNEY: I will not engage in any speculation about personnel announcements. I just won't.

As Wintour worked her way up through the ranks at various fashion magazines, she developed a reputation for an eye for style and a tyrannical management style. She was so well known for her frosty demeanor that she was nicknamed Nuclear Wintour according to one British newspaper.[11]

The movie *The Devil Wears Prada* is about a young woman who comes to New York to get her start in journalism. She is able to land a job with a very powerful, cynical, and ruthless magazine editor played by Meryl Streep, and her suffering and eventual success provides the basic story line. The movie was based on a hugely successful novel by Lauren Weisberger, who wrote the book after spending 11 months working as Wintour's assistant.

The fact that Wintour was so roundly mocked by the press and had so many detractors was not only due to having a resume as thin as the models that appeared in her magazines. She clearly treats her subordinates like serfs—just the kind of ambassador to make an embassy with a staff of a thousand people and more than 20,000 official visitors each year run efficiently.

She was a major donor, however, so despite her reputation and lack of qualifications, she could not be brushed off. Leaking the possibility of an ambassadorship to the press and letting the ensuing reaction run its course would therefore have been one way to handle the problem, even if it did give the White House press spokesman some uncomfortable moments.

In the end, the White House informed Wintour that she would not be going to London as ambassador because Matthew Barzun had gotten the job. Barzun came in ninth on *The New York Times* list, having bundled only $2.3 million, but he had stepped down early as ambassador to Sweden in order to work for the president's reelection and spent 20 "grueling months as finance chairman of the president's national fund-raising campaign" according to the *Times*.[12]

Once again, suddenly discovered business interests appeared in order to lessen the impression that the potential nominee had fallen out of fashion for some reason. *Women's Wear Daily* reported that Wintour could not have taken the job anyhow because Charles Townsend, the CEO of Conde Nast, had recently promoted her to artistic director at the publishing company. Townsend supposedly told her, "If you accept it, you can't then come and tell me you've accepted at a later date a job as an ambassador."[13] Like Marc Lasry, Wintour discovered a pressing business obligation that prevented her from taking the job when it had become clear she was not going to be offered it.

Like Joy Silverman, who was discussed in chapter 3, Wintour was born into a very wealthy family and had no particular use for formal education. She dropped out of high school at age 16 to get her start in the fashion business.[14] Wintour was supposedly being considered for a country that is more important than Barbados, however.

At least it cannot be said that she did not know anything about the country to which she might be appointed ambassador. She was born in London, began her career there, and was decorated by the Queen in 2008 with the Order of the British Empire for her contributions to British journalism and British fashion.[15] She therefore cannot only speak the local language, like Louis Susman (see chapter 1), but she can probably also do so with the proper upper-class accent.

Occasionally the question arises of whether an ambassadorial nominee might know the country too well. Wintour has British, as well as American, citizenship because she was born in London.[16] She did not leave England for New York until 1976, when she was 27 years old.[17] Like Helene Von Damm, she appeared to want to return to the country of her birth as the American ambassador as a way to demonstrate her success despite her limited education.

Although it is considered important for ambassadors to know about the country to which they are appointed, there can be cases of being too informed. If a nominee has spent so much time there that it leads to a close identification with the country, it creates a conflict of interest and makes a bad case of clientitis a much greater possibility. This question cannot be answered in Wintour's case, seeing as she did not get the job.

But it may be answered in the near future. Stories about a nomination to France for Wintour appeared as soon as Lasry dropped out, and she has already shown strong support for Hillary Clinton for president in 2016.[18] In April 2013, *Women's Wear Daily* noted that Wintour "clearly wants to keep her hand in politics," citing as evidence the fact that she had hired Hildy Kuryk as the communications director at Conde Nast.[19] Kuryk worked as a consultant for the first presidential campaign of President Obama and was the finance director of the Democratic National Committee when Wintour gave her the job. If Hillary Clinton is the next president, Wintour will have a very good chance to wear Prada in the ambassador's residence in London, despite the negative press reaction the first time that was suggested.

Wintour or anyone else who survives any press stories about their possible nomination and gets the approval of the president for an ambassadorial post will be confronted with a mountain of paperwork designed to discover potential problems in four different areas—financial, security, tax, and medical. The forms at present include the SF-86 Security Questionnaire, the OGE-278 Financial Disclosure, the IRS Tax Check Waiver, an FBI Name Check, a Contact Sheet, a Biographic Statement, and a questionnaire from the Senate Foreign Relations Committee.

Each administration sets up the vetting process as it wishes, and there is usually a tendency of the staff of a new president to distrust whatever process their predecessors followed. Therefore, changes are often made and the process is reinvented every four to eight years, but the general areas remain the same.

In the security area, a full background investigation is required in order to obtain a top-secret clearance. The purpose of the clearance process is to ensure that "the individual's personal and professional history indicates loyalty to the United States, strength of character, trustworthiness, honesty, reliability, discretion, and sound judgment, as well as freedom from conflicting allegiances and potential for coercion, and a willingness and ability to abide by regulations governing the use, handling, and protection of classified information."[20]

The process of obtaining a security clearance begins with the filling out of Standard Form 86—Questionnaire for National Security Positions, or the SF-86 Security Questionnaire.[21] This 127-page form has sections covering every aspect of the candidate's life, including the circumstances of the person's birth, citizenship, every place of residence for the past 15 years,[22] education after the age of 18, employment, military service, three references, marital status (including information on former spouses and current cohabitation), relatives (whether living or deceased), any close and/or continuing contact with foreign nationals during the past 15 years, foreign financial interests, foreign business or professional activities, contacts with foreign government officials, offices held in foreign governments, voting in foreign elections, foreign travel, police records, any illegal use of drugs during the past 15 years, use of alcohol, prior security clearances, financial records, use of information technology systems, involvement in noncriminal court actions, and any associations with terrorist or criminal organizations. Finally the nominee has to sign forms authorizing the release of his or her medical and credit records.

The State Department's Bureau of Diplomat Security (DS) then begins the process of checking all of this information and interviewing the people that are mentioned in the form, including neighbors, employers, and former spouses. DS is supposed to complete the investigation in about 30 days, but it often takes longer. All questions about any of the information supplied have to be resolved, and if the person has lived overseas for extended periods, that can cause delays. If DS decides the individual is a loyal American and can be trusted with classified information without risk to national security, clearance is granted.

The medical clearance consists mainly of a physical taken at the State Department or administered by a person's personal physician to the nominee and all family members who will accompany the ambassador to the post. The purpose is to ensure that they do not have some health condition that would preclude them from living in the capital in question. This might be because the country does not have adequate medical facilities to deal with a medical condition or because a condition might be aggravated by other factors, such as the city's altitude. For example, parts of La Paz, Bolivia, including the airport, sit at more than 13,000 feet above sea level.

The IRS waiver is needed so that income tax returns for previous years can be carefully reviewed to see if there are any problems on that score. As the case of Zoë Baird demonstrated, the Senate does not take kindly to nominees who have ignored their tax obligations.

The part of the process that takes the longest amount of time is financial disclosure. This requires filling out the OGE-278, which amounts to a mere 19 pages, including instructions. The form requires information on the nominee's

- spouse and dependent children;
- assets and sources of income, including salary, bonus or severance pay, director fees, consulting fees, or honoraria;
- anticipated bonus or severance pay;
- retirement plans;
- deferred compensation;
- investment income;
- bank accounts;
- real estate, except for a personal residence, unless it has been rented;
- stocks, bonds, mutual funds, and so on;
- college savings plans;
- life insurance;
- fixed or variable annuities;
- books and other intellectual property;
- interests in or income from a trust or estate;
- liabilities; and
- outside positions.

The financial disclosure step takes a long time because it involves lawyers at the White House, the State Department, and the Office of Government Ethics (OGE). They all have to examine the information provided to ensure that there are no potential conflicts of interest. The OGE was established in 1978 by the Ethics in Government Act, which was passed in reaction to the corruption of the Nixon administration. Its mission is to foster high ethical standards for employees of the executive branch and to oversee policies designed to prevent and resolve conflicts of interest.

After one survives all of the paperwork and receives the blessing of the security officers, medical doctors, tax authorities, multiple lawyers, and ethics experts, there is one final clearance that has to be obtained—that of the country to which the ambassador will be sent. The State Department sends a message in a very restricted channel to the American embassy in that country with the instruction to send a diplomatic note to the foreign ministry asking for the government's formal acceptance of the individual as the next American ambassador. The approval of the state receiving the ambassador is not just a formality required by protocol but a requirement of the rules governing diplomatic practice.[23]

In diplomatic parlance, the term for this procedure is a request for "*agrément*." This step is a routine feature of diplomatic relations and is normally automatic, but it can add weeks to the process of getting an ambassador to post. Every foreign government has its own procedures for handling these requests, which are sometimes dictated by the country's laws but are always a product of its traditions.

These requests are usually handled without any public disclosure unless the country has a requirement to submit the name to its legislative branch for approval or some other practice that might cause it to become known. The government normally has 30 days to respond, and a lack of a response is taken as a rejection of the candidate, which the foreign government is not required to explain. Because it does not help relations between the two countries, this type of rejection is generally not made public.

An outright rejection can be avoided if the request is never officially made. In August 2013, *The New York Times* reported that Robert Ford was going to be chosen as ambassador to Egypt.[24] Ford, a career diplomat and Middle East expert, had served as ambassador to Syria until the embassy was closed in February 2012 as the security situation in that country deteriorated. Four and a half months later, a story by *Foreign Policy* claimed that Ford had been dropped for the post when representatives of Egypt's military government "quietly indicated that they did not want him in the job because of his stated willingness to negotiate with some of Syria's Islamist militants and political groups."[25] The article said that a spokeswoman at the Egyptian embassy refused to comment on Ford because he had not been officially nominated. The next news on Ford's future came in February 2014, when the press reported he had decided to retire from government service.[26]

Once all of the clearances have been obtained, including the approval of the foreign government, the nomination is publicly announced and sent to the Senate. At this point, the Senate has the opportunity to do more than just review the qualifications of the nominee. As a 1982 Congressional Research Service report noted:

> The requirement for Senate confirmation of nominees serves the primary purpose of keeping up the caliber of appointees by providing a check

on the choices and an opportunity for scrutiny. In the foreign affairs field it provides a means for the Senate to assure that the United States is ably represented abroad. It also provides a channel of communication between Senators and executive branch officials on the problems and goals of U.S. foreign policy. Finally, the hearings on nominations can be a method of overseeing the administration of foreign policy by the executive branch.[27]

The Senate rarely rejects a nominee outright. One Senate Foreign Relations Committee publication in 2000 noted that "available records do not show the last time the Senate rejected a nomination."[28] The committee had to go back more than a century to find an example when it may have happened. In 1889, the Senate refused to confirm Murat Halstead when President Benjamin Harrison nominated him to be minister to Germany. Halstead was not approved apparently because he was a journalist who had written a number of articles in which he denounced the purchasing of Senate seats.[29]

Although it is unclear in Halstead's case whether the Senate actually voted down the nomination or just refused to act, there is one historical example where it did act. In 1831, Andrew Jackson nominated his Secretary of State, Martin Van Buren, as minister to the United Kingdom. After a floor debate, the Senate vote came down to a 23 to 23 tie. At that point Vice President John C. Calhoun cast the deciding vote in favor of rejection. Van Buren soon recovered from this defeat. He first replaced Calhoun as Jackson's vice president in the next election and then became president himself in 1837.[30]

Although a vote against a nominee is extremely rare, there are other ways for the Senate or individual senators to prevent a nomination from being approved. One way is for the chairman of the Foreign Relations Committee to refuse to allow a confirmation hearing to be held. No chairman in recent history has used that power more extensively and ruthlessly than Jesse Helms, a five-term senator from North Carolina who chaired the committee from 1995 to 2001.

Helms had no qualms about frustrating the ambitions of career and political appointees alike. Even fellow Republicans were not safe from his wrath. When President Clinton nominated the Republican governor of Massachusetts, William Weld, Helms single-handedly stopped the nomination even after Weld resigned from the governorship and devoted his energies to overcoming his opposition.[31]

Helms was a staunch conservative and fervent anti-communist who employed every parliamentary maneuver possible to prevent the confirmation of anyone he deemed unworthy. He also used such tactics when he had no objection to the nominee but wanted to attempt to force a change of policy with regard to the country to which the person was named ambassador. President Reagan named a distinguished career diplomat, Melissa Wells, to be ambassador to Mozambique in October 1986, but she did not arrive at post until September 1987 because Helms refused to let her nomination come to a vote. Helms had no problem with Wells, but he opposed the government in Mozambique because he believed it to be communist. He wanted to force the Reagan administration to adopt an aggressive policy similar to the one for Central America. Helms viewed Renamo, an anti-communist rebel group trying to overthrow the Mozambican government, as the same as the Contras, who were struggling to take power in Nicaragua. The fact that Renamo used child soldiers and committed other gross violations of human rights did not deter Helms. After keeping Wells waiting for nearly a year, Helms eventually saw that the policy was not going to change and he allowed the confirmation to go forward.[32]

The combination of a stubborn streak and an indifference to what others, including his Senate colleagues, thought of him, gave Helms tremendous power and the will to use it. Or as then Senator Joe Biden put it, Helms was just "prepared to be mean."[33]

A nomination that is not acted upon during a session of Congress is returned to the president, who then has to decide whether to resubmit it or give up on that nomination. If Congress is not in session, a recess appointment can be made, but appointees know that if their appointment is not confirmed during the next session, they are out of a job.

The question of recess appointments remains a controversial issue, even though it was the subject of a unanimous verdict by the Supreme Court in June 2014. The court decided that the president did not have the power to make such appointments during a recess of fewer than ten days. The problem was not resolved, however, because the Senate had been conducting pro forma sessions, in which no business was done and virtually no senators were present. These fake sessions were designed for the sole purpose of preventing the president from making recess appointments. Conservatives on the court thought the ruling would make the recess-appointment power a weapon that presidents could use against the Senate. The immediate impact of the ruling was unclear, however. What is clear is that, despite the court's unanimous ruling, recess appointments will continue to be an issue over which the executive and legislative branches will clash on occasion when it suits the political interests of one or both of them.[34]

One person who did not get a recess appointment was Hassan Nemazee. The Senate returned his nomination without action seven months after he was nominated by President Clinton in January 1999 to be ambassador to Argentina. The Senate action came after a story about Nemazee appeared in *Forbes* magazine detailing a number of questionable business dealings.[35] Among other things, *Forbes* pointed out that Nemazee, an Iranian citizen, on one occasion obtained a Venezuelan passport so that the business he and his Cuban American partner were running could qualify as 100 percent Hispanic owned.

After he was nominated, Nemazee was so convinced he would be confirmed that he went to Buenos Aires and told embassy officials what kind of furniture he wanted in his office.[36] The furniture was dutifully ordered, but Nemazee never got to enjoy it or the beautiful ambassador's mansion in Argentina. He did eventually get housing provided by the government, however. In 2010, he pleaded guilty to charges of running a Ponzi scheme from 1998 to 2009 that raked in $292 million in fraudulent loans.[37] He was sentenced to 12 1/2 years in federal prison for his crimes.

Nemazee was put forward for an ambassadorship because he was a major fundraiser for a whole series of Democratic presidential contenders, an activity that continued until he was arrested. Clinton nominated him even though he had been a US citizen for only two years. Even the most superficial vetting of his background would have revealed that his business practices were, at a minimum, unethical. And yet his ability to raise money for political campaigns in the end was what mattered most.

Nemazee never made it to a confirmation hearing, and the article in *Forbes* no doubt played a role in ensuring that he did not. Once an appointment is announced and the person nominated is awaiting a confirmation hearing, the best thing to do is have patience, make no speeches, write nothing for publication, and avoid the media at all costs.

Any adverse publicity can derail or at least delay getting the Senate's consent. Timothy Broas was one of 247 people who bundled more than half a million dollars for President Obama's reelection. His reward was the ambassadorship in the Netherlands, but in June 2012 he was arrested for drunk driving and resisting arrest. He then asked that his nomination be withdrawn for "personal reasons."[38] His crimes were apparently not a fatal, self-inflicted wound, however. His nomination was resurrected and resubmitted to the Senate a year later, and on March 13, 2014, he was confirmed by the Senate. He presented his credentials to King Willem-Alexander, finally filling an ambassadorship that had been vacant since September 2011.[39]

Broas lost no time in getting involved in local politics. In his initial meeting with the Dutch press, he took the opportunity to criticize a Right-wing member of parliament.[40] The politician, Geert Wilders, was quoted as saying he would work to ensure the Netherlands had "fewer Moroccans."[41] One Dutch television station explained the ambassador's comments on the country's politics as due to the fact "that Broas is not a seasoned diplomat and that his new position is being seen as a reward for his financial support to Obama's election campaign."[42]

Another nominee who generated some publicity was Brett McGurk, but he did not survive that publicity, even though he had not committed any crimes. President Obama nominated him to be ambassador to Iraq. He was thought by many to be highly qualified for the job because of his extensive experience in that country during the Bush administration.[43] Unfortunately, in a previous tour in Iraq, McGurk, who was married at the time, had affairs with a *Wall Street Journal* reporter, whom he subsequently married, and another State Department employee.[44] When news of this leaked, including texts of salacious emails that he exchanged with the journalist, it provoked strong criticism from several senators. The White House initially stuck with McGurk, but about two weeks after the emails surfaced, his nomination was withdrawn.[45]

The confirmation hearings themselves are usually anticlimactic when they are finally held. The rooms where the hearings are conducted are ornate and impressive, but the senatorial turnout is usually very small. The hearing takes place before the subcommittee for the region where the country is located and not before the full Foreign Relations Committee. Often only a couple of senators show up, in addition to the chairman of the subcommittee, and they might not stay the whole time. Three or four nominees are often dealt with in a single hearing and it can go on for a hour or two.

Often a nominee will ask a senator from the nominee's state to appear at the hearing in order to provide a brief introduction of the nominee to the committee. This can be useful since, given the decorum of the Senate, a senator is less likely to ask tough questions of a nominee who has just been warmly endorsed by a colleague. The tactic does not always work, however, as the case of Mr. George Tsunis demonstrated. His senator from New York, Charles Schumer, appeared and read a lengthly and ringing statement supporting the nomination of Tsunis to be ambassador to Norway that stressed his community involvement and philanthropic contributions. Schumer also noted that Tsunis had been very active in "foreign policy issues."[46] As will be discussed in greater detail, that was not enough to save Tsunis from the grilling he received from Senator John McCain and also from his own inability to respond adequately to even the easiest of questions from friendly senators.

Sometimes the endorsements provided by senators in introducing the nominee to the committee are a bit bizarre. When Kevin O'Malley had his hearing in July 2014 on his nomination to be ambassador to Ireland, he had both his senators, one a Republican and the other a Democrat, show up to tell the committee how qualified he was. Senator Claire McCaskill showed her support for him by pointing out he held Irish citizenship up until his the confirmation process began and that O'Malley would make a good ambassador because he was a lawyer who was as comfortable representing people who were being sued as he was those who were suing.[47] Apparently the senators had no strong objection to the obvious conflict of interest inherent in having as an ambassador someone who had spent his life as a citizen of the country to which he was being sent and O'Malley was confirmed in September.[48]

When the nominee is given the chance to make a few remarks to the committee, in the vast majority of cases, those remarks begin with an introduction of those family members of the nominee that are present. Like the endorsement of a senator, having family attend is both to share in the importance of the moment, but also give the committee members another reason to not be too hard in their questioning. It wouldn't do to have a nominee's spouse burst into tears if the going got rough. The nominee's remarks always includes a bland statement about the country to which he or she is being sent and its importance to the United States. The remarks conclude with the promise that, if confirmed, the nomineewill work to improve the bilateral relationship between the two countries. The senators, for their part, will make some remarks and ask a few polite questions, and then it is over.

There are, however, times when things go spectacularly wrong, and that is more likely to happen with a political appointee than a career nominee. Every time a new presidential term begins, all ambassadors submit their resignations to the president. Those of the political appointees are almost always accepted immediately, and replacements are eventually named during the course of the following year. Those of the career ambassadors are rarely accepted, and they are allowed to serve out the remainder of what is normally a three-year assignment.

Two things happen therefore in the first year of any presidential term. First, the percentage of political appointees is much higher than the 30 percent that has been the case since the Eisenhower administration.

This often leads to comments in the media about the inordinately high percentage, which ignore the fact that the percentage invariably declines during the course of a term because of the front-loading of political appointees. Second, it presents a cluster of confirmation hearings of noncareer appointees who can easily be embarrassed if a senator decides to be aggressive when questioning a nominee.

In early 2014, this perfect storm of potential embarrassment struck for several of Obama's second term political appointees. The gaffes committed by them in their responses to questions in their confirmation hearings generated news stories and editorials, especially in the *Washington Post*. The mistakes were so bad that they also managed to make Jon Stewart's *The Daily Show*, where a segment of the comedy program entitled "The Diplomat Buyers Club" highlighted the fact that the nominees for Argentina, Iceland, and Norway had never been to their respective countries.[49]

Because the hearings were recorded on videotape, television networks also had plenty of fodder for their news programs, which rapidly made their way to YouTube.[50] One story on ABC was entitled "5 Most Cringe-Worthy Blunders from Obama's Ambassadorial Nominees."[51] The top five according to ABC were

- George Tsunis, a highly successful businessman nominated for Norway, who could not come up with an answer to a softball question from a friendly senator about what trade opportunities American businesspeople might find in that country;
- Tsunis's demonstration of his ignorance about the political parties that make up Norway's ruling coalition;
- Noah Bryson Mamet, the nominee for Argentina, admitting he had never been there;
- Colleen Bell, a producer of television soap operas, showing her inability to discuss how she would handle relations with a Hungarian government that has been eroding democracy in that country; and
- Senator Max Baucus beginning his response to a question by saying "Senator, I'm no real expert on China."

With the exception of Baucus, all of the nominees in question were major campaign contributors who had bundled at least half a million dollars. Perhaps out of courtesy to a former colleague, Baucus was rapidly confirmed by the Senate committee and on his way to Beijing. At the same time, dozens of other nominations, mainly of career officers, some of which had been pending for more than six months, continued to languish as the Senate could apparently not find time to confirm them. The Senate Foreign Relations Committee did eventually find the time to approve the nominations of Tsunis, Bell, and Mamet, but it was unclear as of mid- September 2014 when or even whether any of the three would finally be confirmed. Opposition to the nomination of Tsunis was particularly strong from Minnesota, which has a large Norwegian American community. All eight members of congress and both senators from the state opposed the nomination and publicly urged the president to withdraw it.[52] Even that level of opposition might not be enough to derail the nomination, however. After the attention of the media moves on, the interest lessens, the opposition may not be sustained, and what had been controversial appointments often quietly go forward. On the other hand, if one or more senators is intent on preventing confirmation, the issue can persist for many months without being resolved, and the nomination may fail if the White House blinks first and withdraws it.

In addition to demonstrating the need for at least a little preparation before a nominee has a confirmation hearing, the hapless trio showed one other thing—that Woody Allen's dictum that 80 percent of life is just showing up is right.[53] The White House, in a remarkable move toward greater transparency, started putting its visitor access records on its website. This searchable list contains the names of those who have been to the White House for some reason. Searching the available dates, which include the 2010 to 2013 period, it appears Bell visited the White House 20 times, Tsunis 27 times, and Mamet 34 times. The frequency of these visits demonstrates that getting an ambassadorial nomination is not just a matter of donating money and then sitting back and waiting for a phone call from the White House personnel office. It is a campaign that must be waged, and the donations and bundling are just a start.[54]

Even when no major gaffes have been committed by the nominee, there can be one final congressional hurdle following a confirmation hearing. Senators can ask questions for the record (QFRs) and require the nominee to respond to them in writing before the approval of his or her appointment will be passed to the full Senate for a final vote. The QFRs can be on any subject, but they usually concern the country in question or a general topic, such as the need for language training. QFRs are routine and normally few, if any, in number. At other times, they can be another delaying tactic. Jessie Helms had Melissa Wells answer more than 200 QFRs as part of the ordeal that he put her through before allowing her to be confirmed as ambassador to Mozambique.[55]

The responses to the QFRs, like the questions in the hearing, should be an exercise in diplomacy and blandness to the point of banality. The answers have to be responsive enough to satisfy the senator asking the question but at the same time not provide any information that would raise new questions or be offensive to anyone, including the government of the country to which the nominee hopes to go as ambassador. On occasion, that effort fails. In 2010, President Obama nominated Larry Palmer, a career officer, to be ambassador to Venezuela. Following his confirmation hearings, Palmer was sent a number of QFRs and was given the impression that they would be closely held. Believing his responses would not become public, he was a little too candid in his answers to questions regarding the morale of the Venezuelan army and the Venezuelan support for narcotics trafficking and guerrillas in neighboring Colombia. When these observations made their way into the press, the Venezuelan president Hugo Chavez announced on television that Palmer was no longer welcome as ambassador.[56] The State Department revoked the visa of the Venezuelan ambassador in retaliation, but Palmer never made it to Caracas. He was instead appointed as ambassador to Barbados.

Once the hearing is over and the QFRs are answered, a vote is held by the Foreign Relations Committee. If approved by the committee, the nomination passes to the full Senate, where a vote is eventually held. That can involve some additional delay if the Senate is dragging its feet on such approvals, as was the case in 2014 when dozens of nominations had been pending for months. Such delays are usually a function of the gridlock that affects much of what Congress does and not a result of a problem with a particular nominee. It is therefore usually just a question of time until this final step is taken, but it can be a long wait.

When the confirmation vote is finally held, the secretary of the Senate will attest to a "resolution of confirmation," which is then sent to the White House, and the president formally appoints the person. At that stage in the process, all that is left for the ambassador-designate to do is have a ceremony in which he or she is sworn in.

A senior State Department official usually administers the oath, but how senior that person is depends on the wishes of the new ambassador and the availability of the official. One of the reasons Colin Powell was a popular secretary of state was that he made a point of trying to be present for swearing-in ceremonies whenever he could. Being a good general, he realized that such consideration, and the signal it sent, would strengthen morale and be greatly appreciated by the rank and file.

Although Secretaries Rice and Clinton followed Powell's example to a degree, most secretaries of state rarely make the time to attend swearing-in ceremonies, and even an under secretary can often be hard to find. The default choice is the assistant secretary for the region. That distinction is probably lost on most people attending the ceremony, seeing as they are there at the invitation of the person being sworn in to celebrate the moment. They are more likely to notice what is being served to eat and drink afterward. (The menu is entirely up to the newly minted ambassador, because the individual being sworn in picks up the catering tab for the event.)

Particularly for career officers, the ceremony usually takes place on the eighth floor of the State Department in the Benjamin Franklin state dining room. The monumental room has "free-standing scagliola Corinthian columns along long walls and engaged columns along the short walls," and the area is decorated with several million dollars' worth of early American furniture.[57] It is an elegant venue in which to end the long journey to an ambassadorship. For the career officers, it is the culmination of at least 20 years of hard work. For the political appointees, it marks being rewarded by the White House for a political, economic, or personal relationship to the president. And for both, it brings to an end what is usually a year's worth of paperwork, congressional scrutiny, anxiety, and waiting.

Once the title is officially bestowed, the new ambassador simply has to go to post and present his or her credentials to whatever official of the foreign government is designated to receive them. The credentials are formal letters signed by the president (or by the machine that replicates the president's signature), which officially announce that the term of the previous ambassador has ended and that of the new ambassador has begun.

With that last act, the process is complete and the job begins. What country it will begin in depends on the kind of ambassador the person is because as chapter 6 will explain, political appointees and career officers go to different kinds of countries. What the ambassador actually does in the position and how well those duties are carried out will be the subject of the next chapter.

Given the partisan divide between the two major political parties, broad agreement on anything is rare. One thing on which there is general agreement, though, is that the appointments process is broken. It takes too long, puts the nominees in limbo for an indefinite period, and leaves positions unfilled for months on end.

At the same time that Senator Baucus was being rapidly confirmed, 50 other ambassadorial nominees were still awaiting a vote. Eleven of the 28 ambassadorships in Latin America were vacant, as were 10 out of the 40 in sub-Saharan Africa. Aside from the three or four who had put on a poor performance in their confirmation hearings, none of the appointments had any hint of controversy associated with them. And yet the Senate proceeded at a pace that could not even be considered glacial.

Ironically, some attributed the senatorial slows to an attempt to speed up the appointments process. At the end of 2013, the Democratic majority, angered by the stalling of Republicans on a range of issues and appointments, exercised the so-called nuclear option. That is the name given to the change made by Democrats to what had been Senate practice for at least 40 years. Instead of requiring 60 votes for a final confirmation vote, a simple majority was deemed sufficient. In retaliation, Republicans started insisting that each individual nomination be debated instead of allowing large numbers of them to be approved at the same time by unanimous consent.[58] As a result, what had been a slow process became an even slower one. The Senate did manage to confirm a new under secretary of state for arms control around this time, however. That nominee had only been waiting for 540 days.[59]

Although few can remember a time when the process was this slow and the number of those awaiting a vote was this high, the problem is not new. There have been almost as many studies to solve it as Washington has monuments. The Senate Committee on Governmental Affairs held hearings in 2001 on the presidential appointments process and wrote a historical summary of the recommendations of previous studies on how to improve the process.[60] The earlier reports numbered ten, with one from 1935 and the other nine written between 1985 and 2001. The 9/11 Commission, which investigated the terrorist attacks on that day, also addressed the need to improve the process in one of its recommendations.

All of the recommendations boil down to attempts to make the process faster and more efficient and to reduce the number of positions that require Senate confirmation. In 2012, Congress passed and the president signed a bill designed to address at least the last recommendation. Public Law 112–116, the Presidential Appointment Efficiency and Streamlining Act, eliminated the requirement for Senate confirmation for appointees to 163 positions. None of them were ambassadorial positions, however, and the number of those will not be reduced, given that the Constitution stipulates that the Senate must provide its advice and consent for such appointments. Whether the Senate will ever do so efficiently or quickly enough is a debate that will never be resolved. One historian described the Constitution as "an invitation to struggle." The confirmation of ambassadors will always remain just one more opportunity for that struggle to be acted out.

CHAPTER 5

What an Ambassador Does

The embarrassing performances of the nominees to be the ambassadors in Norway, Argentina, and Hungary in their confirmation hearings in early 2014 did not only become the fodder for satirical reports on *The Daily Show*. They also set off a flurry of critical articles in the media and another round of debates about what qualifications are necessary to be an ambassador. This chapter will discuss the qualifications question—what an ambassador actually does and how well those duties are performed.[1]

At the same time that the controversy was playing over the three hapless nominees, an earlier political appointee ambassador passed away. Shirley Temple was a child movie star who won an honorary Academy Award when she was only six years old.[2] Although Hollywood found little use for her talents once she became an adult, her career did not end. Her obituary in *The New York Times* describes her life after stardom:

> After marrying Charles Alden Black in 1950, she became a prominent Republican fund-raiser. She was appointed a delegate to the United Nations General Assembly by President Richard M. Nixon in 1969. She went on to win wide respect as the United States ambassador to Ghana from 1974 to 1976, was President Gerald R. Ford's chief of protocol in 1976 and 1977, and became President George H. W. Bush's ambassador to what was then Czechoslovakia in 1989, serving there during the fall of Communism in Eastern Europe.[3]

The obituary also reported that during her time at the United Nations, she did well by all accounts and tackled a wide range of issues. Her service at the United Nations during the Nixon administration may have increased her interest and experience in international affairs, but it did not translate into a prestigious ambassadorship the next time a

Republican was elected president. At the time, being sent to Ghana as ambassador was unusual for a political appointee and especially for a woman. Such an assignment would seem to indicate that her relationship with fellow movie star Ronald Reagan was not all that strong.

Although the appointment may not have been much of a reward from the White House, it upset some career diplomats because the embassy in Accra was one the Foreign Service could count on as almost always being given to a career officer. To the surprise of many, Temple Black again did well, and some observers even considered her performance outstanding. One senior officer in the Bureau of African Affairs said she "turned out to be one of the best ambassadors we've ever had."[4]

Following her time in Ghana, she become the chief of protocol in the State Department, the first female to hold that position. For a number of years, she also ran the two-week charm school that all new ambassadors, career and political alike, attend before they go to their posts. This brief orientation course covers a wide range of issues and is all the formal training that many political appointees receive before going to post.

Because her work in the department gave her broad exposure to many officials and ambassadors on their way to their embassies, Temple Black is often mentioned in the oral histories of retired diplomats, and she has received a generally positive review from them.[5] She is described as having worked hard, trusted her subordinates, and relied on a strong deputy chief of mission to take care of the internal management of the embassy.[6]

Ambassador Temple Black may have succeeded in Africa and gotten positive reviews for her work in the department, but her second posting abroad was more problematic. She became ambassador to Czechoslovakia in 1989 and held that position until 1992. At the end of 1989, the communists were forced out by demands for a democratic government and Vaclav Havel was elected president. According to the deputy chief of mission at the time, the ambassador was popular on the street because of her charm and celebrity, but she was regarded by the leaders of the Velvet Revolution that brought Havel to power as politically naïve and having been too cozy with the communist regime in its final months.[7]

It would have been a challenging environment for any ambassador. Although the country had democracy again after years of domination by the Soviet Union, it did not have unity. In 1992, the Parliament voted to dissolve the union, and on January 1, 1993, the Czech Republic and the Slovak Republic were simultaneously brought into being.

As the inevitability of the breakup became apparent, Temple Black was reluctant to report the news to Washington. She knew it would not be welcomed because of the fear that the division of Czechoslovakia would result in a civil war, as it had in Yugoslavia. Although one of an embassy's most important functions is keeping Washington abreast of local political developments, she feared the messenger would be blamed for not keeping the country together.

She therefore did not want to be the bearer of bad news because she feared it would affect her tenure. She knew well from her years running the orientation course for new ambassadors that ambassadors served for three years and were then replaced. It was a rule that was rarely violated, but she hoped to convince Washington that she was worthy of an exception, and having the divorce of Czechs and the Slovaks occur on her watch would not help her case.

When the instruction came to request *agrément* for her successor, Temple Black went to see President Havel alone and did not bring along anyone to take notes for a written record of the conversation. She returned from the meeting claiming that Havel did not want her to leave.[8] If Havel actually said that, he was merely being diplomatic about the news of her departure. He was at the time already using his channels to Washington to make it clear he wanted a new US ambassador as soon as possible.[9]

Washington listened to the president instead of the ambassador. The request for *agrément* was finally delivered to the foreign minister when he visited Washington. Ambassador Black left Prague shortly thereafter.

If a former child movie star can have mixed results as ambassador even after years of government service, what are the qualifications for a good ambassador? That is a question that will never have a definitive answer. The four appointees who did not cover themselves in glory during their confirmation hearings in 2014 come from a wide range of backgrounds: George Tsunis is the CEO of a hotel chain, Colleen Bell is a producer of television soap operas, Noah Mamet is a political operative and consultant, and Max Baucus is a politician and senator.

If there are qualifications to become an ambassador other than having a relationship with the president (as was discussed in chapter 3), the State Department does not know what they are or is at least unwilling to spell them out with any clarity. The following exchange took place at the February 7, 2014, noon press briefing at the department between a reporter and Jen Psaki, the department spokesperson:[10]

Q: What, in a nutshell, are the central qualifications to be named U.S. ambassador?

MS.PSAKI: Well, fortunately the United States has diplomatic relationships with many, many countries around the world, as you know. And we have ambassadors who are from political backgrounds, who are from financial backgrounds, who have run companies large and small, but our process has continued to be—or our approach has continued to be approximately a 70/30 balance of career employees, so people who have been working through the Foreign Service and serving around the world, building that level of experience, and then about 30 percent from outside the private sector.

Over the course of history, there have been many, many ambassadors who have come from outside of the career path who have been very successful. And just to point you to a few—Sargent Shriver, former Vice President Mondale, Pamela Harriman—there are many who have been very successful serving in these roles in countries around the world, and that's a part of the reason why this will continue.

Q: So as you know, there's been some criticism that—of the specific qualifications of some of the recent nominees. I mean, George Tsunis didn't seem to even know what type of government Norway has, called one of the members of the ruling coalition a fringe element. So I'm wondering: Does an ambassador have to have at least some basic knowledge of the country that he is going to?

MS.PSAKI: Well, I think ambassadors go to countries. Obviously, that's the goal. But the ambassadors go to countries to represent the United States, to be a resource to people on the ground. We've seen those reports, we've all read them. But I would encourage people to give those who have had tougher hearings a chance to go to their countries and see what their tenure will entail. And the judgment can't be made about how effective they'll be or how appreciated they'll be by the government until we have that happen.

Q: So right now, you have—the percentage is 37 percent, which is considerably more political appointees than George Bush had, considerably more than Bill Clinton had. And I'm going through the list. I mean, most of these gave hundreds of thousands of dollars or raised hundreds of thousands of dollars for the Obama campaign. How much does it cost to become an ambassador, to be named ambassador, in the Obama Administration?

MS.PSAKI: We don't name ambassadors from the State Department. The White House names ambassadors, so I would certainly point you to my old colleagues across the street for that. What I was conveying is that from the State Department point of view, there have been many, many political ambassadors, people who have come from a range of histories and backgrounds who've been very successful and worked very effectively in these roles.

The press enjoys putting the department spokesperson on the spot and likes pushing for responses to loaded questions, which can then be used to exploit any inconsistencies the next time the issue arises. If Psaki had attempted to list the qualities required of an ambassador, the press would have evaluated every nominee in light of those qualities and asked follow-up questions that would have been even more difficult to answer.

Although the State Department is unwilling to describe the qualifications for a good ambassador in the midst of the controversy over the Tsunis, Bell, and Mamet nominations, there are others that have described the qualifications or at least have expressed an opinion as to the suitability of those three nominees. The American Foreign Service Association (AFSA) was established in 1924 and is the professional association and labor union of the Foreign Service. AFSA represents more than 31,000 active and retired employees of the Department of State, US Agency for International Development (USAID), Foreign Agricultural Service (FAS), Foreign Commercial Service (FCS), International Broadcasting Bureau (IBB), and the Animal and Plant Health Inspection Service (APHIS).

As the Tsunis-Bell-Mamet controversy continued, AFSA's Governing Board passed a resolution expressing its concern about their qualifications but only said it was going to examine their credentials further.[11] Fifteen former presidents of AFSA were not as diplomatic as its Governing Board was. They wrote a letter to Senate Majority Leader Harry Reid urging him to oppose their confirmation. They went on to say: "Although we have no reason to doubt that the nominees are conscientious and worthy Americans, the fact that they appear to have been chosen on the basis of their service in raising money for electoral campaigns, with minimal demonstrated qualifications for their posts, has subjected them to widespread public ridicule, not only in the U.S. but also abroad."[12]

But what are the qualifications to be an ambassador? Certainly knowing the language, history, and culture of the country to which one is sent is important, but is that enough and is it absolutely necessary? As pointed out in the introduction, John Davis Lodge spoke beautiful Spanish and knew a lot about Argentina, but many considered him a pompous fool. His successor, Robert C. Hill, after having served as ambassador to five Spanish-speaking countries, could still not manage a complete sentence in the language, but he was regarded by many as remarkably effective.

As the controversy continued, the AFSA made an attempt to at least describe the necessary qualifications by issuing the "Guidelines for Successful Performance as a Chief of Mission."[13] That document listed the following four general guidelines and suggested they ought to be used in the assessment of all future nominees for ambassadorships:

- *Leadership, character, and proven interpersonal skills*: The nominee has demonstrated the interpersonal skills necessary to represent the United States, including utmost integrity, honesty, moral courage, fairness, empathy, an appropriate measure of humility, awareness of personal strengths and weaknesses, overall judgment and decisiveness, and the ability to inspire, as well as a proven ability to be effective in taking on new challenges. A demonstrated understanding and mastery of working in a complex environment where the objectives of multiple and sometimes competing organizations must be balanced. A key skill is the ability to listen in order to better understand the host country's perspectives, as well as the mission staff's views and concerns. These skills can be demonstrated through leadership and management of government organizations, private sector companies, or non-governmental and private volunteer organizations.
- *Understanding of high-level policy and operations and of key U.S. interests in the country or organization of prospective assignment*: The nominee possesses the knowledge and capacity to lead the operations of a diplomatic mission effectively; participate constructively in the formulation of policy and implement policy in a creative manner that yields positive results where possible; the ability to communicate persuasively with government stakeholders (White House, State Department, other executive agencies and Congress), host nation officials, political leaders and civil society. He or she demonstrates the capacity to negotiate, and has the proven ability to take on various challenges, including working with U.S. and foreign business communities and other nongovernmental interests, and providing services to U.S. citizens.
- *Management*: The nominee has relevant management experience. He or she possesses a commitment to team building, the ability to innovate, problem-solving skills, experience in setting goals

and visions, ability to manage change, strategic planning skills, experience in allocation of resources, and commitment to mentoring and career development. He or she has the capacity to work well with a deputy and other members of a team, and to delegate effectively.

- *Understanding of host country and international affairs, ability to promote/advance U.S. interests*: The nominee has experience in or with the host country and/or other suitable international experience and capacity, has knowledge of the host country culture and language, and/or of other foreign cultures or languages. He or she has the ability to manage relations between the U.S. and the country/organization of assignment in order to advance U.S. interests, including the interests of U.S. commercial firms as well as individual U.S. citizens and nationals. The nominee skillfully interacts with different audiences—both public and private.[14]

The guidelines did not end the debate, however. A group described as ten retired ambassadors assembled the guidelines. Although seven of those ambassadors had been career officers, the other three consisted of a fraternity brother of George W. Bush, a man whose diplomatic experience consisted of one year as ambassador, and a major Obama bundler who had run the Office of Presidential Personnel. In other words, they were men who had benefited from the way that ambassadorships are handed out to political appointees and therefore were unlikely to challenge the status quo.

Although a majority of the AFSA Governing Board approved the guidelines, every former ambassador on the board voted against them. But even if a set of guidelines upon which everyone agreed could be constructed, it would do little to improve the quality of ambassadors. Expecting that those who cannot meet the guidelines are going to decide not to apply for the job is the equivalent of thinking that describing virtue will rid the world of sinners.

Another AFSA effort was a request made under the Freedom of Information Act for the copies of the "certificates of demonstrated competence" of the nominees. One of the reforms brought about by the Foreign Service Act of 1980 was a requirement for the State Department to send such a document to the Senate for each nominee. The White House and State Department complied with the law, but it changed little. The certificates became one-page summaries of the nominees' backgrounds with the same kind of basic biographic information that any Google search would uncover.

Because they reveal so little and nothing that is not already known, a certificate of competence is not going to be the smoking gun that proves a nominee's incompetence. Jen Psaki admitted as much at the March 7, 2014, noon press briefing when she was asked about AFSA's request. She responded: "These documents that they're asking for are about a page or two pages long. They are certainly not reflective of the qualifications or even that extensive of a background of any of the individuals."[15]

At least AFSA's request has resulted in an agreement that in the future the certificates will be posted on the State Department website.[16] It was not retroactive, however, and the certificate of George Tsunis was not posted.[17] According to a brief biography on AllGov.com, Tsunis's only foreign policy experience was being a member of the Brookings Institution Foreign Policy Leadership Committee and the Business Executives for National Security (BENS). A search of the Brookings website revealed only two references to that committee, and neither gave any indication of what it does other than perhaps provide an addition for the résumés of donors to Brookings. A search of the BENS website likewise gave no indication that Tsunis did anything other than belong to the organization. BENS, which counts a significant number of defense contractors among its ranks, describes its mission as applying good business practices to national security problems, but how it carries that out is unclear.[18]

The thinness of Tsunis's résumé when it came to foreign policy credentials drew little notice before his confirmation hearing train wreck. Because his performance on that occasion was so bad, however, that it created significant opposition when members of the Nordic American community in Minnesota organized a petition asking their two Democratic senators to block the nomination.[19] As mentioned in chapter 4, both senators and all 8 of the state's congressional representatives subsequently voiced their opposition to Tsunis's confirmation.[20]

Although the confirmation hearing focused attention on Tsunis's credentials, his case is the exception, and there would not have been much reaction to them if there had not been a videotape of his pathetic performance. One reason why the qualifications of a nominee are usually not questioned is that there is no way to know in advance who will fail as an ambassador. An anemic résumé when it comes to international experience does not guarantee failure as an ambassador. Despite his answers to the questions he received at the hearing, Tsunis could go on to be a good ambassador if he eventually gets confirmed by the Senate.

On the other hand, extensive experience in foreign affairs does not guarantee success. Those who fail as ambassadors come not only from the ranks of political appointees but from those of career officers, as well. The internal auditor of the State Department is the Office of the Inspector General (OIG). It periodically dispatches a team to inspect each embassy and the team writes a thorough evaluation after interviewing dozens of people at a post and dozens more in Washington who have anything to do with that embassy. In addition, everyone who works in the embassy fills out a "Workplace and Quality of Life Questionnaire," in which they rate the effectiveness of the management of their workplace and quality of life on a scale of one to five. An example of the questionnaire is found at appendix K.

The scores generated by the questionnaires guide the inspection team and provide indicators of problem areas. Once the team completes its work, it writes up an extensive assessment, including recommendations on ways the embassy can improve its management and ensure its compliance with the many rules and regulations that govern how the embassy does its work. Thanks to the Inspector General Reform Act of 2008, the reports are posted on the OIG's website with minimal redactions. Reports dating back to 2004 are available.

Each embassy is supposed to be inspected once every five years, but Congress routinely waives that requirement, and due to insufficient resources, the average in reality is every eight years. The reports make interesting reading for anyone who wants to learn about the bureaucratic mechanics of an embassy. But they do not really answer the question of what the requirements to be an ambassador should be, and they even do not provide an easy answer as to whether career ambassadors do a better job overall than political appointees do. Those who have served on inspection teams know that both good and bad ambassadors can come from both groups.[21]

The latter seems like a question that, although not easy to answer, could perhaps be at least partially resolved by a bit of social science. To test the question of whether there is a measurable difference between political appointee ambassadors and career ones, four graduate students in the School of International Affairs at Penn State were asked to read the 139 inspection reports that the inspector general at that point had posted on the IG's website. They included 98 embassies with career chiefs of mission and 41 with political appointees.

The students were tasked with assigning two grades to each ambassador: one for internal mission management and the other for external relations. Although the average grades for the career officers were slightly higher in both categories, the difference was not statistically significant. The career ambassadors were more tightly clustered around the average, whereas the political appointees had a flatter distribution—in other words, there was a larger standard deviation in their scores. This tends to confirm what many believe based on anecdotal evidence—that political appointees are more likely to be either good or bad, whereas career officers tend to fall more in the middle.

Bad ambassadors, career and political alike, could be avoided if there was a way to determine in advance what the qualifications for success are. Other professions have sought an answer to that question. The American Bar Association does a thorough review of the background and experience of judicial nominees and declares each of them to be either highly qualified, qualified, or unqualified.

The clearest measure of the performance of a judge is how often a higher court overrules his or her decisions. A recent study found little difference in the reversal rates of judges regardless of which of the three ABA categories they had been assigned.[22] An a priori indicator that some deem a true determinant of success may not work for ambassadors any more than it does with judges. And a résumé that is declared too thin or a couple of flubbed questions in a confirmation hearing are usually not going to be enough to derail a nomination.

In addition, every chief of mission (COM) has a career officer for a deputy (DCM). The deficiencies of a COM can be compensated for if the ambassador is smart enough and trusting enough to make good use of the DCM. If there is an indicator of future ambassadorial success, it is probably based on personality and the ability to effectively manage people, and that is as true for career COMs as it is for political ones. Managerial skills and personality traits are not readily conveyed by basic biographic information, however.

The importance of the personality traits of an ambassador was well described by Charles Schmitz, a retired State Department official:

> Ambassadors really are almost kings overseas. Unless a person comes with a very strong internal compass, it is easy to go wrong as ambassador. It doesn't have anything to do with political versus career. It has to do with the inner character of the person taking the job. I think career people are as much given to the egomaniacal quality of being ambassador as some of the worst of the political appointees.[23]

Schmitz also did some work with AFSA, and he talked about how the certificates of competency had been required by law, but the Senate never really had much interest in them. They became one-page bio-graphic summaries to which no one really paid any attention, including the people assigned to prepare them. He describes in his oral history how the State Department nevertheless classified them to keep them from becoming public and how AFSA had to threaten to sue to get them released. The department relented before the case could go to court and turned them over to AFSA, but the department would admit to no wrongdoing. Apparently that agreement did not last, seeing as the date of Schmitz's oral history interview was 1993 and AFSA had to threaten to sue again in 2014 to get the certificates. History has repeated itself thanks to AFSA's efforts, and the certificates are now being posted on the State Department website. Given the difficulty in defining the essential qualifications for being an ambassador, it unlikely the certifi-cates will ever have any effect on keeping the White House from put-ting forward a nominee who many will regard as unqualified nominee for confirmation as ambassador.

Although the qualifications necessary to be an ambassador cannot be precisely described, what that person actually does and the responsibili-ties he or she has can be described, but only up to a point. The formal structure of the job is laid out in writing, but how that job plays out in real life may be quite different as there are many functions to perform and they never come together in exactly the same way from one embassy to the next.

The formal structure consists mainly of the provisions in the *Foreign Affairs Manual* (FAM), which covers the authority of the chief of mis-sion and also the president's letter of instructions to his ambassadors. The relevant sections of the FAM, along with the letters of instruction from the last four presidents, are contained in the appendices.

The letters of instruction were begun during the administration of President Kennedy in order to reaffirm the authority of ambassadors. Doing so was necessary because in the midst of the Cold War, the grow-ing number of Defense Department and intelligence community per-sonnel working in embassies had led to questions of who was in charge. It is an issue that periodically arises and has been renewed by the so-called war on terror.[24]

The letters of the four presidents have much in common and list some of the challenges that ambassadors have faced over the decades, including the issue of who is in charge of federal government employees overseas. They differ in that they typically start with a few paragraphs reflecting the broad foreign policy concerns of the day and the prior-ities of the president that signed them. Written in 1990, 1996, 2003, and 2009, respectively, they represent snapshots of Washington's view of the world at that time, and they all make reference to the uniqueness of that moment in history.

President George H. W. Bush, writing in 1990 (appendix H), noted that the postwar era was drawing to a close and a new, exciting time of change in international relations was beginning. He added: "As leader of the democracies, our Nation faces an historic opportunity to help shape a freer, more secure, and more prosperous world, in which our ideals and our way of life can truly flourish."

President Clinton, in 1996 (appendix G), also spoke of the post–Cold War era, which had yet to acquire a name. He listed three main foreign policy goals: renewing and adapting America's security alliances and structures; rebuilding and revitalizing the American economy; and promoting democracy, human rights, and sustainable development. Clinton also stressed the challenges posed by global problems, such as arms proliferation, terrorism, human rights, the environment, refugees, migration, and humanitarian assistance.

There are different versions of the letter even from the same president as it is updated as necessary to respond to changes in the world and America's response to it. The letter of George W. Bush before the terrorist attacks on 9/11 was very different from the one drafted in mid-2003 (appendix F). After 9/11, for Bush 43 the three most important tasks for ambassadors were

- waging a relentless global war against terrorism, to defeat those who seek to harm us and our friends;
- overcoming the faceless enemies of human dignity, including disease, starvation, and poverty; and
- assisting American citizens, institutions, and businesses as they pursue their charitable and commercial interests.

The letters can also be an opportunity to make an indirect critique of the previous administration by stressing how things will change under a new president. The letter from President Obama in July 2009 (appendix E) speaks about the need to "renew America's security and standing in the world" and to "rebuild traditional alliances." The implication is clear that all that reconstruction would not be necessary if the previous administration had done a better job.

The Obama letter goes on to talk about the key common challenges of the twenty-first century, including weapons of mass destruction, terrorism, poverty, pandemic disease, dependence on fossil fuels, and global climate change. It also stresses the importance of another twenty-first-century issue—the use of the tools and technology to pursue diplomacy and public outreach.

The issues that seem to show up in every letter of instruction include the recurring challenges that ambassadors face, and they generally have to do with the control of US government personnel and resources. The ambassador is in charge of all government employees in his or her country, regardless of their location or employment category. There are exceptions, however, with the notable one being armed forces personnel who are under the direction of the military commander for that region. Other exceptions include Americans on the staff of international organizations and Voice of America journalists.

The exception for military personnel has been complicated by the effort to combat terrorism. In the past, members of the armed forces who fell under the jurisdiction of the ambassador worked in the embassy and those who did not were largely located on military bases. Now with the antiterrorism fight being a global struggle, there can be hundreds of American soldiers in a country helping the local government improve its ability to deal with that threat. This requires close collaboration and communication between military authorities and the embassy to avoid embarrassing situations.

That collaboration and communication does not always happen. In one incident in Paraguay in 2006, an American special operations team quickly left the country after its members shot and killed a robber. Senior embassy officials had not been told that the team was in the country and they were unaware of it because it had operated out of a hotel and not out of the embassy.[25]

This failure was in part a result of the scramble by various sections of the government to respond to the threat of terrorism. As the Department of Defense (DOD) under Secretary of Defense Rumsfeld tried to increase its bureaucratic turf in the war on terror, it entered into operational and intelligence areas that were traditionally the CIA's and State Department's responsibilities. Both agencies worried about whether there was sufficient coordination of such efforts by the DOD with other parts of the government.[26] Although Rumsfeld's successor, Robert Gates, improved things by establishing procedures for how such operations were to be handled, much depends on the military commanders of the region and the ambassador of the country in question, how well they get along and how well they communicate with each other.

Another area often mentioned in the letters of instruction is the chain of command and communication. Ambassadors are told that they should report to the president through the secretary of state and that they will receive their instructions from the secretary unless the president personally orders the use of a different channel. A career ambassador would likely never go outside of these rules, but others do on occasion. As was the case with Ambassador Lodge, there are from time to time political appointees who believe they can communicate directly with the president and do not have to bother with going through the State Department.

Ambassadors are also told that they have the right to see any communications being sent from or arriving at their embassies. That was a lot easier in the days when the only secure way to pass a message was to put it in the form of a cable or telegram and send it through the communications technicians in an embassy. Now with fax machines, email, better telephone connections, and a host of other ways to get messages to and from Washington, it has become a lot harder. The sheer volume is one thing. Another is whether the ambassador is aware enough to know that there are things that he or she should be seeing. And there is also the question of how much the ambassador wants to know. There are occasions when ambassadors might want to be able to say they were uninformed.

The letters also stress that the ambassador is responsible for the security of the government employees under his or her jurisdiction and for the proper and efficient use of other government resources. The security question is never an easy one. An embassy and the people who work in it have to interact with the people in the country in which the embassy is located, even when some of those people would like nothing better than to murder a representative of the United States. Deciding how much security is enough and how much is too much are questions that never have satisfactory or definitive answers.

When the decision is made that security is inadequate, a request has to be submitted to Washington for the funds necessary to beef it up. Such requests almost never elicit a prompt approval, given that resources are always limited, improving security is expensive, and requests from posts with greater threats will be attended to first. With 275 diplomatic missions around the world, there are many targets for terrorists and a huge number of buildings that have to be protected to a necessary degree in response to an ever-changing security situation.

Not only do the buildings need protection, but the people who work in them do as well. That raises another challenge that is a staple part of the letters of instruction. Within an embassy, there are usually more people working for different government agencies and departments than there are working for the State Department. Those other agencies often want to expand the number of people they have overseas, but they are often reluctant to pay for the full cost. The ambassador is given the authority to deny requests to increase staffing at an embassy, and even to reduce it, if a case can be made that the government employees in question are not needed or are at too high a risk to warrant them being there. The State Department is almost always trying to limit the number of non–State Department personnel, but the demands for increasing it are constant and can come from any number of different directions.

Sorting out the bureaucracy in an embassy and determining how much comes out of each of the various budgets involved to cover the cost of running the embassy is no small exercise. Working in the embassy in London, for instance, are permanent staff members from nine cabinet-level agencies, along with numerous other federal agencies. The cost of keeping them there is divided between 41 different budget accounts.[27]

Managing so many different bureaucrats from so many different parts of the government can be like the proverbial attempt at herding cats. They will all always stand up when the ambassador enters the room and say, "Yes, sir," but the reality is that if they are not from the State Department, they have a boss back in Washington whom they care about more than they care about the ambassador. That boss determines their prospects for promotion and their next assignment—things over which an ambassador will have little influence.

The letters of instruction usually end with the admonition that the ambassador is expected to maintain the highest standards of ethical conduct and should ensure there is equal opportunity and no discrimination or harassment in the embassy. That would seem like an unnecessary warning, but it is a useful reminder that the job has many different aspects and a much greater level of scrutiny than nearly any position an ambassador may have held previously did. It is also a reminder that there is a lot more to an ambassador's work than ignoring parking tickets and attending endless cocktail parties, even though it is hard to describe what the qualifications for it are or what it consists of with any precision.

Thanks to the OIG reports, although the qualifications and duties of an ambassador can be somewhat uncertain, how well he or she is doing the job is not. And with the reports posted online, that report card is there for the world to see. The reports provide dozens of case studies of both good and bad examples of ambassadorial leadership. The following pages outline some of them that illustrate the Dos and Don'ts of being an ambassador.

Woody Was Right—Showing Up Matters

If Woody Allen's rule of thumb that 80 percent of life involves just showing up is true, then that would be a good place to start for any ambassador who wants to do the job properly. Trying to spend less time in an unpleasant country would be understandable, but the Bahamas? Tropical paradise notwithstanding, the ambassador there managed to be somewhere else for 276 days during a 670-day period from November 2009 to September 2011. That works out to being gone an average of 12 days a month or, put another way, being there less than 60 percent of the time. And when she was at post, she apparently preferred working from the residence instead of going to the office.[28]

The ambassador was Nicole Avant. In announcing her nomination, the White House described her as follows:

> Ms. Avant serves as Vice President of Interior Music and Avant Garde Music Publishing. A businesswoman, philanthropist and activist, she has been recognized for her tireless efforts to mobilize the younger generation towards greater charitable and political involvement. She has worked as an academic counselor at The Neighborhood Academic Initiative, a USC mentorship program for high school students. Ms. Avant serves as a board member for the Bogart Pediatric Cancer Research Program, the Center for American Progress and Best Buddies, and was named one of the American Cancer Society Next Generation Leaders in 2007.[29]

Avant's father is a Democratic Party activist and music executive, and her husband is the chief content officer at Netflix. She and her husband bundled more than half a million dollars for President Obama.[30] Her father bundled another hundred thousand and over the years has donated nearly $700,000 to various federal candidates, parties, and political action committees. She was also finance cochair of the presidential campaign in southern California.[31] That is an important position, given that celebrities and the entertainment industry in general are a very rich source of funds for Democratic candidates.[32]

According to the inspection report, Avant was in charge during "an extended period of dysfunctional leadership and mismanagement, which caused problems throughout the embassy."[33] One of the reasons for those problems was her overreliance on a DCM who was described as having an intimidating management style. But being out of the country more than 40 percent of the time did not help. During one of those absences, she attended a Democratic National Committee event in Los

Angeles for President Obama. In his remarks, the president made the following comment:

> A couple of people I just want to mention who are here. The governor of the great state of California, Jerry Brown is in the house. (Applause.) And our ambassador to the Bahamas—(laughter)—Nicole Avant is in the house. (Applause.) It's a nice gig, isn't it? (Laughter.)[34]

Living in Beverly Hills and occasionally dropping by an embassy in the Caribbean would be a gig many would like to have. But it is a real job. The embassy in Nassau has 154 Americans and 61 locally employed staff working for five different cabinet departments. It is also a critical threat post for crime, which means that it does not get much worse in terms of being a place where common criminals are a problem for diplomats and their families.

It is also an embassy that has to deal with issues like drug and human trafficking and money laundering. Despite these concerns, the inspectors also found that many of the cables coming from the Nassau embassy "show little political reporting or analysis on international crime, drug smuggling, and illegal migration or on prevention of terrorism."

Clearly even countries largely known for their beach resorts have a role in helping protect America's national security and other interests. As the inspection reports notes, "the Bahamas is a critical partner in ongoing efforts to ensure the security of the south-east flank of the United States." Avant resigned shortly after the inspection report was released, apparently preferring to return to Los Angeles rather than protecting that flank.

Don't Beat the Staff

Internal management of an embassy, whether it involves coordinating efforts to protect the homeland or mentoring junior officers, is a vital part of being an ambassador. The number two person in any embassy, the deputy chief of mission, is always a career Foreign Service Officer. The DCM ideally works very closely with the ambassador and the usual division of labor is that the DCM concentrates on the internal management of the embassy, whereas the ambassador attends to the external relations and constituencies. That by no means suggests that each focuses exclusively on those respective areas, but there is usually enough work on both fronts to keep them each occupied. Even in a small embassy, a division of labor of that kind makes for better management.

A 2009 inspection report on the embassy in Port of Spain, Trinidad and Tobago, indicates what happens when it does not work out that way:

> The Office of Inspector General (OIG) inspection took place just days after the Ambassador departed. This noncareer envoy, who served from 2001 to 2009, had left a distinctive stamp on the Embassy, in part because of a management style that precluded deputies from acting in the traditional DCM role of chief operating officer for the Embassy's internal activities. Those who resisted, departed. The Ambassador went through five DCMs, the longest serving were two who had been elevated from the ranks and thus were mindful of the limited authority the Ambassador would afford them.
>
> OIG's previous inspection in 2003 found that the DCM had a distinctly subsidiary, often mediating, role in Embassy Port of Spain's direction and coordination. This constrained DCMs, invariably career officers, from systematically addressing long-standing administrative problems. Further, in 2003 the OIG inspection team highlighted the Ambassador's hands-on role in personnel matters, including the hiring of local employees, and advised the Ambassador to move away from too great an involvement that undercut the Embassy's supervisory officers and created as many problems as it solved. The Ambassador did not take this action. The latest OIG team still found palpable tension between the American and local employees, amplified in part by the former Ambassador's ill-considered, semi-public criticism of his consuls, his management officer and even his DCM.[35]

The report also noted that "the Ambassador had empowered local staff explicitly or implicitly to the point that the spouse of one local employee was viewed as more of a confidant of the Ambassador than his own DCM. The Ambassador also entertained complaints directly from local staff, bypassing their American supervisors." One reason for the overly accommodating approach to those hired locally may have been the fact that the ambassador was born and raised in Kingston, the capital of Saint Vincent and the Grenadines, another island nation in the Caribbean. He may have identified with the local employees because of his background and, as a result, been overly sympathetic to them, making it difficult for those in the embassy who had to supervise them directly.

The ambassador in question was Roy Austin, a friend of George W. Bush and fellow member of the Skull and Bones secret society at Yale. The normal tour of duty for ambassadors and DCMs is three years, so to go through five DCMs in seven years is an indicator of a major management malfunction. Although his DCMs lasted only a little more than a year on average, Austin got to stay more than twice as long as normal because of his friendship with Bush. That friendship also spared him from correcting any of the problems in his performance, even though those failings had been pointed out in the earlier inspection report in 2003.

The State Department clearly did not have the stomach to deal with the situation partly because the ambassador was a friend of the president but also perhaps because the nation in question was not all that important. When it comes to the Caribbean, if the ambassador sinks his island, few in Washington will notice or care. But unimportant does not mean that such an embassy has no importance. The description of the embassy in the inspection report makes that clear:

> Port of Spain includes 44 direct-hire Americans, roughly 20 long-term, but temporary duty military special operations personnel, and 119 locally employed staff. Among agencies represented at post are the Department of Defense, the Department of Justice, the Department of Agriculture, and the Department of Homeland Security. Reflecting the flow of drugs and visitors to the United States, the mission has comparatively large consular and Drug Enforcement Administration operations. These and other mission elements operate out of four scattered and generally run-down facilities in downtown Port of Spain, a cumbersome arrangement, which frustrates efficient work within the Embassy.

Embassy offices were not the only things that were in bad shape. The report notes that the ambassador's residence also had a feeling of neglect and disrepair, in part because the ambassador viewed repair activities as intrusive.

Really—Don't Beat the Staff

Although many inspection reports contain some mild criticism of the deficiencies uncovered, there are a few that read like a Stephen King novel. One that might be considered to belong to that category, and considered by many to be the worst report card ever given an embassy, is a 2011 report on the embassy in Luxembourg. It is difficult to find on the OIG website and was not listed on their list of inspection reports.

Such a bad report deserves to be more than summarized. Here is an extended excerpt from the section on post management:

> Embassy Luxembourg is a small, resource-poor mission that has under-performed for the entirety of the current Ambassador's tenure. At present,

due to internal problems, it plays no significant role in policy advocacy or reporting, though developments in Luxembourg are certainly of interest to Washington clients and other U.S. missions in the NATO and EU communities. Since the Ambassador's confirmation, most of the senior staff, including two deputy chiefs of mission (DCM) and two section chiefs, has either curtailed or volunteered for service in Kabul and Baghdad. Other U.S. staff members have also departed early. At the time of the inspection, additional members of staff were contemplating curtailing. The OIG team believes and in some cases knows for certain that these early departures are because of the Ambassador's management style. The mission does not provide an environment that nurtures, supports, or trains entry-level or recently tenured officers. Management resources have been skewed toward front office priorities to the detriment of the performance of core responsibilities and the fulfillment of Foreign Affairs Manual (FAM) policies and requirements.

The current Ambassador is not responsible for the management cuts in 2008 that crippled general services operations before her arrival. However, the bulk of the mission's internal problems are linked to her leadership deficiencies, the most damaging of which is an abusive management style. She has followed a pattern of public criticism of colleagues, including DCMs, who have not performed to her satisfaction. The team believes that a climate of acute stress exists in the mission, which is especially evident among officers and local staff who have been here more than 3 or 4 months. Those who have questioned or challenged some of the Ambassador's actions state that they have paid a heavy price in the form of verbal abuse and been threatened with dismissal.

This appraisal will not be news to the Bureau of European and Eurasian Affairs (EUR), which has been forthcoming about its concerns regarding management issues at Embassy Luxembourg. It is unfortunate that an impression is being created among officers and local employees at this mission that this kind of behavior may be routinely tolerated by Department of State leadership, particularly for noncareer ambassadors.

With the exception of the consular section, toward which the Ambassador is hands-off, there has also been a chronic communications problem between the front office and the rest of the mission. This is partly the natural result of the absence of a permanent DCM at the mission; of the seven permanent and temporary staff who served in this position since the Ambassador's confirmation in November 2009, only one has remained for longer than 6 months. This group includes a DCM who had been in the job for only 4 months, and who the Ambassador decided to replace only weeks before her arrival at the embassy. The situation is further complicated by the fact that the Ambassador maintains total control over her own calendar, which renders the role of the office management specialist ambiguous to the staff and deprives the Ambassador of an important element of the management process.

Coordination of access to the Ambassador and of the ordinary flow of information to mission employees is lacking. An even bigger problem is the Ambassador's lack of confidence—or perhaps trust—in her staff, which leads to a near total absence of regular guidance and advance planning. The OIG team found no evidence that the Ambassador used the Mission Strategic and Resource Plan (MSRP) as a management tool. She did not provide a COM statement to the OIG team as required by OIG procedures, making it difficult for the team to assess the Ambassador's policy and program priorities.

The Ambassador believes her major contribution is in the area of public diplomacy. This generally takes the form of responding to representation opportunities in this highly pro-American society or attending diplomatic community events. The OIG team was told that the Ambassador has expressed on various occasions the importance she attaches to the perquisites of a COM. Much of her focus has been on the COM's residence (CMR) and official residence staff.[36]

The report noted the ambassador indicated that she wanted to start again, saying that she would welcome the department's help in resolving the major problems that beset her first year. Apparently, that sentiment did not last long. She resigned two weeks before the report was made public.[37]

The ambassador was Cynthia Stroum, a venture capitalist and the daughter of a wealthy Seattle businessman, who had bundled more than $500,000 for President Obama's election campaign. She was also on the finance committees for both of the current Democratic senators from Washington, Maria Cantwell and Patty Murray. In announcing her resignation, she cited a desire to focus on her family and personal business.[38]

One thing the ambassador did trust her staff to do was look for temporary housing for her when the ambassador's residence was being repaired. The few staff members in the small embassy spent a great deal of time screening more than 200 possibilities and visiting between 30 and 40 during the search. Only four met her criteria, and she rejected them all.

One other issue had to do with the mattress in the residence where she did stay. She did not like the king-sized one that the State Department provided, so she bought a queen-sized version. She twice put in a claim for reimbursement, and it was rejected both times. Unfortunately, although a personal representative of the most powerful man in the world can do many things, getting the US government to pay for a new mattress is not one of them when that mattress is just a question of personal preference. The rules on how money is spent and the bureaucracy involved often come as a shock to those who have not experienced it previously, especially those not used to dealing with the red tape of government.

The Job Is Not What You Make It

Another surprise for some of those who come to an ambassadorship from outside of government is that there are things you cannot do, like buy a new mattress, and things you must do. Into the latter category falls all manner of obligations that the government expects an ambassador to handle, even if it means devoting less time to other things the ambassador would like to do.

A case in point is Douglas Kmiec, who became Obama's ambassador to Malta in 2009. Kmiec might have seemed an unlikely choice. He is a prominent Catholic academic and constitutional lawyer, a Republican who served in the Justice Department during the Reagan administration, and a vocal opponent of abortion. Even though he is pro-life, he supported Obama because he believed the president's policies would be more effective at reducing abortions. For his efforts he got the ambassadorship, but he was also denied communion at Mass by a priest who used the occasion to denounce Kmiec's endorsement of Obama.[39]

Kmiec nonetheless took the job, but he only lasted a year and a half. His vision of what his responsibilities were and how he should spend his time clashed with the views of the State Department. He apparently thought he was more than just Obama's ambassador to Malta. He spent much of his time writing articles for religious publications, whereas projects like the transfer of embassy operations to a new building received little of his attention. Again, the inspection report lays out the problem without pulling any punches:

> The Ambassador's outside activities have detracted from his attention to core mission goals. The Ambassador should focus on embassy priorities and refrain from outside activities, including writing and speaking engagements that do not pertain directly to strengthening maritime security, promoting U.S. trade and investment, and other mission goals.
>
> Based on a belief that he was given a special mandate to promote President Obama's interfaith initiatives, he has devoted considerable time to writing articles for publication in the United States as well as in Malta, and to presenting his views on subjects outside the bilateral portfolio. He has been inconsistent in observance of clearance procedures required for publication. He also looks well beyond the bilateral

relationship when considering possible events for the mission to host in Malta. His approach has required Department principals, as well as some embassy staff, to spend an inordinate amount of time reviewing his writings, speeches, and other initiatives. His official schedule has been uncharacteristically light for an ambassador at a post of this size, and on average he spends several hours of each workday in the residence, much of which appears to be devoted to his nonofficial writings.

At the same time, he has not focused sufficiently on key management issues within the embassy, including the new embassy compound. The Ambassador pursues an active public diplomacy program and while he is popular with the Maltese Government and public, he meets infrequently with senior government officials, business executives, and diplomatic colleagues outside social events.

The Ambassador advised the inspection team that he intended to discontinue his outside writings and focus on matters that directly pertain to the embassy and priorities outlined in the Mission Strategic and Resource Plan (MSRP). Within weeks of the team's departure, however, he resumed drafting public essays that addressed subjects outside his purview as Ambassador to Malta and detracted from his core responsibilities.[40]

Kmiec was unwilling to accept the State Department's opinion of what his job entailed, however. When the White House did not endorse his view of how he should be spending his time, he resigned. In his letter to the president and secretary of state announcing his decision, Kmiec asserted that the OIG report was flawed and had a narrow vision of the embassy's mission. He also claimed: "My voice has been prevented from speaking: my pen has been enjoined from writing."[41]

Apparently, the White House chose not to intervene to save him, and Kmiec left Malta in May 2011. Kmiec's interest in a government job did not disappear, however, and his 20 months as ambassador seem to have provided him the experience for higher office, at least in his own mind. In a lengthy Facebook post in early 2014, he let it be known that he is interested and available to be presidential hopeful Hillary Clinton's vice president.[42]

You Can Do Too Much as Well as Too Little

Kmiec and Stroum wanted to spend too much time doing things outside of the embassy. The flip side of that is doing too much inside the embassy and becoming such a micromanager that the embassy does not function as well as it should.

The ambassador in Denmark from 2009 to 2013 is a good example of this, even though there was also praise for things she had done well. The inspection report lauded her effective dialogue with the Danes and said she had been the driving force behind major initiatives on women's issues and counterterrorism. She was also complimented for fostering a high degree of collaboration among the various agencies at the embassy.

But the report went on to point out:

> The reporting, analysis, and outreach functions are operating below potential, due to the concentration of decision-making in the hands of the Ambassador. The embassy staff perceives that the Ambassador is unwilling to delegate authority, and that this weakens the chain of command and disempowers section leaders, making it difficult for them to organize their work and to hold officers within their sections accountable. The Ambassador has, in effect, become a first-line supervisor, and can be harsh in dealing with any lapses she perceives.[43]

A follow-up inspection issued a second report noting that there had been some improvement. But it also stated:

> As was the case at the time of the inspection, the Ambassador prefers to run a relatively flat organization; the Ambassador reaches out to individual officers for information or to assign them tasks. Often, section chiefs are unaware of assigned tasks until advised by their subordinates. While it is the prerogative of the Ambassador and DCM to operate a relatively flat organization, including reaching out directly to any member of the mission, the absence of a clear system to keep supervisors informed about those contacts hinders section chiefs' ability to maintain oversight and quality control over their officers' work. This practice also results in a loss of accountability, and in the case of some entry-level officers, their involvement with special projects may have limited their exposure to the core programs that they need to master.[44]

The ambassador was Laurie Fulton, a lawyer who belonged to a high-powered Washington firm. She was a low-six-figures bundler for Obama who has contributed tens of thousands of dollars of her own money to a variety of Democratic candidates over the years. She is also the former wife of Senator Tom Daschle.[45] Although her insistence on dealing directly with lower-level subordinates undercut their immediate supervisors and caused some confusion in the chain of command, it was apparently not sufficiently serious to cut short her time in Copenhagen. She served three and a half years and departed in early 2013.

You're Not in the Army Now... or the Air Force

Ambassadors bring to the job the management style that they develop during their professional lives, but sometimes that style is not appropriate to the situation. In the case of Kenya, the challenge for a manager is considerable. The embassy in Nairobi is the largest in Africa, with 1,300 employees working for 19 different federal agencies. Because of its location, relatively good transportation links, and generally pleasant environment, it is a popular place for regional offices that cover a number of the neighboring countries from Nairobi.

In 2011, Scott Gration stepped into this challenging role. He is the son of missionaries who grew up in Kenya, and he speaks fluent Swahili. He had a highly successful career in the Air Force, rising to the rank of Major General. He became an early supporter of Obama and one of few campaign advisors with experience in the military.

Stroum and Avant received their ambassadorships because of an economic relationship with the president. They bundled hundreds of thousands of dollars for his election campaign and threw in tens of thousands more in personal contributions. Kmiec, on the other hand, was an example of a political relationship, because he may have helped convince a few Catholics to vote for the pro-choice candidate. Austin was purely a personal friend of President Bush. Gration is an example of a person who gives time, not money, to the president and wins votes through the hard work of an electoral campaign rather than through political influence. And being a former high-ranking military officer, he helped deflect criticism about the president's lack of military experience.

Despite his success as an Air Force general, he was a poor choice to lead the embassy in Kenya. A management style that worked in the armed forces was not transferable to herding bureaucrats from 19 different agencies. Once again, the inspection report pulled no punches:

> The Ambassador has lost the respect and confidence of the staff to lead the mission. Of more than 80 chiefs of mission inspected in recent cycles, the Ambassador ranked last for interpersonal relations, next to last on both managerial skill and attention to morale, and third from last in his overall scores from surveys of mission members. The inspectors found no reason to question these assessments; the Ambassador's leadership to date has been divisive and ineffective.
>
> The Ambassador has damaged the cohesion of Embassy Nairobi's country team by underscoring differences between offices working directly with Kenya and those with regional responsibilities. Unless corrected there is a risk that the country team will become dysfunctional.

The Ambassador needs to broaden his understanding of why various agencies are part of his mission, cease avoiding contact with them, and work with the assistance of a senior Department of State official and the next deputy chief of mission to restore country team harmony.

The Ambassador's efforts to develop and focus the mission's work around what he calls "mission essential tasks" have consumed considerable staff time and produced documents of unclear status and almost no value to the Department in approving priorities and assigning resources.

The Ambassador's greatest weakness is his reluctance to accept clear-cut U.S. Government decisions. Notwithstanding his talk about the importance of mission staff doing the right thing, the Ambassador by deed or word has encouraged it to do the opposite.

The Ambassador does not read classified front channel messages and has not established a system to have his staff screen incoming cables relevant to Kenya and U.S. interests in the region.[46]

Under Gration, as was the case with Stroum, embassy staffers were volunteering to serve in Iraq and Afghanistan to avoid having to work for him further. When interviewed by the Associated Press, three embassy employees described the general as having a "my way or the highway" military leadership style. Gration resigned after being shown a draft of the inspection report.[47]

Planning Counts, Even When It Isn't Easy

All of the examples thus far have been political appointees. There are, of course, career officers that do not succeed as ambassadors, as well. They sometimes do so under more difficult circumstances, and Bahrain is one example of such a challenge. It is a country with a repressive government that has been brutally suppressing pro-democracy demonstrators and violating human rights. The human rights NGO Freedom House places Bahrain firmly in its "not free" category. At the same time, it provides a major port for the US Navy providing a home for the Fifth Fleet and is therefore an important military ally. Although there are differences with all countries on any number of issues, few present a starker conflict of interests for the United States. To deal with this situation, a career officer, Thomas C. Krajeski, was sent as ambassador in 2011. It did not go well according to the inspection report from March 2014:

The embassy has two competing policy priorities: to maintain strong bilateral military cooperation and to advance human rights. The Ambassador has forged strong relationships with U.S. military leaders based in Bahrain to promote common goals.

The Ambassador has not focused sufficiently on planning processes and implementation as a way to keep staff focused during turbulent times. His belief that reactive "seat of the pants" leadership works best in Bahrain's challenging environment has left staff members who do not have access to him on a regular basis confused about mission goals. Disdain for planning has trickled down to section heads, leaving most sections without the tools to make the best use of their programs and resources.

The Ambassador's failure to maintain a robust planning and review process has led to confusion and lack of focus among some staff members and sidelined economic/commercial activities and public diplomacy programs.

The embassy has not developed a comprehensive strategy to improve the Ambassador's negative media image. The Ambassador has agreed to increase his participation in noncontroversial programs and events with potential to generate positive publicity. Public affairs activities suffer from a lack of strategic planning.[48]

It is not clear how the ambassador could have gotten good press in a country with no press freedom. If he pushed even slightly on the human rights question in a public way, the media, which is entirely under the government's thumb, would attack him.

The media at the State Department brought the question of the report up at the Daily Press Briefing, which led to the following exchange, where the deputy spokesperson read a prepared response:

Q: Do you have a reaction to the inspector general report on the ambassador to Bahrain?

MS. HARF: I do. We have, obviously, received the report. The State Department values the oversight provided by our inspector general and we take IG recommendations seriously and rely on them to make improvements in how we operate. With regard to this specific inspection report, Department officials are reviewing the report and its recommendations and will respond to the inspector general formally. While we agree with some of the recommendations, we disagree with others. I'm not going to outline those today. We'll do that in a formal report. But we believe the report contains a number of factual inaccuracies and take issue with several of the report's assertions.

Our ambassador in Bahrain is qualified, highly capable, and we have full confidence in his leadership of the mission. He has served with distinction for over 35 years in some of our most challenging missions, including in Iraq and as our ambassador in Yemen; has repeatedly been recognized for his service and leadership, including multiple Superior Honor Awards and the President's Distinguished Service Award.

Q: But just because he—did all those wonderful things in the past doesn't mean—doesn't necessarily have anything to do with the complaints—

MS. HARF: With his leadership now?

Q: Well, with the—

MS. HARF: Well, I think it matters. Absolutely.

Q: Well, it matters in the sense that he has leadership capabilities—

MS. HARF: Yes.

Q: —but that doesn't mean necessarily that what is being applied to this particular case in Bahrain really doesn't have much bearing.

MS. HARF: I think it's an important fact to note. I also—as I said, we will respond formally, but we do disagree with some of the recommendations. We take issue with several of the report's assertions and believe the report contains a number of factual inaccuracies. We will be responding formally to the IG.[49]

So although the inspection reports provide great insight, accountability, and measurement of performance, they are not without controversy or criticism. The need for planning is one of the things that consumes a great deal of time and effort in an embassy, but it is essential to keep all of the different members of the country team working together to achieve the goals that have been set. Rarely will those goals be as difficult and more in conflict with each other than in Bahrain. That is a challenge that is not likely to be faced by a political appointee ambassador. Of the 14 men who have been the American ambassador to that country, only 2 were political appointees.[50] Why that is the case will be discussed in chapter 6, which concerns how not just career or noncareer status but also gender, race, religion, and sexual preference can matter in where someone goes as ambassador.

CHAPTER 6

Where Ambassadors Go

There are around 170 different places in the world where one can be an American ambassador. Who gets that job in a particular country is a decision driven by many factors. How those factors come into play is not easily understood given the lack of transparency in the personnel process and can be surprising. The first and foremost is whether the person is a career officer or a political appointee. There are other elements that influence ambassadorial assignments, however, and they include gender, race, sexual orientation, religion, and one's position on abortion. This chapter will look at each of these factors and how it affects who gets sent where as ambassador.

The division between career and noncareer officers will be considered first, given that it is by far the most important overall. At the State Department's two-week charm school for new ambassadors, the divide between career ambassadors and political appointees becomes immediately obvious to all of the participants. The ambassadors and their spouses sit around a large U-shaped table listening to lectures on subjects that range from the mundane to the momentous. There is a lot of advice about how to handle the media. Speakers also talk about everything from filling out forms to get reimbursement for official entertaining to what to do if taken hostage.

Many of the career officers in this seminar will know each other, whereas the appointees will probably know few if any of the other participants. To make it easy for everyone to get to know their classmates, a placard is placed on the table for each ambassador and spouse that lists their names and the country to which they are going. The Foreign Service Officers (FSOs) look around the room with envy at the destinations of the noncareer ambassadors who are going to places like Denmark and Mexico. At the same time, the political appointees will ponder the places to which the career people are going and will ask themselves, "Just where are Niger and Malawi?"

Gary Trudeau, the creator of *Doonesbury*, captured the essence of much of the process of getting an ambassadorship and portrayed this difference brilliantly in a comic stip. It consisted of four frames:

- In the first frame, an auctioneer in black tie at a microphone says, "Our next lot is a most challenging posting—the Republic of Rwanda!"
- The view in the second frame looks over the shoulder of the auctioneer as he continues to speak to a large audience in formal attire. He says, "What am I bid for this distinguished appointment? Shall we start with $50,000? Do I hear $30,000? $20,000?"
- In the third frame, the auctioneer tries again to coax a bid out of anyone in the audience by saying "$10,000?" A man in the audience wearing a tuxedo turns to his elegantly dressed wife and asks, "Where the hell is Rwanda?" His wife responds, "It's in deepest darkest dear. It's not for us."
- In the final frame, the auctioneer brings his gavel down with a "BAM" and says, "No bid! Rwanda goes to a career diplomat!" The man in a tux shouts "Hear hear! Good for him!" His wife, looking at her program and holding a flute of champagne, sighs and says, "Yes, those people are so good in the sticky countries!"

The strip ran on August 24, 1989, well before April 1994, when Rwanda became synonymous with genocide. Ironically, despite what the strip implied, of the 16 men and 1 woman who have served as ambassadors to Rwanda, two have been political appointees. One, who was appointed by George H. W. Bush, was serving when the cartoon ran. The other was his predecessor, who was appointed by Reagan.

The fact that to date only 12 percent of the ambassadors to Rwanda have been political appointees, and neither of them were significant campaign contributors, does indicate the division between the "sticky" countries where career ambassadors are sent and the countries to which political appointees are dispatched. It also demonstrates that within the ranks of political appointees, distinctions are made depending on whether the ambassador's relationship to the president is economic, political, or personal.

Table 6.1, which was compiled by the American Foreign Service Association (AFSA), demonstrates how different the regions of the world are when it comes to ambassadorships.

Table 6.1 History of Ambassadorial Appointments by Continent

Continent	Career	Political	Political since 1960 (%)
Western Europe[1]	104	275	72.6
The Caribbean[2]	44	114	72.2
Oceania[3]	79	73	48.0
North and Central America[4]	88	63	41.7
South Asia[5]	87	32	26.9
East Asia[6]	152	52	25.5
South America[7]	167	48	22.3
Eastern Europe[8]	158	45	22.2
Africa[9]	652	112	14.7
The Middle East[10]	236	39	14.2
Central Asia[11]	51	0	0

Source: American Foreign Service Association, updated May 9, 2014.

Note: [1] Western Europe includes Andorra, Austria, Belgium, Cyprus, Denmark, Finland, France, Germany, Greece, Holy See, Iceland, Ireland, Italy, Liechtenstein, Luxembourg, Malta, Monaco, the Netherlands, Norway, Portugal, San Marino, Spain, Sweden, Switzerland, and the United Kingdom.

[2] The Caribbean includes Antigua, Bahamas, Barbados, Barbuda, Dominica, the Dominican Republic, Grenada, Haiti, Jamaica, St. Kitts and Nevis, St. Lucia, St. Vincent and the Grenadines, and Trinidad and Tobago.

[3] Oceania includes Australia, Fiji, Kiribati, Marshall Islands, Micronesia, Nauru, New Zealand, Papua New Guinea, Samoa, Solomon Islands, Tonga, Tuvalu, and Vanuatu.

[4] North and Central America include Belize, Canada, Costa Rica, El Salvador, Guatemala, Honduras, Mexico, Nicaragua, and Panama.

[5] South Asia includes Afghanistan, Bangladesh, India, Maldives, Nepal, Pakistan, and Sri Lanka.

[6] East Asia includes Brunei, Burma, Cambodia, China, Indonesia, Japan, Laos, Malaysia, Mongolia, Palau, Philippines, Singapore, South Korea, Thailand, Timor-Leste, and Vietnam.

[7] South America includes Argentina, Bolivia, Brazil, Chile, Colombia, Ecuador, Guyana, Paraguay, Peru, Suriname, Uruguay, and Venezuela.

[8] Eastern Europe includes Albania, Belarus, Bosnia and Herzegovina, Bulgaria, Croatia, Czech Republic, Estonia, Georgia, Hungary, Kosovo, Latvia, Lithuania, Macedonia, Moldova, Montenegro, Poland, Romania, Russia, Serbia, Slovakia, Slovenia, and Ukraine.

[9] Africa includes Angola, Benin, Botswana, Burkina Faso, Burundi, Cameroon, Cape Verde, the Central African Republic, Chad, Comoros, Congo (DR), Congo (Republic of), the Côte d'Ivoire, Djibouti, Equatorial Guinea, Eritrea, Ethiopia, Gabon, Gambia, Ghana, Guinea, Guinea-Bissau, Kenya, Lesotho, Liberia, Madagascar, Malawi, Mali, Mauritania, Mauritius, Mozambique, Namibia, Niger, Nigeria, Rwanda, São Tomé and Principe, Senegal, Seychelles, Sierra Leone, Somalia, South Africa, South Sudan, Sudan, Swaziland, Tanzania, Togo, Uganda, Zambia, and Zimbabwe.

[10] The Middle East includes Algeria, Bahrain, Egypt, Iraq, Israel, Jordan, Kuwait, Lebanon, Libya, Morocco, Oman, Qatar, Saudi Arabia, Syria, Tunisia, Turkey, United Arab Emirates, and Yemen.

[11] Central Asia includes Armenia, Azerbaijan, Kazakhstan, Kyrgyz Republic, Tajikistan, Turkmenistan, and Uzbekistan.

Clearly not all regions are created equal. Although the overall ratio since 1960 has been about 30 percent political appointee ambassadors and 70 percent career officers, that ratio is reversed for Western Europe and the Caribbean, where more than 72 percent of the ambassadors have been political appointees. At the other extreme is Central Asia, which has had independent countries, and ambassadors to them, only since the breakup of the Soviet Union. It is nonetheless notable that there has not been a single political appointee among the 51 ambassadors who have gone there.

So why the pronounced pattern of assignments? No social science theory would be able to explain it, nor would any official admit it, but there is a somewhat cynical explanation: political appointees, many of whom give lots of money to buy their titles, want countries that their friends will recognize and come to visit, that have few risks, and where the quality of life is good. That means Western Europe and the Caribbean and a few other English-speaking island nations in the Pacific, such as Australia and New Zealand.

Being close to the United States is also a plus. There have been other ambassadors besides Nicole Avant (see chapter 5) who have not been all that interested in spending much time on the job, and a shorter flight home makes that easier. A map provided by Max Fisher in his blog on the *Washington Post* website demonstrated perfectly the geography of ambassadorial appointments by showing the countries where the bundlers went, where other political appointees went, and where career ambassadors went.[1] The clustering of the bundlers in their two favorite regions was evident, as were the less desirable destinations of the career officers.

Another feature of this peculiar geography is that the more money an appointee gives, the better the country he or she gets as measured in terms of gross domestic product per capita, the standard measure of economic development, and in terms of the number of international tourists that visit each year. The data analyzed by my colleague Johannes Fedderke in an article we wrote together shows a very strong correlation between such factors.[2] In other words, the wealthier the country, the more likely it is that it will have a political appointee as an ambassador. And the wealthier the country, the more that appointee will have contributed to political campaigns to get the job.

So why is such a system tolerated if the wealth of the country and the wealth of the ambassador are what matter most? It can hardly be expected to produce optimal results in terms of the effectiveness of foreign policy. The reason is that, in the end as the constitution says, the president gets to appoint ambassadors. Even though the president is the most powerful person in the world, there are a limited number of ways to reward those who helped with the election. Since the cost of presidential campaigns has surpassed the one billion dollar mark, the president needs a lot of helpers, and some of them will help because they want to be rewarded with an ambassadorship. To satisfy some of them and encourage others to contribute, this implicit quid pro quo is part of the American way of government.

This system may not be as dysfunctional as it seems. Relations with the countries in Western Europe are typically as strong as they are complex. Communication with and travel between them and the United States are not difficult. And they have large embassies with capable staffs and also usually a competent ambassador from them in Washington. It is therefore easy enough to work around a political appointee, either in the foreign capital or in Washington, if the ambassador turns out to be lazy or a disaster. And these countries are well accustomed to the peculiar American tradition and manner of sending amateur envoys. Some have even complained privately when their ambassador gave less in campaign contributions than one sent to a neighboring country.

As for the Caribbean, the tropical paradises not far from the southeastern United States, relations are also usually very good and not that important from Washington's perspective. If the ambassador runs the embassy poorly, no one in Washington is likely to notice or care very much. Not every island is equally attractive however. Haiti has not had a political appointee ambassador in the last 50 years. But some island nations can become more attractive as the country on the other half of Hispaniola demonstrates. The last 6 ambassadors to the Dominican Republic have been political appointees. The 10 ambassadors before that were all career officers. Clearly the country has come a long way from 1965 when President Johnson order its occupation by 22,000 American troops in order to prevent it from being taken over by what he claimed would be a communist dictatorship.

Besides island nations and rich countries, there is another pool of plum assignments that are given to political appointees. Although most ambassadors are appointed to specific countries, there are a number that are named to serve as the US representatives to multilateral organizations, such as the specialized agencies of the United Nations. Almost all of these jobs are located in major cities in the developed world, including Brussels, Geneva, and Rome. It is therefore not surprising that political appointees hold 14 out of the 19 ambassadorships to such multinational organizations.[3]

Each of these jobs comes with a title and a nice house in a European capital. With the exception of the International Atomic Energy Agency, which tracks how nations are using their nuclear programs, the work is usually not specialized or difficult enough to require much experience. There are also career people in the delegations to these organizations that an ambassador without relevant experienced can be compensated for and worked around if necessary.

The more pleasant a country is in terms of its appeal to tourists, the more likely it is that a political appointee will be running the embassy.

That is not the case in the "sticky" countries, which often have pay differentials to make staffing them at all levels easier. These incentives refer to additional pay given to those who serve in embassies in countries that are dangerous, unhealthy, or generally unpleasant. Political appointees of any description are very rarely found in such countries, and major campaign contributors never are.

Appendices I–J include lists of the countries that had danger pay and hardship allowances in 2011. The lists change often because conditions at these posts are periodically reviewed to see if the differential is still justified, should be maintained as is, or increased.

Danger pay is compensation for just what the name implies. It is a bonus of at least 15 percent of the employee's base pay, but it can be as high as 35 percent, for serving in places where a threat to embassy personnel exists because of civil unrest, terrorism, drug traffickers, or some other form of violence. In only 2 of the 18 embassies with danger pay, Afghanistan and Saudi Arabia, were there political appointee ambassadors in 2011. Both of them were retired generals, and neither of them made any significant campaign contributions.

Hardship pay is awarded where the local conditions differ substantially from the environment in the United States and warrant additional compensation as a recruitment and retention incentive. This allowance is meant to compensate for spending a few years in a country known for crime, disease, poverty, poor health care, isolation, or other local features that make it a particularly difficult place to live. The hardship allowance is an addition to base pay that starts at 5 percent and can be as high as 35 percent.

Of the more than 165 embassies, 127 have conditions sufficiently difficult to warrant some level of hardship pay. Of the 77 percent of posts with hardship pay, only 13, or 10 percent, have political appointees as ambassadors. And of those 13 appointees, only 4 made campaign contributions in the six-figure range and only 1 made contributions in the mid-five figures. In the cases of two of those four significant contributors, the posts had a hardship allowance of only 5 percent, and in the cases of the other two, it was 10 percent.[4]

Although political appointees rarely go to embassies with hardship and danger pay, they do go to Washington. But again it is a place where big donors almost never go. An analysis of the 141 State Department officials who required Senate confirmation of their appointments from January 2001 through October 2013 (from the beginning of the George W. Bush administration into the second term of Obama's presidency) showed very few big contributors. Of the 141, only 40 were career officials, who traditionally do not make campaign contributions. Of the remaining 101, only 3 had given or bundled in the six-figure range and only 4 had made it into the five-figure category. The one who gave the most, having bundled in excess of $500,000, came to his Washington job after being ambassador in Paris.

One reason for this discrepancy is that more than half of these officials came predominantly from political or government backgrounds. Among the remainder there were only 15 with business backgrounds and a few each from the media, academia, think tanks, nongovernment organizations, law, and the military. A crowd like that is probably not going to have the financial resources to contribute large sums to an election campaign in order to buy a title. And Washington jobs are generally for policy wonks who have an interest in and the qualifications for work that is heavy on substance and short on glamor.

The titles that go with thosed kinds of jobs are of more limited valued than ambassadorships for résumé-building purposes. No one puts "assistant secretary" or "under secretary" on their business cards after they leave government, but most former ambassadors do add their positions. As with reaching the rank of colonel or general, it is an honorific that stays with a person for the rest of his or her life. Washington jobs are also for those who are interested in policy making and willing to work very long hours, a description that does not fit the average megadonor.

Aside from the wealth and touristic value of countries, there are other determinants as to who goes where as an ambassador. In the early days of the country, the men who were in charge of America's diplomatic missions abroad were the founding fathers or looked just like them. They were white, male, Anglo-Saxon, and Protestant, with the occasional Catholic. As the country's overseas interests, economy, and population grew, the ranks of diplomats gradually became more diverse.

More recently in the nation's history, it has been said that the diplomats who are supposed to represent America should be as diverse as the American people. The reality is that the makeup of America's ambassadors reflects the prejudices and social values of the moment and will never be an exact replica of the demographics of the population of the country as a whole. Although it is less true than in the past, gender, ethnicity, religion, and sexual orientation all have an effect on who becomes an ambassador to what country. The following sections will discuss each of these factors and how they affect ambassadorial assignments.

Women

For nearly a century, the State Department employed no women in full-time positions. It began to hire them in 1874 but only for clerical work. The attitude of the department reflected the patronizing, condescending view of the era. For example, in 1905, Assistant Secretary Frederick Van Dyne is quoted in the Short History on the State Department's website as saying: "The greatest obstacle to the employment of women as diplomatic agents is their well known inability to keep a secret."[5]

The effort to win women the right to vote, which culminated in the ratification of the Nineteenth Amendment in 1920, helped prompt a different attitude in the State Department, as well as society at large. Things began to change, but progress came slowly to such a tradition-bound institution like the State Department.

The first woman to enter the Foreign Service, Lucile Atcherson, did not do so until 1922. She was sent to Switzerland in 1925 and resigned two years later in order to get married. Unlike men, women could not enter the Foreign Service if they were married and had to leave it if they acquired a spouse. That requirement was not abolished until 1972. That same year, the requirement for supervisors to comment on the suitability of the wives and other family members of male officers was eliminated from annual evaluation reports.

Ruth Bryan Owen was the first woman to be chief of a diplomatic mission. A former congresswoman, President Roosevelt named her envoy extraordinary and plenipotentiary to Denmark in 1933.

Helen Eugenie Anderson was the first woman to have the title of ambassador. Active in the Democratic Party, she was appointed by President Truman as ambassador to Denmark in 1949. In 1962, President Kennedy sent her to Bulgaria, making her the first female ambassador to a communist country.

Frances Willis became the first career diplomat named as ambassador when she was appointed to Switzerland in 1953. Within the State Department, promotions to high-level positions took longer than the ones overseas did. A woman did not fill the role of an assistant secretary until 1973 and one did not become an under secretary until 1977.

These success stories were the exceptions. In the 1960s, only 7 percent of new officers brought into the Foreign Service were women, and they held only 2.5 percent of the senior positions. By 1990, the Senior Foreign Service was still only 19 percent female. By 2005, that number had risen to 30 percent, but it has not risen much since then.[6] At least at the entry level, things are better than ever before. Today, 40 percent of those taking the written exam for the Foreign Service and 40 percent of those hired are women.

Even though the number of women in the senior ranks seems to have plateaued at 30 percent, the Foreign Service is still far ahead of other sectors of American society. Only 4 percent of the CEOs of Fortune 500 companies are women, and less than 17 percent of those who sit on the boards of those corporations are.[7] Only a quarter of university presidents, a supposedly enlightened group, are women.[8]

Progress has also been made with regard to the effect of gender on ambassadorial placements, but there are still patterns that are pronounced. Table 6.2 indicates some of them. The first three columns cover all ambassadorial appointments from the beginning of US diplomatic relations through May 2014.[9] The second set of three columns cover the current president and his immediate predecessor.

The historical data show that female ambassadors have been typically underrepresented in Western Europe, North and Central America, East Asia, South America, and the Middle East. With the exception of the first region, the explanation could be that there was a reluctance to send a female ambassador to parts of the world where local attitudes toward women might make her job more difficult. In the case of Western Europe, it can probably be attributed to the fact that the region is popular with big donors and women have typically not had the financial wherewithal that men have had to allow them to make large

Table 6.2 Female Ambassadorial Appointments

Region	Historical total			January 2001–June 2013		
	Total	Women	%	Total	Women	%
Western Europe	993	51	5.1	89	14	15.7
The Caribbean	237	37	15.6	23	9	39.1
Oceania	184	39	21.2	26	8	30.7
North and Central America	414	15	3.6	34	9	26.5
South Asia	148	19	12.8	30	8	26.7
East Asia	332	22	6.6	56	11	19.6
South America	580	20	3.4	45	11	24.4
Eastern Europe	346	26	7.5	99	21	21.2
Africa	810	125	15.4	169	53	31.3
The Middle East	435	21	4.8	73	14	19.2
Central Asia	53	12	22.6	20	7	35.0
Total	4,532	387	8.5	664	170	25.6

Source: The data for this table and the others in this chapter were gathered from the AFSA website, State Department, and White House announcements and was put together by my research assistants.

campaign contributions. All of this is largely speculation, given that the motivation for such decisions is rarely admitted or spelled out in historical documents.

The regional distribution for the last two presidents does not show much deviation from the mean. Female ambassadorial representation in Western Europe is still the lowest, probably for the same reason it has always been. The areas where it is higher than average—the Caribbean, Oceania, Africa and Central Asia—read like a list of the less important regions of the world. So although progress has been made in treating female diplomats as equals to their male counterparts, further improvement is possible.

Race and Ethnicity

African American diplomats have a longer history than female diplomats but much slower progress in being treated fairly. The only reason for the longer history lies in the fact that there were two predominantly black nations where it was thought to be appropriate to send African American envoys—Haiti, the second country to win its independence in the western hemisphere, and Liberia, which was founded by freed American slaves and dates its independence to 1847.

The first African American diplomat, Ebenezer Don Carlos Bassett, was sent to Haiti as minister resident and consul general in 1869. Lester Aglar Walton, the first African American chief of mission, was sent to Liberia in 1935. Edward Dudley, the first African American to have the title of ambassador was assigned there in 1949.[10]

Clifton R. Wharton, Sr. was the first African American to have a professional position in the State Department. He was also the first African American FSO and the first African American appointed as chief of a diplomatic mission to a European country. But his road to Europe had to lead through Liberia.

Wharton was a lawyer who entered the State Department as a law clerk in 1924. The passage of the Rogers Act that year opened the opportunity to enter the Foreign Service through a competitive exam. Wharton took the exam along with 144 other candidates. He was among the 21 who passed, but the chairman of the State Department's personnel board at the time, Joseph Grew, was openly hostile to the idea of accepting African Americans into the department's professional ranks. He wrote: "Only twenty passed, including one Negro who will go at once to Liberia." The day after Wharton entered the Foreign Service, Grew announced he was being assigned to Liberia and was in such a hurry to get him there that Wharton was denied the training that other new diplomats were given.[11]

Wharton went on to be chief of mission in Romania in 1958 and then ambassador to Norway. He died in 1990, just three years before he would have been able to see his son sworn in as deputy secretary of state, which was the highest level achieved by an African American in the department until Colin Powell became secretary in 2001. The tenure of Clifton Wharton, Jr., was short lived, however, as he held the position for only ten months. His resignation prompted a number of editorials and opinion articles claiming that Wharton was being made the scapegoat for the foreign policy failures in places like Bosnia, Haiti, and Somalia that occurred during the first year of the Clinton administration.[12] His letter of resignation after such a short tenure could not avoid referring to the reasons for his departure. He clearly agreed with the editorial writers, because he said in his resignation letter to President Clinton: "The process to which I have been subjected, in the long run, damages the Presidency and government more than the individual involved."

Joseph Grew was not the only department official to put into writing his views on where African Americans should be assigned. In 1949, Christian Ravndal, wrote a memorandum to the deputy under secretary for administration with the subject line "Countries to which an outstanding Negro might appropriately be sent as Ambassador." Ravndal was director general of the Foreign Service at the time, the State Department's most senior personnel officer who is always an FSO.[13]

Ravndal had three sets of countries to suggest. Romania or Bulgaria came first because "the appointment of an outstanding Negro as Ambassador to one of the iron curtain countries should serve to counteract the communist propaganda that Americans are guilty of race discrimination." The second choice was Afghanistan or Ethiopia, but he did not give any justification for suggesting either country. The third group of choices included Haiti, Paraguay, Guatemala, El Salvador, and Honduras, even though Ravndal worried that they would require the ambassador to "overcome the initial hostility with which he would be met." As for other possibilities, Ravndal thought that Middle Eastern countries and Portugal would be offended by an ambassador of color and that Ecuador, Bolivia, and the Dominican Republic had not "evolved enough socially to overcome race prejudice." He suggested that Switzerland, Norway, and Denmark were civilized and enlightened enough and "generally without the race prejudice found in other places."[14]

It is not clear the degree to which Ravndal's thinking reflected the attitudes of others in the department or its effect on personnel decisions, but the fact that he put such views in an official memo would support the idea that his was not an atypical attitude. It is also strange that he did not mention Liberia, but perhaps that was an obvious choice. Less than three months after he wrote the memo, Dudley was named ambassador to Liberia. Over the next decade, five more African Americans would reach ambassadorial rank. Four of them would be sent to Africa—two to Liberia, and one each to Guinea and Niger—and one to Europe—Wharton to Norway.

The regional distribution of ambassadorial appointments for African Americans is much more unbalanced than it is for women, as is shown in table 6.3. The figures in the first few columns for the historical totals, in effect 1949 to 2013, can be compared with those for the most recent years.

The dominance of Africa as a destination for African American ambassadors is plain to see. Historically, more than 72 percent of them have gone to Africa. Even in the last dozen years, the percentage remains high—at 60 percent—in a region that has a little more than a quarter of all the US embassies in the world.

In earlier times, as John Grew demonstrated, there were prejudices within the State Department that had a profound effect on where African American diplomats were sent. Ravndal's memo demonstrates

Table 6.3 African American Ambassadorial Appointments

Region	Historical total			January 2001–June 2013		
	Total	African Americans	%	Total	African Americans	%
Western Europe	993	9	0.9	89	2	2.2
The Caribbean	237	10	4.2	23	5	21.7
Oceania	184	8	4.3	26	4	15.4
North and Central America	414	2	0.5	34	1	2.9
South Asia	148	2	1.6	30	1	3.3
East Asia	332	3	0.9	56	2	3.6
South America	580	4	0.7	45	3	6.7
Eastern Europe	346	3	0.9	99	6	6.1
Africa	810	118	14.6	169	41	24.3
The Middle East	435	5	1.1	73	2	2.7
Central Asia	53	1	1.9	20	1	5.0
Total	4,532	164	8.5	664	68	10.2

Source: American Foreign Service Association, State Department, and other public sources.

another kind of bias. Trying to anticipate the prejudices of the country to which a diplomat might be sent and letting that drive the assignment process is another way that options have remained limited for African American diplomats.

There is a third, more benign, explanation for this geographic pattern of assignments at least as it exists today. Because of their heritage, African American diplomats could be choosing to serve in Africa because they want to learn more about their roots or because they think their ethnicity might be an advantage in dealing with African officials. Or perhaps they believe they will be less welcome in other parts of the world and therefore less effective.

Political and economic officers tend to specialize in one particular region of the world, and that region is mainly a question of personal preferences. For career officers, having established one's identity and gained experience and language ability in a region makes it highly likely that when the possibility of a subsequent ambassadorship arises, it will be in that same region.

If self-selection is today the most important determinant of where an African American might go as ambassador, then the same might be true for other minorities. Table 6.4 shows the figures for Hispanics.

As the size of any sample gets smaller, the more tenuous are the conclusions that can be drawn from it, but the same sort of geographic concentration that is drawing African American ambassadors to Africa seems to also apply to Hispanics and Latin America.

There are other factors that may enter into the question of ethnicity. Recruiting of minorities by the State Department has been uneven over the years and can receive greater or less emphasis depending on the priorities placed on the small number of people who actively seek recruits. With 20,000 people a year signing up to take an exam for a job for which there usually around 350 openings, there is no shortage of applicants to the Foreign Service.

One reason that minorities may be underrepresented in admissions to the Foreign Service and at the ambassadorial level is the question of family income. According to the Census Bureau, the median income for white families in 2009 was nearly $52,000, whereas for blacks and Hispanics, it was $33,000 and $38,000, respectively.[15] Those minorities are less likely to attend college than whites are, and they are also less likely to graduate even if they do. As one May 2014 *New York Times* article about college graduation rates states: "Rich kids graduate; poor and working-class kids don't. Or to put it more statistically: About a quarter of college freshmen born into the bottom half of the income

Table 6.4 Hispanic American Ambassadorial Appointments, 2001–2013

Region	Total	Hispanic Americans	Hispanic (%)	Hispanic American Ambassadors (%)
Western Europe	89	2	2	9
The Caribbean	23	3	13	13
Oceania	26	0	0	0
North and Central America	34	6	18	26
South Asia	30	1	3	4
East Asia	56	2	4	9
South America	45	5	11	22
Eastern Europe	99	0	0	0
Africa	169	4	6	18
The Middle East	73	0	0	0
Central Asia	20	0	0	0
Total	664	23	3	100

Source: American Foreign Service Association, State Department, and other public sources.

distribution will manage to collect a bachelor's degree by age 24, while almost 90 percent of freshmen born into families in the top income quartile will go on to finish their degree."[16]

With the competition to pass the written exam to enter the Foreign Service, having a good college education is essential despite the fact that it is not a formal requirement to apply. And even if it were possible to somehow correct for the disadvantage that minorities face because of lower family income and graduation rates, change would be slow. Admitting more minority officers means that it will be at least 20 years before that change reaches the level of the Senior Foreign Service.

Sexual Orientation

One might not think that sexual preferences would have an effect on who gets to be an ambassador and where they are sent, but it has always been the case and, despite the remarkable progress made with regard to gay rights in recent years, it will continue to have some effect in the future.

Since Thomas Bayard became the first American diplomat to be given the title of ambassador when he was sent to London in 1893, there have been more than 4,500 people who have had that honor. Until 2013, only three of them had been openly gay.

The first was James Hormel, a prominent philanthropist and the grandson of the founder of the meat company that created Spam.

Before it became synomous with unwanted emails, Spam was known as a canned, precooked meat product made up mostly of pork that was widely eaten but rarely enjoyed. When President Clinton put Hormel forward for Luxembourg in 1997, it created a firestorm of congressional opposition. The Senate Foreign Relations Committee approved his appointment, but a number of Republican senators, responding to pressure from conservative Christian groups and Catholic organizations, blocked the nomination.[17]

In arguing against Hormel, Senator Trent Lott of Mississippi labeled homosexuality a sin and compared it to alcoholism and kleptomania. Also among those senators opposing Hormel was Chuck Hagel, who said that being "openly, aggressively gay" would limit his effectiveness as ambassador. Fifteen years later, facing his own confirmation struggle to become secretary of defense, Hagel apologized for the remark.[18]

When the full Senate failed to act on Hormel's nomination, Clinton bypassed the Senate and gave him a recess appointment in 1999. That only allowed him to serve until the beginning of 2001. At that time, a new session of Congress began and his nomination as ambassador was not resubmitted for consideration because of the opposition to his appointment.

Over the next 12 years, there were only two more openly gay ambassadors. The first one to be confirmed by the Senate was Michael Guest, a career diplomat whom George W. Bush named as ambassador to Romania. When Guest was sworn in on September 14, 2001, Secretary of State Colin Powell spoke and commented explicitly and positively on the presence of Guest's life partner. President Obama named one openly gay ambassador in his first term, David Huebner for New Zealand, without any significant Senate opposition.

In June 2013, Obama nominated five more gay men who were confirmed without controversy within two months: Rufus Gifford for Denmark, John Berry for Australia, James Costos for Spain, James Brewster for the Dominican Republic, and Daniel Baer for the Organization for Security and Cooperation in Europe (located in Vienna). All were political appointees and all were named to wealthy nations or, in the case of Brewster, the Caribbean.

The congressional treatment that openly gay nominees receive today stands in stark contrast not only to the reaction to Hormel's appointment in 1997, but it is even more remarkable when compared to the 1950s. Back then, when State Department officials would make their annual appearance before Congress to discuss the budget, the chair of the committee that handled the department would ask, "How many homosexuals has the Department fired this year?" In that era, homosexuality was grounds for dismissal and security officials in the department devoted considerable time and effort to investigating anyone accused of being a homosexual. One security officer, in fact, was employed full time to follow up on such allegations.[19]

Even in the 1980s, homosexuality was considered reason enough to revoke one's security clearance, because it was thought that it made the employee vulnerable to blackmail by foreign agents. Loss of one's clearance made any meaningful work in the department or career advancement impossible. Secretary of State George Shultz stopped the practice during the Reagan administration.

As the country's attitudes have changed, the approach of the State Department toward issues of race, gender, and sexual orientation have evolved. Recently society's evolving approach to gay rights has been reflected in dramtic progress in the way the department treats homosexuals. After the 2013 Supreme Court decision striking down the Defense of Marriage Act was announced, the State Department and other federal government agencies moved quickly to expand benefits to same-sex married couples. A majority of Americans now support allowing gay marriage and do not believe that homosexual relationships between consenting adults are morally wrong. And gay men and lesbians are now welcome in the military, even by Secretary of Defense Hagel.

Governments in some other parts of the world are not so enlightened, however: 76 countries criminalize homosexuality and 5 of those allow the death penalty for such an offense. In nearly all of Africa and the Middle East, there are harsh legal restrictions against it. And the trend recently is not necessarily heading in the right direction. In December 2013, India's highest court reinstated a colonial-era law criminalizing same-sex acts, and in February 2014, Ugandan President Yoweri Musevani signed a bill into law that toughened sanctions against homosexuality, including the possibility of life sentences for gay sex and same-sex marriages.[20] The bill was later struck down by Uganda's Constitutional Court because it was passed by the parliament when it had lacked a quorum. Supporters of the bill said they would push to have it properly approved.[21]

Even in parts of the world where homosexuality is not criminalized, strong negative reactions can be provoked by the naming of an openly gay ambassador. Brewster's appointment to the Dominican Republic was denounced as "an insult to good Dominican customs" by Reverend Cristobal Cardozo, leader of the Dominican Evangelical Fraternity. And Nicolas de Jesus Lopez, Santo Domingo's only Catholic cardinal, scoffed that "you can expect anything from the U.S." Despite such opposition, the Dominican government accepted the appointment, and the embassy's website mentions that Brewster's husband has accompanied him to post.[22]

Sending openly gay ambassadors to countries where homosexuality is condemned and criminalized will therefore continue be an issue the State Department has to deal with in the future. It is a new variation of an old problem, however. Although the State Department reflects the United States (the country it represents), it cannot completely ignore the attitudes in a country to which an ambassador is sent. It was because of racism abroad, as well as at home, that for so many years it was rare that an African American ambassador was assigned outside Africa or Western Europe. And there were no doubt prolonged debates about sending women as ambassadors to the Middle East. Although Americans like to ignore their own prejudices and insist that the rest of the world should be as enlightened as the United States, the reality is that it is not going to happen. A country that imposes harsh penalties on its own citizens for homosexuality is not going to accept an openly gay ambassador with enthusiasm, and it would not be receptive to a request for a diplomatic visa for an ambassador's same-sex spouse or life partner. And no dilomatic visa means no diplomatic immunity from things that are considered crimes locally.

That question would seem to be likely to arise less often if one were to believe the media reporting on the subject. A number of articles in 2013 listing the current openly gay ambassadors noted that, with the exception of Guest, all were political appointees, and they put the total number at eight. There have been other career ambassadors in recent years that made no secret of their homosexuality but have not advertised it to a level where it attracted media attention. For career officers, the approach has been similar to a version of the "Don't Ask, Don't Tell" policy that was attempted for a time by the military. The public scrutiny that comes with being nominated as ambassador can be intense, and opposition can come from any quarter. Given the number of hurdles that one must overcome to get the title, no one who has spent a career getting there would want to create another one.

Career officers know that senators can place a hold on a nomination without even identifying themselves or offering a reason. And if opposition is aroused, significant support from the White House is unlikely. The president might expend political capital in a confirmation fight for a political appointee but would be far less inclined to do so for a career officer, where there is less at stake.

Discretion might also be the watchword for some career officers, because being openly gay limits the number of potential countries to which they can be assigned. Those who specialize in regions of the world where there are laws against homosexuality or widespread, endemic intolerance of gays risk limiting their ambassadorial opportunities. Another aspect of the geography of ambassadorial appointments is that the more developed a country is, the less likely it is to have such laws, but those are also the countries that are more likely to go to political appointees. That further limits the possibilities for an openly gay career ambassador.

In those parts of the world where LGBT rights are advancing, there is more of an opportunity for gay career officers to be ambassadors. In May 2014, the White House announced the nomination of an openly gay career officer, Theodore Osius, to be ambassador to Vietnam. Although it is one of the most politically repressive countries in Asia, Vietnam has been one of the most accepting when it comes to gay rights and marriage.[23] Osius is married to another FSO, and they have a son.[24]

The articles, mainly in the gay press, about Osius's nomination did not mention what role his husband would play in Vietnam. That question relates to one of the traditions of the State Department, which, although anachronistic, could still have an effect on the prospects of gay career officers becoming ambassadors. There has been a long-standing practice of treating an ambassador's spouse as an unpaid employee, which may not be entirely a thing of the past. Every career officer who becomes an ambassador first serves as deputy chief of mission. Ambassadors get to choose their DCMs and, although no one would admit it today, a male ambassador might not pick someone to be DCM if he thought that meant increasing the workload on his wife for "representational social events"—the euphemism for all of those diplomatic cocktail parties.

Such an attitude could be a case of "domestic" politics determining who eventually becomes an ambassador. The Obama White House's nomination of five openly gay ambassadors represents domestic political considerations of another kind. Costos and Brewster both bundled more than a million dollars for Obama's reelection campaign, and Gifford served as the campaign's finance director. And even those who were not significant donors or fundraisers still represent a payback to a key Democratic constituency. The president and Governor Mitt Romney evenly split heterosexual voters in 2012, but Obama won the gay vote by 76 percent to 22 percent—an even greater gap than the one among Latino voters.[25]

Hormel was also a major donor to the Democratic Party.[26] He gave so much that according to his autobiography, Bob Farmer, the national treasurer of the party, urged Hormel to seek an ambassadorial appointment. Hormel writes that although he was intrigued by the idea, he did not think that having been a contributor without having gone to any great lengths to get Clinton elected would put him seriously in the running for a high-level position. Farmer urged him to look over a copy of the "Plum Book," a government publication listing some 7,000 federal jobs for political appointees. Hormel took the advice and described what he found:

> I skimmed through the Cabinet jobs, the senior level department appointments, and the presidential commissions. There was assistant secretary of this and under secretary of that and memberships on commissions relating to every aspect of public policy. In most cases, my qualifications weren't suitable for a given position, or else I knew of someone higher in the pecking order than me. The best fit, it seemed, was an ambassadorial post.[27]

The implication would seem to be that the qualifications for an ambassadorship are not that great when compared to other government jobs, but Hormel demonstrated that once he made the decision, he was going to work hard to get the job. He goes on to detail how much time, effort, and networking he had to do in the fight to overcome the opposition that his nomination created. Although the Senate never acted on his nomination, it took a lot of work on his part to push the president into giving him a recess appointment. Nearly two years passed from the time his name was sent to the Senate in October 1997 until he presented his credentials in Luxembourg, but he persisted and made history in the process.

All of the openly gay ambassadors named thus far have been men. The lack of lebians may reflect the fact that they have less money to contribute to political campaigns or the possibility that when it comes to equal rights for LGBT community, gay men are at this point in the evolution of societal attitudes more equal than the rest.

Religion

One of the concerns the founding fathers had when they were drafting the Constitution was the separation of church and state. That concern was reflected in Article VI, which states "no religious Test shall ever be required as a Qualification to any Office or public Trust under the United States." There have been religious tests, however. Belonging to a certain religion has precluded some diplomatic assignments and has been a requirement for others.

Up until the 1970s, Jews were not assigned to the embassy in Tel Aviv. Martin Indyk was the thirteenth ambassador to Israel and the first Jew to get the job, but that was not until 1995. Samuel Lewis, who had the job from 1977 to 1985, described the reason for this policy in his oral history:

> I have a feeling that the Israelis also think it's wiser for a non-Jew to be there. I think, frankly, it is better for everybody concerned that our ambassador not be Jewish. I'm sure there's some Jewish ambassadors who could do the job very well and would handle the pressures very well, but the Israelis are past masters at putting all sorts of psychological pressures on foreigners who[m] they're trying to influence. It's hard enough to remain objective and not to be overly influenced by "localitis," let's say, if you're non-Jewish. I think if you're Jewish, it just adds one more dimension of potential conflict, emotional conflict. The ambassador is in the toughest spot. The emotional spotlight of the public and the government is on you just continuously, and you are so much a public figure there, that I think the strain of being Jewish, especially if you were openly Jewish, practicing Jewish, Orthodox, or just "religious," subject to all of the emotional tensions that conflicts between Washington and Jerusalem inevitably produce, argue that the U.S. shouldn't put people into that situation if you can avoid it. I'm sure some could handle it very well, but I think on the balance, it's probably wiser not to.

Lewis later amended his oral history to note that he had supported Indyk's getting the job because Indyk was the most qualified candidate at the time. Since Indyk, there have been five men who have been ambassador to Israel, and two of them have been Jewish. Today it would be unlikely that many nations would openly reject an American ambassador because he or she was Jewish. That was not the case in the past, but there have been some countries where it was never a problem. In Turkey, for instance, there is a much higher percentage of ambassadors who have been Jewish because the Ottoman Empire was one part of the world that had no problem accepting Jews.

Although in the past Jews were excluded from some ambassadorships, there is at least one at present where the right religion is an absolute requirement. Not only is there a "religious test" for this particular ambassadorship, but it automatically draws the person into the debate about one of the most divisive social issues in America today. That ambassadorship is to the Holy See, and it is unique in that it is a city-state as well as a religious group. Here is how the State Department describes the relationship:

> The Holy See is the universal government of the Catholic Church and operates from Vatican City State, a sovereign, independent territory. The Pope is the ruler of both Vatican City State and the Holy See. The Holy See, as the supreme body of government of the Catholic Church, is a sovereign juridical entity under international law. The United States and the Holy See consult and cooperate on international issues of mutual interest, including human rights, inter-religious understanding, peace and conflict prevention, development, and environmental protection.
>
> The United States maintained consular relations with the Papal States from 1797 to 1870 and diplomatic relations with the Pope, in his capacity as head of the Papal States, from 1848 to 1868, though not at the ambassadorial level. These relations lapsed in 1870 with the loss of all papal territories during the unification of Italy. From 1870 to 1984, the United States did not have diplomatic relations with the Holy See. Several U.S. presidents, however, designated personal envoys to visit the Holy See periodically for discussions of international humanitarian and political issues. In 1984, a revised Concordat was signed defining the relations between the government and the church within Italy. The United States and the Holy See announced the establishment of diplomatic relations in 1984.[28]

The State Department summary gives the impression that relations lapsed in the mid-nineteenth century because of the loss of papal territories, but it actually happened after Congress passed a ban in 1867 against spending federal funds on diplomatic missions to the Vatican. The congressional action was prompted by a rumor that the Pope was going to forbid American Protestants from holding services in their homes within Rome's city walls.[29]

Congress repealed the prohibition in 1984, making relations at the ambassadorial level possible again, and President Reagan quickly elevated his special envoy to the Vatican, William A. Wilson, to ambassadorial rank. Wilson was a very close friend of Reagan and a member of his "kitchen cabinet," his collection of wealthy supporters and advisors. Since then, there have been ten ambassadors to the Vatican. All were political appointees and all were Catholic. They were also all antiabortion or, if not, did their best to avoid discussing the issue.[30]

During Obama's first term, stories in the conservative media claimed that the administration had three candidates for the position who were rejected by the Vatican for being insufficiently pro-life. An article in the *Catholic News Service* suggested otherwise. It quoted a Vatican official who maintained that the Vatican did not vet the personal beliefs of those put forward as ambassadors. The article went on to state, however, that marital status did matter and that the Vatican had rejected two ambassadorial candidates in recent years—one a divorced man from Argentina with a live-in partner and the second an openly gay man from France who was in a union with another man. Both were Catholic, but apparently they were not Catholic enough.[31]

Wilson had no such problems, given that he was married to a woman. In addition, she was the heir to a fortune from the Pennzoil petroleum company. He also became known for more than being the American ambassador to the Holy See. In 1986, the Libyan dictator, Muammar el-Qaddafi revealed to the media that Wilson had made a secret trip to Libya to meet with him, despite there being prohibitions on travel to the country and contact with the Libyan government.[32] The meeting came just a few weeks after the terrorist attacks on the airports in Rome and Vienna that killed 20 people and were supposedly carried out by agents of Qaddafi.[33]

In Secretary of State George Shultz's memoir, there is a section entitled "Free-Lance Diplomacy," in which he lays the blame for the trip on Wilson.[34] At the same time, he admits that White House officials had authorized Wilson's contact with Qaddafi and had been sending messages to the Libyan leader via the Italian foreign minister asking him to receive a White House emissary. Although Italian officials confirmed that they had been asked to arrange the meeting, three White House officials denied that any contact had been authorized. Clearly someone was lying.[35]

What is beyond dispute is that as the State Department was going around the world trying to gain the cooperation of America's allies in stopping Qaddafi's support for terrorism, Ambassador Wilson was engaging Qaddafi in conversation. Apparently the chat had little effect other than giving Qaddafi the opportunity to report the visit of a White House emissary to the media. Shultz notes that Wilson resigned in May 1986, a few weeks after Reagan had ordered air strikes in an attempt to at least coerce, if not kill, the Libyan leader.

If Shultz is correct, the duplicity and double dealing of the White House in this affair would be on a par with that of the Iran Contra scandal. Yet Shultz accuses Wilson of pulling "strings inside the

White House" and obsequiously asserts that Reagan "was not going soft on terrorism or on Colonel Qaddafi." According to another newspaper article in 1987, however, Reagan knew about Wilson's trip in advance.[36]

This was not Wilson's first interaction with Libyan officials. After the State Department learned from a foreign intelligence service that he had held meetings with Libyan officials in 1982 in Rome, he was warned to stop such contacts. He had also been admonished for inserting himself into two criminal investigations of his business friends.

Nevertheless, Wilson was allowed to stay on and, for nearly his entire time in Rome, keep his seat on the Pennzoil board. Shultz, who termed Wilson's private diplomacy an "embarrassment," could do nothing about it because of Wilson's friendship with Reagan. According to one account, it took the intervention of Nancy Reagan to convince her husband that Wilson finally had to go.[37]

When Wilson left Rome, he gave a press conference, but he refused to discuss the trip to Libya and denied he had ever had his wrists slapped by Washington.[38] Even stranger was his assertion a couple of months later that he had been tricked into going to Libya by "someone friendly" who was part of the US government but not with the CIA. He claimed that he therefore had no reason to be suspicious and explained he thought he was flying on a corporate jet to see Fiat executives in Turin. One might think from such statements that he might have been kidnapped by the Department of Commerce were it not for the fact that Wilson piloted the aircraft himself and a flight plan for Tripoli had been filed before he took off.[39]

Sometimes it is an ambassador's lot to take the fall for the folly of a policy dreamed up in Washington or between the ambassador and officials in the White House. As a good friend of Reagan, Wilson may have agreed to do just that without protest. Whether or not he was engaging in a freelance effort for his own business interests, he should have been fired immediately. Keeping him on for months after the trip was made public seriously undermined American credibility in its efforts to combat Qaddafi's support for terrorism. It is sometimes argued that having a close friend of the president as an ambassador is an important advantage. Mr. Wilson demonstrates that there can just as easily be disadvantages to such a relationship. The closer the ambassador is to the president, the harder it is to fire the ambassador even when there ample cause to do so.

The Vatican is not the only embassy where being Catholic matters. Ambassadors to Ireland have been overwhelmingly Irish, Catholic, and, for nearly half a century, political appointees. The last time an FSO presented credentials as ambassador in Dublin was 1965.[40] The Irish are therefore used to noncareer ambassadors, and they do not like it when there is a prolonged gap between them.

The first one appointed during by Obama to Dublin was Dan Rooney. He gave the exceedingly modest amount of $30,000 to Obama's campaign, but having the endorsement and support of the owner of the Pittsburgh Steelers football team was apparently contribution enough. Following the departure of Rooney in December 2012, a year and a half passed without a replacement being announced. The most plausible explanation for such a long gap is that candidates must have been considered during that time but failed to survive the background investigations and other parts of the clearance process.[41]

Another article called into question the assumption that clearance problems had derailed candidates. It quoted a senior White House official as saying that reports that candidates had failed the background checks were "not right." The official offered no excuse for the long gap between ambassadors, however. In this case, as with most questions surrounding personnel decisions, the truth is elusive and facts are hard to come by given the secrecy that surrounds the process.[42]

Finally, in June 2013, the White House announced that Kevin O'Malley, a Missouri lawyer, was being nominated for the post. According to media reports, he is a devout Catholic and Irish American. According to Federal Election Commission records, he donated twice to Obama's campaign for a total of $4,600 and made another 42 donations to various Democratic candidates over the past decade that add up to a little less than $30,000. He is according to one media report an ex-seminarian and a prominent parishioner in the St. Louis diocese so apprarently he is Catholic enough for the post. In September 2014, the Senate confirmed O'Malley's appointment.[43]

One thing O'Malley was not was a significant bundler. One news story interpreted the lack of major contributions as a sign that the embarrassment caused by Tsunis, Bell, and Mamet (see chapter 4) might have caused bundlers to be avoided for a time. The theory proved to be short-lived, however. The next day the announcement was made that Jane Hartley, an economic and political consultant who is married to an investment banker, was being nominated as ambassador to France. She was among the top 50 bundlers for the 2012 campaign, and she gathered up more than half a million dollars for the election effort. According to press reports, she speaks "conversational" French, which was the same description that was used for Mamet's ability to speak

Spanish. Although the term gives no real indication of how well she can speak the language, it is clear that, despite any earlier bundler embarrassments, money is still able to talk when it comes to ambassadorial appointments.[44]

Personal Preference

The desires of an aspiring ambassador can also play a determining role in the decision about who gets a particular country. Career officers are usually happy, or at least willing, to take any embassy they are offered. Political appointees, on the other hand, can have very specific ideas about where they want to go. *You Can't Go Home Again* is the title of a novel by Thomas Wolfe, but it also might be good advice to a person who wants to return to the country of his or her birth as the American ambassador. For example, Helene Von Damm received mixed results, despite the rave reviews she gave herself. Anna Wintour may well have the opportunity to employ her managerial talents as ambassador to London in 2017 regardless of whether that is in the national interest.

It is generally not a good idea for an ambassador to attempt to go home, though however. He or she will be subjected to pressures and expectations, especially if they still have family there, which a person without such ties does not have. It will not be long before a distant relative asks for help getting a visa or for some other favor.

Sometimes it is the ambassador's spouse that wants to go home again. That was true in the case of Vera and Donald Blinken. Vera had left Hungary as a child and he, years later, was able to go there as ambassador. In their coauthored memoir, he describes how he helped raise five million dollars at a single dinner in New York for Bill Clinton's election in 1992. She goes on to describe another reason why it is not a good idea to go home again:

> For the first time in our marriage, in his capacity as ambassador to Hungary, Donald was obliged to keep secrets from me. A red folder on his desk contained intelligence reports, and it was allowed to be there only when he was alone in his office. What disturbed me more than the curiosity about the contents of the red folder was not being able to share this part of Donald's life.
>
> Being a wonderful husband, Donald applied for and obtained a security clearance for me from the State Department. Now, when I was with him escorting officials on diplomatic missions, I could accompany them into the [sic] "The Bubble," the secure enclosure in the Embassy where sensitive information was discussed.[45]

It is hard to know where to begin with such a bizarre admission. Access to classified material is always based on a person having an appropriate security clearance and a need to know the information in question. Security clearances take time and money to grant, so there is also the question of the appropriate use of government resources in this case, even though the amount of resources expended would depend on the level of clearance. What is clear is that the ambassador's wife had no need to know what was in the red folder or what was said inside The Bubble.

If she were a banker's wife, would she have wanted access to the financial records of her husband's clients? Or if she were the wife of a businessman, would she have wanted to read confidential corporate documents? Knowing the Hungarian political scene, did she have favorites whom she wanted to assist and impress with her access to classified information? Sharing state secrets simply because one's spouse feels left out is not something that is defensible though the it is probably far more common than State Department security officials would care to admit.

Another case of an ambassador returning to his roots may be that of John Estrada. He was nominated to be ambassador to Trinidad and Tobago in 2013. He gave only about $1,000 to political causes, but he did endorse Obama for president in 2008.[46] That was after his retirement from being the sergeant major of the Marine Corps, the highest-ranking enlisted man in the Corps. His college degree is from an online, for-profit university, and his management style is unknown at this point, although it was presumably shaped by his years in the military. If he tries to run the embassy like boot camp, it will not be a happy experience for anyone involved. Ambassador Gration proved in Kenya that managing civilian bureaucrats takes a more subtle style than the one required to run a battalion of infanty. Presumably Ambassador Estrada will some day get to try his hand at it, but he was still awaiting Senate confirmation over a year after his nomination.

His success, although commendable, plays into what is often another part of the "going home again" narrative: in America, anyone from the humblest beginnings can succeed with hard work. Well, not really anyone. With income inequality being the highest on record and social mobility being lower than nearly every other developed country, the odds are long for bootstrap success stories. They still have their appeal nonetheless, and they can occasionally translate into ambassadorial appointments.[47]

There are other factors that can play a role in who goes where as ambassador, but they have a more random impact, and it often boils down to sending someone to whatever country is available when a place is needed for someone on short notice. When Chase Untermayer described how he solved the personnel problem caused by the inability of Bruce Gelb, the director of the US Information Agency, and Richard Carlson, the director of Voice of America, to get along, he said that he fired both and had to come up with a couple of open ambassadorships, preferably in Western Europe or a tropical paradise. Belgium and the Seychelles, the "country club islands," were available. So Gelb went to the former, Carlson went to the latter, and the problem was solved.[48]

In addition to granting *agrément*, countries can make clear what kinds of ambassadors they are willing to accept. Saudi Arabia wants ambassadors who do not speak Arabic and who have a close personal relationship with the US president so career officers are usually not in the running. Japan likes high-profile personalities and was thrilled when Caroline Kennedy was sent there in 2013 as ambassador, that is, until she took to Twitter to criticize the country for the way it treats dolphins. Kennedy proposed the Tweet to the State Department and, while the wording was worked out jointly, it seems hard to believe that Washington thought it was a great idea. In a culture where "face" matters a great deal, public humiliation via social media is not the best way to encourage cooperation from the Japanese government. And it is safe, even if somewhat painful, to say that Japan and the United States have bigger fish to fry.[49]

There are therefore many reasons why a particular ambassador winds up in a specific country. As described in this chapter, many of them have so little to do with ability and experience of an ambassador that it is fair to wonder whether it matters gets to be one. Why it does will be the subject of chapter 7.

CHAPTER 7

Why It Matters and
How It Might Be Changed

The previous chapters discussed the history of the title "ambassador" in American diplomacy, who gets to be one, how one gets to be one, and what factors come into play in determining the country to which a particular ambassador will be sent. What an ambassador does and how that performance is measured was also considered.

This chapter will look at why it is important to put capable people in such positions, even though the process described thus far does not seem designed to produce the best result in every case. It will conclude with some recommendations on ways that process might be improved within the constraints of the American political system as it operates today and how globalization makes those changes even more important than in the past.

Those recommendations will not include a plea for eliminating all political appointee ambassadors or even ones who are major campaign contributors. Noncareer ambassadors can and do make important contributions to the way American foreign policy is conducted.

There are several arguments offered for why there should be political appointee ambassadors, but most of them fall apart in practice. For instance, it is said that political appointee ambassadors reflect the president's foreign policy better than career ambassadors do. If that were really the case and really important, it would be an effective argument for making all ambassadors political appointees. Career officers know that they serve the president in power, and it would be rare for one of them to attempt to implement his or her own foreign policy. Those who get an ambassadorship because they bundled half a million dollars or more are not in a position to reflect the president's foreign policy, assuming they know what it is, as effectively as professional diplomats, who know how the bureaucracy works in Washington and how to make the best argument to overseas audiences. Ambassador Kennedy's use of social media to hector the Japanese government shows an ignorance of local custom as well a lack of understanding of what matters most in dealing with an important ally.

Besides, ideological litmus tests do not produce the best results. Even many of the examples of unprepared political appointees discussed in earlier chapters are from the Obama administration, it is only because there is greater transparency now than there was in the past. The reports of the inspector general are there for anyone to read, and the assessments of the performance of the ambassadors, career and political alike, are laid out in detail, but they are online only for the current president and some of the appointees of his immediate predecessor. In the Obama administration, the names of visitors to the White House and bundlers are also publicly available, unlike the Bush administration approach to visitor information and Governor Romney's refusal to reveal who his contributors were. When Vice President Cheney, for instance, called together a group of oil company executives to draft a national energy plan, the Bush adminstation went all the way to the Supreme Court in a successful effort to prevent the public from knowing who was involved.[1]

No poll of experienced foreign policy professionals has been asked the question, but if one were done, the Reagan administration would certainly win the prize for the worst political ambassadors in recent history. Not only were there were more of them, 38 percent as opposed to the average of around 30 percent, but ability was a secondary consideration. As Lyn Nofziger, Reagan's political advisor, suggested ideology was what mattered. Without the declassification of the inspector general's reports for previous presidencies, which administration had the worst ambassadors will be a debate without resolution.

Tevi Troy, who served as director of domestic policy during the Romney Readiness Project, in an article about presidential transitions, made an observation that could explain why many perceive Reagan's ambassadorial appointees to have been worse than those of other presidents. In the article, Troy wrote, "George H. W. Bush's intra-party transition of 1988 angered conservatives who felt that they were not getting the same respect they had from the Reagan team. Whereas Reagan had sought to tap into an ideological movement, Bush and his people preferred pragmatists who would solve the specific policy problems affecting their constituents."

Diplomacy, like politics, can be described as the art of the possible. Ideologues are not the best diplomats, because they start by assuming that they are always right and that differing points of view have no validity. That may be a useful approach if the goal is to wage jihad, but it does not work if the objective is to negotiate a solution to a problem that everyone can not only accept but also support.[2]

Another argument offered for political appointees is that when an ambassador is a friend of the president, the ambassador can get the White House to do things a career person cannot. The problem with that argument is that very few political appointee ambassadors have a relationship with the president that is significant enough to be able to get their phone calls to the White House returned. In those cases where there is a relationship, as with Reagan's close friend and financial advisor William Wilson, it can mean keeping on an ambassador who should have been fired immediately. In addition, foreign policy is best implemented by the regional assistant secretary and secretary of state rather than some uncoordinated operation within the White House or National Security Council staff, as Wilson again demonstrates. On occasion, however, it is useful to have an ambassador who is not worried about his or her next promotion or assignment, like a career person always is. That kind of independence can lead to an ambassador doing something he or she knows the State Department will not like but that needs to be done. The occasions when that happens are rare, though they do occur.

There is one good argument for political appointees. Those with enormous wealth can use their personal fortunes to supplement the always meager amounts of money that Congress provides for representational entertaining—the wining and dining of foreign elites. In cities like London and Paris, the embassy's annual budget for such entertaining could easily be exhausted in a month or two. Often noncareer ambassadors dig into their own pockets to cover the costs.

There have been outstanding ambassadors who did not spend their careers in the Foreign Service. But the fact that it turned out well in some cases is not an adequate defense of the way in which many ambassadors are selected today.

As mentioned in chapter 5, when asked what the qualifications to be an ambassador were, State Department spokesperson Jen Psaki cited three examples of noncareer ambassadors whom she said had been very successful—Sargent Shriver, Walter Mondale, and Pamela Harriman.

Shriver served in Paris in the late 1960s, and Mondale served in Tokyo and Harriman in Paris in the mid-1990s. Shriver was director of the Peace Corps and married to President Kennedy's sister, and Mondale was a senator and vice president. Harriman was a Washington socialite and prolific fundraiser for the Democratic Party who had affairs with a number of rich and powerful men and even married some of them.

The absence of any recent examples of outstanding noncareer ambassadors from Psaki's list does not strengthen her argument. And it is, of course, hard to judge just how good the three on her list were. All three undoubtedly had fans who thought they were great ambassadors, but then again, so did John Davis Lodge.

Mondale and Shriver at least had extensive managerial and government experience but were both probably selected for their political connections more than anything else. Although there are political appointee ambassadors who have performed well, there are few cases in which it seems clear that the person was selected only because of experience and qualifications. It is impossible to sort out all of the reasons for a complex personnel decision, such as who gets an ambassadorial appointment, but there always seems to be elements that can be traced back to a personal, economic, or political relationship to the president that could have come into play as the real motivation.

For instance, was Jon Huntsman sent to China because he had experience in the country or because it was part of some domestic political strategy? Was Karl Eikenberry sent to Afghanistan because he had experience in the region or because his background as a retired general gave the Obama administration protection from criticism by Republicans of Obama's lack of military experience? Whatever the case, the choice would seem to have been one that did not work out well. At the same time the White House was wrestling with a decision about how many additional troops to send to Afghanistan, someone leaked two cables in which Eikenberry cautioned against such a move. Eventually Obama went ahead with a surge of 30,000 troops anyhow despite the ambassador's recommendation. The flap over the leaked cable and Eikenberry's reportedly poor relationship with Afghan president Hamid Karzai had some observers calling for Eikenberry to be fired.[3]

Eikenberry and Huntsman at least had highly relevant experience. It would be hard to argue that political appointees whose main attribute is their ability to gather money for election campaigns are given ambassadorships mainly on the basis of their qualifications. The three who bombed their confirmation hearings in early 2014 are prime examples of that (see chapter 4). Sending a hotel owner to Norway when he has never visited and apparently knows little about the country clearly shows he got his nomination for some other reason than relevant experience. Dispatching someone who speaks "conversational" Spanish to a troublesome country like Argentina, which has defaulted on its debt and flirted with Iran, is certainly not. And relying on a soap opera producer to deal with the resurgent anti-Semitism in Hungary and extreme Right-wing political factions there is not either.

Perhaps in the cases of these three, it is not such a bad thing that ambassadors have such little power in some areas, especially compared to their private-sector counterparts. The full title of the job is "ambassador extraordinary and plenipotentiary." The last word has two different meanings—a person who has full powers and, in the case of a diplomat, a person who is fully authorized to represent his or her government.

When it comes to ambassadors, the second definition is definitely the one that applies. They lack full powers in two areas in particular. First, ambassadors have almost no control over the budgets of their embassies. The many agencies represented in the embassy's staff provide funds to support their programs from dozens of different budgets. And the decisions about how much will be spent and on what to spend it are made in Washington. The ambassador can make recommendations for which programs to expand or cut, but that opinion will just be one of many as battles over budgets are fought each year in Washington. Once these struggles are over, the results are passed to the embassy for implementation.

Second, ambassadors have almost no control over who works in an embassy. They are allowed to pick their DCMs and their secretaries, but beyond that, the other employees come out of the assignment process in their respective agencies in Washington. An ambassador can ask to have someone removed from the embassy for cause or for incompetence, but that recommendation will not be greeted with enthusiasm in Washington. It is a bit of a "nuclear option," where the ambassador using it can do as much damage to himself or herself as to their intended target.

Because ambassadors lack full powers in key areas, the second definition of plenipotentiary is therefore the one that applies. Ambassadors are fully authorized to represent their governments. And that is why they still matter today, even if their authority is limited. The following sections outline some of areas in which the role of the ambassador is as important today as it ever was.

Resources and Efficiency

Even though ambassadors do not have control over budgets or personnel, they still must supervise and coordinate the actions of a large bureaucratic organization. As anyone who has suffered an incompetent boss knows, the person in charge is important regardless of the amount of power that person wields.

In an embassy, it is even more important. Although the ambassador does not decide how resources are spent, he or she can have great impact on whether they are spent efficiently. If people are not motivated and well led, they will underperform.

This is even more important overseas. Government employees at home get a salary, benefits, and a place to do their job. Abroad it is a much more expensive proposition. The employee costs not only what a person working in the United States does, but there are other expenses, as well. The employee, spouse or partner, and other family members must all be transported to the country and back again, usually several times during a tour of duty. They must be provided housing at government expense, and it either comes furnished or the household effects of the employee must be shipped to post, as well. Education must be provided for the employee's children, which means paying for a local school that meets US standards. That almost always requires an expensive private school that is as costly as the private ones at home. Health care must also be adequate, and that can mean trips to a medical facility in another country when the country in which the embassy is located does not have acceptable facilities.

Another expense is providing a secure place to work, which is never easy when that place is a high-profile target for anyone who has a problem with American foreign policy. The embassy must be secure from attack by terrorists and from attempts to intercept its communications. That kind of building can be expensive even in the friendliest of capitals. The embassy now under construction in London, for instance, will cost in excess of one billion dollars.[4] The employees must also be provided with all of the support and supplies necessary for a bureaucracy, including a means to communicate with headquarters rapidly and securely.

All of this adds up to a US government employee overseas costing far more than an employee of equivalent rank in the United States. If those employees have such bad leadership that they request a move to Kabul instead of serving out their time in a comfortable Western European country like Luxembourg, then the cost of that move to the government is considerable. Public service requires sacrifice no matter where in the world one serves, but one of the sacrifices made should not include having to work under an insecure and defensive ambassador who compensates for a lack of experience with an aggressive and abusive attitude.

Public Diplomacy

As democracy has spread over the course of the past century, the importance of public opinion has grown. Economic development, higher literacy, and communications technology have amplified its importance, as both the Arab Spring and Tiananmen Square in China have shown. In this new environment, social media has become an important means of communications for reaching out to the public in other countries. Embassies and ambassadors have Twitter accounts and Facebook pages, as well as websites to compete in the battle to influence public opinion.

This requires ambassadors who are not only capable of dealing with the traditional media and journalists but are also able to use the new media to spread messages. An ambassador who does not like either public speaking or socializing, as apparently was the case when John Louis was in London, will be unable to communicate with all of the audiences that need to be informed about American policy and the reasons for it. And an ambassador who arrives after a Senate confirmation hearing reveals that ambassador's ignorance of the country to which he or she is being sent will never be fully credible.

American Exceptionalism

Another challenge for today's ambassadors is the concept of American exceptionalism. Prior to each presidential election, the two major political parties put together their platforms, which are explanations of their beliefs and the policies they would put in place if in power. The platforms are designed to attract and energize certain groups of voters.

The word "exceptionalism" had never appeared in any of these policy statements before 2012. That year, it not only made its debut in the Republican platform, but there was an entire 8,000 word section devoted to the concept and its implications for American foreign policy. The first paragraph from that section of the platform reads:

> We are the party of peace through strength. Professing American exceptionalism—the conviction that our country holds a unique place and role in human history—we proudly associate ourselves with those Americans of all political stripes who, more than three decades ago in a world as dangerous as today's, came together to advance the cause of freedom. Repudiating the folly of an amateur foreign policy and defying a worldwide Marxist advance, they announced their strategy in the timeless slogan we repeat today: peace through strength—an enduring peace

based on freedom and the will to defend it, and American democratic values and the will to promote them. While the twentieth century was undeniably an American century—with strong leadership, adherence to the principles of freedom and democracy our Founders' [sic] enshrined in our nation's Declaration of Independence and Constitution, and a continued reliance on Divine Providence—the twenty-first century will be one of American greatness as well.[5]

It was not that American politicians did not know that America was different from other nations prior to 2012. The concept of American exceptionalism can be traced back at least as far as Alex de Tocqueville, the French historian who traveled throughout the country in the 1800s. Louis Hartz, a liberal political scientist, is believed by some to have been the first to coin the phrase in the 1950s.[6]

American exceptionalism can be defined in different ways but seems to imply that the country benefits from divine inspiration, a unique place in human history, and a sunny optimism about its ability to solve its own problems without much reference to the rest of the world. It can be seen in the assertion that it was the country's "Manifest Destiny" to expand westward to the Pacific Ocean during the nineteenth century without any particular regard to the Native Americans and Mexicans that were encountered along the way. Today it can be used to justify most anything America does abroad, and that can be a problem.

The real reason American exceptionalism became an issue in American foreign policy in 2012 is domestic politics. When Obama made his first overseas trip as president, he was asked whether he believed in American exceptionalism. He responded by stressing his belief in the values enshrined in the Constitution and said he was enormously proud of his country and its role and history in the world. But he also added: "I believe in American exceptionalism, just as I suspect that the Brits believe in British exceptionalism and the Greeks believe in Greek exceptionalism."[7]

The last comment was seized upon by Republicans as demonstrating that the president did not understand America or somehow viewed the country differently than they did. The charge had as much validity as the claim that he was a Kenyan-born, Muslim socialist, but it was another way to undermine the president's policies without offering a coherent argument against them. Accuracy, or a debate about the country's role in the world, was not the purpose of thumping the tub of American exceptionalism. The intent was to motivate people to vote out of fear and loathing for someone supposedly different from them.

That tactic did not work well enough to win Governor Romney the presidency, but it is one that keeps being relentlessly recycled by the Right. When Obama obtained the release of an American serviceman, Bowe Bergdahl, in exchange for the freeing of five Taliban prisoners from Guantanamo, *Fox News* trotted out its forensic psychiatrist to explain the move. According to Keith Ablow, Obama made the decision because he "doesn't affiliate with patriotism" and does not have "Americanism in his soul." In case that failed to rally the target audience, Ablow also brought up the fact that Bergdahl had danced in a ballet. That reference was supposed to demonstrate Bergdahl's narcissism, but it was probably also meant to fire up the homophobic.[8]

Whatever the intention, the tactic has worked. Obama feels obligated to periodically defend his belief in American exceptionalism. In a foreign policy speech at West Point in May 2014, he said: "I believe in American exceptionalism with every fiber of my being. But what makes us exceptional is not our ability to flout international norms and the rule of law; it's our willingness to affirm them through our actions."[9]

In 2013, in the president's annual address to the United Nations General Assembly, Obama vigorously defended American exceptionalism, saying: "Some may disagree, but I believe America is exceptional—in part because we have shown a willingness through the sacrifice of blood and treasure to stand up not only for our own narrow self-interests, but for the interests of all."[10]

One of the purposes of the speech was to encourage other nations to become more involved in Syria. It did not appear to have much of a result other than to encourage Vladimir Putin, the president of Russia, to write an opinion piece in *The New York Times* that criticized Obama's assertion by saying that "it is extremely dangerous to encourage people to see themselves as exceptional, whatever the motivation."[11]

Putin, although not a master of public relations, has a point. It would be hard for an ambassador to have a productive conversation with the representatives of another country by beginning with assertions that the country the ambassador represents has the benefit of divine inspiration, moral superiority, and a unique role in the world that implies all others must follow its leadership.

Even though it makes for bad foreign policy, American exceptionalism may be good domestic politics. A poll by the Brookings Institution in 2010 found that nearly 60 percent of Americans agreed with the statement that "God has granted America a special role in history."[12] But it is bad foreign policy to be heavy-handed in such assertions, and American ambassadors will have to find a path between offending politicians at home and alienating audiences abroad when the subject arises. That may be difficult for a hotel owner who could not name what opportunities American businessmen might find in Norway or a soap opera producer who could not describe America's strategic interests in Hungary.[13]

Globalization

If a word is typed into Google's Ngram Viewer, the resulting graph shows how often that word appears in books published between 1800 and 2000. If the word is "globalization," the graph looks like the proverbial hockey stick. The word barely appears before 1970, and then in 1990 it takes off in a dramatic rise that almost appears vertical. Today the word is in the news constantly, and its effects seem to touch virtually every aspect of life, whether it be cultural, economic, or political.

For a concept that has become so common, however, globalization is a word that is hard to define. As the Ngram graph so clearly indicates, the number of books that mention the word is increasing exponentially, and many of them are dedicated solely to explaining its impact. Most of these books, either explicitly or implicitly, view that impact positively or negatively and yet only rarely do they attempt a concise definition of what it is they are describing.

So here is a two-sentence attempt at defining the term: globalization refers to people, things, and ideas crossing national boundaries with greater speed, frequency, impact, and reach. Usually driven by technology, it is neither new nor reversible.

This definition will not satisfy everyone, as it does not state whether globalization's impact is positive or negative. That is because it has good effects as well as bad ones. Getting into an argument about which matters more is as much a distraction as it is a moral dilemma that is impossible to resolve definitively. The people, things, and ideas that cross borders can be positive—business people, tourists, international trade, and a greater appreciation for democracy and human rights. On the other hand, they could also be terrorists with weapons and ideologies of hate.

One thing that observers of globalization could probably agree on is that it weakens anything constrained by national borders and strengthens anything that can ignore those borders. National governments and labor unions lose strength, whereas multinational corporations and international organizations are at an advantage. What is also clear is that the most serious problems the world faces today—terrorism, health threats, climate change, refugees, and civil wars—all are facilitated by globalization. And because of that, no nation, not even the world's only superpower, can effectively deal with those problems alone.

If the United States is to deal effectively with those problems in concert with other nations, it must have the best diplomatic representation possible. Ambassadors who know little about the language, culture, and history of the countries to which they are accredited will not be effective envoys. Those who are commonly seen to have bought their ambassadorships through bundling campaign contributions will have difficulty being taken seriously by opinion leaders in those countries. In particular, they will have difficulty explaining and defending the position of the United States when it comes to treaties that attempt to deal with the problems that globalization presents. One of the things they will have to explain is the American reluctance to enter into international agreements designed to address those problems and why that reluctance has increased. Voting to approve treaties has been a normal part of Senate business since Congress began. In its first two centuries, the Senate approved more than 1,500 treaties. It rejected only 21, and another 85 were withdrawn because the Senate did not take action on them.[14]

If a treaty is not withdrawn or is rejected and not acted upon, it can remain in limbo indefinitely. As of May 2014, there were 34 treaties awaiting action by the Senate. One had been submitted for consideration in 1949 and has yet to be acted upon.[15] The framers of the Constitution purposefully made it difficult for the United States to enter into a treaty by requiring a two-thirds majority of the Senate to approve such an action. The founding fathers feared that the executive branch would abuse the power to enter into entangling alliances more than they worried that the requirement for a supermajority would result in congressional inaction. They did not anticipate the rise of political parties or appreciate that partisan politics could become so strong that national interests would be of secondary importance in Washington.[16]

These treaties deal with everything from the protection of albatrosses and petrels to the testing of nuclear weapons. In general, they are all designed to help foster the international cooperation required to deal with the problems that are a result of globalization. That goal has not prevented some politicians from preventing their ratification in order to advance their own personal interests at the expense of the national interest. In the process, they have lowered America's standing in the world, made its claims to leadership more tenuous, and put American ambassadors in a difficult situation when it comes to explaining their country's actions. The following sections identify some of the worst examples.

Tax Treaties

Five of the 34 pending agreements are tax treaties with Chile, Hungary, Switzerland, Luxembourg, and Spain. The United States has such treaties with more than 60 countries, and they are used to prevent the double taxation of income and profits and to make cheating on taxes more difficult. The five that are pending have strong support from business groups and law enforcement officials, but a single senator has blocked action on all of them. Although it takes 67 senators to approve a treaty, it takes just 1 to prevent approval without some extraordinary parliamentary maneuvering on the part of the rest of the senators.[17]

The single senator is Rand Paul, who is said to be considering a run for the presidency in 2016. He wrote to the Senate majority leader, Harry Reid, saying that although he does not condone cheating on taxes, he cannot support a law that "endangers regular foreign investment and punishes every American in pursuit of tax cheats."[18]

The law to which Paul objects is the Foreign Account Tax Compliance Act, which will force foreign banks to provide more information about American account holders than was required in the past. The tax treaties are essential to the law's implementation and effectiveness. Swiss bankers have routinely rejected American requests for the information that a tax treaty is designed to uncover, and it is estimated that 22,000 Americans have more than ten billion dollars in Swiss banks. According to one economist, worldwide that figure is closer to eight trillion dollars, which means that 8 percent of the world's personal financial wealth is stashed in tax havens.[19]

Although Senator Paul's tactics are designed to keep all of that money hidden in the name of privacy, the result could be that Americans who use tax havens will bring at least part of it home. They will have a candidate to support in 2016 and will want to contribute to his election campaign. If nothing else, it might win Paul the support of Mitt Romney, who has reportedly parked millions of dollars in the Cayman Islands in order to avoid taxes.[20]

Law of the Sea

Drafted more than 30 years ago, the Law of the Sea Treaty is designed to help regulate activities that take place over, under, and on the world's oceans. It defines a country's rights when it comes to navigation, offshore fishing, and deep-sea mining. It has been ratified by 162 countries and is supported by the oil and gas industry, the Pentagon, environmentalists, and past presidents from both parties. If the United States were to ratify it, it would strengthen US claims to sovereignty over the full outer continental shelf off American shores.[21]

The treaty would also lessen the chance for conflict in the South China Sea and other hot spots by establishing a legal framework that could be used to resolve maritime disputes. As an editorial in *The New York Times* noted, "few aspects of China's dynamic emergence as a global power have generated as much insecurity and danger in its neighborhood as its mounting campaign to control the South China Sea, a vital waterway for international commerce."[22]

Despite these benefits and widespread support, a 2012 attempt to get it approved failed when 34 senators said they would oppose it. Criticism of the treaty was based on the claims that it would oblige the United States to reduce greenhouse gas emissions, force the transfer of billions of dollars of royalties to less-developed countries, and infringe on US sovereignty. According to Senator Orrin Hatch of Utah, the treaty would also cost jobs and sink America's economy, although perhaps not in his state, given its lack of a coastline.[23]

Despite the overwhelming scientific evidence of the growing impact of climate change, there are those who continue to argue against reducing greenhouse gas emissions. Failing to do so will certainly create jobs for those who work to repair the damage of natural disasters. As for the argument about a possible infringement on US sovereignty, that can be said of any agreement, treaty or any other form of international involvement. Clarifying the status of the outer continental shelf would extend US sovereignty to an area where it could be contested.

Rights of the Disabled

The Convention on the Rights of Persons with Disabilities is another treaty that has failed to win approval in the Senate. Veterans' groups, the United States Chamber of Commerce, major corporations, and a number of Republican senators, including John McCain, support the treaty, which has been ratified by 141 countries.

Opposed to it were former Senator Rick Santorum, the Heritage Foundation, and some groups of people who school their children at home. They argued that it would open up the United States to global enforcers, threaten the chance for children with disabilities to be educated at home, and ease access to abortion.

When the treaty came up for a vote in December 2012, former senator and Republican presidential candidate Bob Dole was on the floor of the Senate, in his wheelchair, urging his former colleagues to vote in its favor. The convention is based on the Americans with Disabilities Act and would extend the standards contained in that law to those nations who ratified the convention. Mr. Dole said he went to the Senate to urge its passage not to advocate for the United Nations but in order to encourage other countries to treat the disabled the same way as the United States does. Dole's former colleagues greeted him warmly, and then 38 of them voted against the measure, thereby preventing its ratification.[24]

Rights of Children

One of the most popular and respected human rights treaties in history was the Convention on the Rights of the Child. It was negotiated during the Reagan and George H. W. Bush administrations with major input from American diplomats. The UN General Assembly unanimously approved it in 1989, and within months nearly every country in the world and the Vatican had ratified it, but it has not even been sent to the Senate for consideration. The only countries that belong to the United Nations that have failed to accept the treaty are the United States and Somalia.

Some might think that the failure to accept a treaty the rest of the world has embraced shows that the Somalia and the United States have much in common. The arguments offered by those who oppose the treaty is that it would undermine traditional families, the rights of parents, and American sovereignty. They invoke the image of an out-of-control government that would secretly remove the children of a mother in the armed forces who went on a month-long deployment, would begin mandatory sex education at age four, and would imprison parents who failed to get their children vaccinated.[25]

That the treaty would do none of those things does not matter, unless one considers American participation in an international agreement of any kind to be an infringement on sovereignty. The treaty contains no mandates, and no treaty can override the Constitution. Instead, this international agreement calls for things like freedom from violence toward, abuse of, and exploitation of children, adequate nutrition and health care, free primary education, and equal treatment regardless of gender, race, or cultural background.[26]

One of the features of globalization is that it has made it easier for people holding the same views to connect and interact. It does not matter whether those views are based on fact or fiction. The only thing that does matter is whether someone can profit from marketing those ideas and spreading the alarm. For many yeares there have been people who believe the United Nations operates a fleet of black helicopters and is out to rob the American people of their freedom and their guns. Now thanks to globalization, such people can connect with one another and become even easier targets for those seeking to cash in on their fears.

One example is Dick Morris, who for 20 years was a political consultant to President Clinton. He has found a new line of work in addition to being a commentator on Fox News. He and his wife wrote a book entitled *Here Come the Black Helicopters!—UN Global Governance and the Loss of Freedom*, which begins with the following sentences: "There is a growing threat to our freedom and autonomy as a nation. Here's why: The United Nations and its globalist allies in the United States are determined to take away our national sovereignty."[27] Morris's career as advisor to Clinton was cut short when it was revealed that throughout an entire year he allowed a prostitute to listen in on his telephone conversations with the president.[28] He also predicted a landslide victory for Mitt Romney in the 2012 election. That would seem to indicate he might not be the best source to listen to when considering the fate of Western civilization. And yet, 93 of the 117 people who wrote reviews of his book on Amazon.com gave it a 4- or 5-star rating.[29]

Failed politicians like Rick Santorum and Newt Gingrich, as well as pundits like Morris, have found a ready market and responsive audiences for those who believe that American exceptionalism means that America can exempt itself from the problems created by globalization. As the inability of Santorum or Gingrich to get reelected indicates, such people are a small minority of the general population. Unfortunately, they are large enough in number and passionate enough in their fears that they can effectively block international efforts to deal with those problems. Leaving it to hotel owners and soap opera producers to explain this phenomenon to foreign audiences will make it even more unlikely for solutions to be found in the future and will make American assertions of global leadership as ridiculous as the arguments of the opponents of these treaties.

If it is important to have diplomats who can work with other nations to find solutions to global problems, then it is important to find the best diplomats. The current method of auctioning off major embassies cannot possible produce ambassadors who best serve the national interest. Depsite the fact that the corrupting influence of money on politics is here to stay, improving the process is possible. But change is not without its challenges as the status quo always serves someone's interests.

How It Might Be Changed

The president of the United States may be the most powerful person in the world, but the president does not have the power to reward all of those who help with the election. With elections having become a multi-billion dollar business and a host of consultants like Dick Morris, pollsters, lobbyists and others making a living off that business, change will be difficult. Just as President Eisenhower warned against allowing the military-industrial complex to distort national priorities, there is an electoral-industrial complex dedicated to preserving the profits reaped from a dysfunctional political system.

For those eager to blame Washington for the gridlock and every other problem in the world, a look in the mirror might be helpful. The problems that America faces are, as in any democracy, traceable to the American electorate. Voters consist of three groups—those on either end of the political spectrum who are engaged in politics and see the other end as the problem and the disinterested, unengaged, and uninformed middle.

According to a Pew Research Center poll, partisan antipathy between liberals and conservatives is deeper and more extensive than at any point in the past two decades. As a result, 92 percent of Republicans are ideologically to the right of the median Democrat and 94 percent of Democrats are to the left of the median Republican. Half of the consistently liberal Democrats think Republican policies jeopardize the nation's well-being, whereas nearly two-thirds of consistently conservative Republicans believe the same about Democratic policies.[30]

That degree of polarization makes it hard to formulate a foreign policy that serves the interests of the nation, because each end of the political spectrum thinks the other is a threat to those interests. One example of that inability is reflected in the attitudes toward climate change, its implications, and what ought to be done about it. A Yale University study of Democrats, Republicans, Tea Party members, and Independents found the following:

- A majority of Democrats (55%) say that most scientists think global warming is happening, whereas the majority of Republicans (56%) and Tea Party members (69%) say that there is a lot of disagreement among scientists about whether or not global warming is happening.
- A large majority of Democrats (72%) worry about global warming, compared to 53 percent of Independents, 38 percent of

Republicans, and 24 percent of Tea Party members. More than half (51%) of Tea Party members say they are not at all worried about global warming.

- Nearly half of Democrats (45%) say that global warming is already harming people in the United States, whereas 33 percent of Republicans and 51 percent of Tea Party members say it will never harm people in the United States.
- Tea Party members are much more likely to say that they are "very well informed" about global warming than the other groups are. Likewise, they are also much more likely to say they "do not need any more information" about global warming to make up their mind.[31]

That degree of skepticism certainly provides incentive for inaction on the part of Congress. And it may be why in the past year, the House Science, Space, and Technology Committee has held 15 hearings on space exploration, at least three of which have considered the search for extraterrestrial life. In the same time period, the committee held only two hearings that were devoted to climate change. It would be too easy here to comment on the possibility of intelligent life inside the beltway around Washington, but it must surely be a question in the minds of overseas audiences as well as most Americans.[32]

One of the further effects of globalization is that there are now so many sources of information that people can believe whatever they want to believe, and they can find evidence and information to confirm those beliefs on the Internet. The difficulty of making coherent policy in such a partisan environment filled with misinformation may be impossible to overcome.

Another problem that will not be easily overcome is the impact of money on politics. The conservative majority on the Supreme Court has shown in recent rulings that corporations have free speech rights, just as people do, and that "free speech" includes pouring unlimited amounts of anonymous money into groups that sponsor attack ads and utilize other political tactics.

To the extent that there is regulation of the political marketplace, it is ineffectual and also politicized. A *New York Times* editorial observed, "It is an open scandal in Washington that the Federal Election Commission (FEC) is completely ossified as the referee and penalizer of abuses in national politics." The editorial went on to describe how Crossroads GPS had simply rejected an FEC request for the details of how it spent more than 50 million dollars during the fourth quarter of 2012, including who donated that money.[33]

Crossroads GPS was organized by Karl Rove, the former political advisor of President George W. Bush. Because it is a nonprofit organization and not a political action committee (PAC), it does not have to reveal who its donors are. Crossroads GPS and a sister organization gathered more than 300 million dollars in the 2012 election cycle. Despite the fact that Crossroads spends huge sums of money, the FEC demonstrated just how toothless it is when its legal staff concluded that Crossroads had probably broken election laws. The commission, which is evenly divided between three Republicans and three Democrats, deadlocked on whether to do anything about that violation and has been unable to act for years on many such issues because of that divide.[34] The FEC is a typically Washington solution to a problem. Create a toothless watchdog to give the appearance of action while at the same time there will be no effective oversight.

One way to address the problem of money in elections, and the failure of regulatory bodies to do anything about it, would be to enhance the influence of small donors. John Sarbanes, a Maryland Democrat, has introduced a bill in Congress that would provide a $50 tax credit per donor per election cycle. The bill also includes a system of matching funds where federal funds would be provided at a rate of nine federal dollars to every private one if the candidate agrees to the full disclosure of all donations and to limit them to a maximum of $150.[35]

The prospects for the bill are uncertain as there are many politicians who will resist limitations of their ability to sell out to the highest bidder even while they decry the amount of time they have to spend on fundraising. One thing that is certain is that Rove and others will fight any efforts to diminish the political power they wield because of the hundreds of millions of dollars they control. The impact of this money spreads beyond pollsters and political consultants like Rove. Television stations in swing states, for instance, are much more valuable than those in states that are clearly red or blue. The ad revenue from political contests in states that can go either way in an election makes those stations extremely valuable.[36]

Although there will be strong resistance from the advocates of anonymous, corporate free speech, full disclosure and greater transparency would be a significant step toward being able to figure out who receives an ambassadorship because of their efforts to harvest campaign cash for their favorite candidate. The Obama administration is largely doing that already by releasing the names of its major bundlers. A Romney administration would have refused to provide that information and could have kept it secret because no law requires such disclosures.

In addition to ambassadorships, increased transparency would also make clearer who else is benefitting from contributions to the electoral process. As of July 2012, a mere 196 Americans had given more than 80 percent of the money spent at that point by super-PACs. That kind of political action committee can raise unlimited sums of money from corporations, unions, and individuals, but it is supposed to be independent and is not permitted to contribute to or coordinate directly with parties or candidates. Of course, such limitations are more restrictions that the FEC does not bother to enforce.[37] And it is safe to assume that it is not a simple love of democracy that motivates those 196 people to donate huge sums of money.

In addition to greater transparency in campaign contributions, there could be greater congressional interest in who is appointed as ambassadors. The only reason that there has been any controversy about Tsunis, Bell, and Mamet is because Senators McCain and Rubio showed up at their hearings and asked some questions that were not the usual fluff. That plus the resulting recordings of their inadequate answers created enough interest and media attention to at least make their nominations controversial, although at this point in time it remains to be seen whether it will ultimately prevent their confirmation.

Tsunis bundled or contributed $1.3 million for President Obama's reelection effort and other Democratic candidates. He had contributed $50,000 to Senator McCain's campaign in 2008 but then switched horses and parties the following year.[38] It is probably no coincidence that McCain was the one who provided Tsunis with his most difficult questions. Whether or not it was mere payback, Congress should take a greater interest in the process and not simply because a senator or two might find it a useful part of the gotcha politics of Washington.

Greater congressional interest is not a call for greater congressional obstruction. There is already enough of that. In November 2013, the Democrats in the Senate exercised the nuclear option and changed the rules so that a simple majority could end a filibuster instead of a 60 vote supermajority. In retaliation, the Republicans have used other parliamentary maneuvers to block appointments, including, as of early June 2014, some 42 ambassadorships. Those tactics prompted Senate Foreign Relations Committee Chairman Bob Menendez to assert that the Republican obstruction of ambassador nominations was crippling the US global agenda and damaging national security.[39]

Holding up nominees to ambassadorial posts is not only damages national security. It is also particularly wasteful. Those people generally leave their previous jobs in order to prepare for Senate confirmation, and they cannot go to their embassy before that confirmation happens. As a result, about all they can do is brush up on their language skills and do busy work as they wait for months to years for the Senate to act.

Nominees for Washington positions have the advantage that they can begin to act in a limited fashion in the jobs to which they are appointed even in the absence of confirmation, as long as they keep a low profile. In June 2014, the *Wall Street Journal* reported that Carlos Pascual was stepping down as the senior energy policy advisor in the State Department. The article's headline noted that Pascual, who had previously served as ambassador to Ukraine and Mexico, was "instrumental in U.S. efforts in Ukraine and Russia over [the] past several months." What the article did not mention was that he had been waiting at that point for 852 days without even getting a hearing on his nomination as assistant secretary of state for energy resources. The lack of confirmation apparently did not prevent him from being instrumental, but it undoubtedly made him less effective, given that he had to carry out his duties without giving the appearance that he was assuming the Senate would confirm him.[40]

In addition to stopping the obstructionism that is damaging American foreign policy and national security, there is one other thing Congress could do to improve the process for selecting ambassadors. It could insist on knowing the language abilities of the nominees. The two people put forward in 2014 for Argentina and France are said to speak the languages of those two countries at a "conversational" level. It certainly matters whether that level is a primary school, high school, or college level. The Foreign Service Institute (FSI) is responsible for training State Department personnel in a wide variety of languages and it tests all of its language students in reading and speaking and awards them a grade from zero to five. To stay in the Foreign Service, career officers have to reach a 3/3 level in at least one language.

The two nominees in question are no doubt spending some time brushing up their conversational language ability at FSI. Even if they are not, the test takes less than half an hour, and the resulting score is something that Congress should require prior to confirmation.

Language test scores would provide a precise measure of the ability of the nominee in a critically important area for any ambassador today. Having accurate measures of performance is always difficult on an individual level and for the government as a whole. As described in chapter 5, in an embassy, the report done by the State Department's Inspector General (IG) is the best measure of how well it is being run. Even though the law says each post should be inspected every five years, on average inspections occur only every eight years because they are so expensive and time consuming. An ambassador's term is usually three years, which means that most of them will serve their time without a thorough review of their performance.

As part of the inspection of an embassy, every employee is required to fill out a Personal Questionnaire (PQ), where they are asked to rate the work environment and management of the post. Instead of this happening only when an embassy comes up for an inspection, an abbreviated PQ could be sent electronically to everyone at every post every year. The embassies with the most serious problems could then be easily identified and a small team could be sent to do a rapid review. A similar system could also be used in Washington to rate the effectiveness of each bureau and the assistant secretary who runs it. And the results could be added to the IG's website.

This system would apply to career officials as well as political appointees. Although none of the four ambassadors who resigned was a career officer, career ambassadors may be failing just as often as political appointees. That is in part because they face bigger challenges than their political counterparts do given that they are sent to countries that are more difficult for several reasons. Morale problems are typically worst at embassies with hardship and danger pay allowances—places where political appointees rarely tread.

Holding career ambassadors up to such scrutiny could pose a challenge for the American Foreign Service Association (AFSA), which is both a professional organization and the labor union of the Foreign Service. AFSA will have to decide whether it is more important to protect all of its members, including the incompetent, or to make its first priority improving the profession of diplomacy as it is practiced in the United States. Drafting guidelines for successful performance as an ambassador is not going to have any practical effect or improve performance as it makes no provisions for accountability.

A system of measuring performance on a timely basis would have an effect, and such a system should also be applied to everyone in a position of responsibility, including both ambassadors overseas and senior officials in the State Department in Washington. When faced with the prospect of becoming a public failure, some of those who want to become ambassadors and whose primary qualification is the size of their checkbook might then reconsider buying the title.

For many years after the country was founded, the United States benefitted from have oceans to its east and west and a single benign neighbor to its north and south. That allowed the country to ignore the rest of the world when it chose to do so. That tradition continues today in the minds of some and is utilized by politicians who like to appeal to voters who are xenophobic.

That can make even the most practical measures impossible. For instance, there are only three countries in the world that currently fail to use the metric system on a regular basis. Two of them, Liberia and Myanmar, are moving ahead with adopting the way that the rest of the world measures things. The only country that is not doing so is the United States. When an effort was made in the mid-1970s to have the country go metric, the National Cowboy Hall of Fame sued to block the move. The reason was because the West was won by the inch, foot, yard, and mile.[41] Whether any court was convinced by that argument or not, the United States continues to go it alone mile by mile.

Following World War II, the United States emerged as the preeminent power on the globe. Although the end of the Cold War reduced the threat to America's survival, new threats have emerged in this increasingly globalized world. These threats cannot be met without the cooperation of other nations, and that means the United States cannot afford to ignore the rest of the world. America is an exceptional country in many ways, but exceptionalism does not mean that the country can act like a cowboy and not suffer the consequences.

Effective efforts at dealing with today's problems requires skillful diplomacy. If the best diplomats are not chosen to conduct that diplomacy, America proceeds at its own peril. Hopefully this book, by explaining how ambassadors are chosen and why the selection procedure matters, will make a small contribution to improving that process.

Appendices

Appendix A: Questionnaire for Presidential Appointees, Obama Administration, November 2008

I. Professional Background

(1) Please furnish copies of all resumes and biographical statements issued by you or any other entity at your discretion or with your consent within the past ten years.

(2) If you are a member of any licensed profession or occupation, please specify the following: the present status of each license; whether any such license has ever been withdrawn, suspended, or revoked; whether any disciplinary action of any kind has ever been taken in connection with your license. Please also list any applications for professional licenses or certifications that [may] have been denied, and the reasons for denial.

(3) Please provide the names of all corporations, firms, partnerships, trusts, or other business enterprises, and all non-profit organizations and other such institutions with which you are now, or during the past ten years have been, affiliated with as an advisor, attorney or consultant.

(4) Please chronologically list activities, other than those listed on your resume or biography, from which you have derived earned income (e.g., self-employment, consulting activities, writing, speaking, royalties and honoraria) for the past ten years.

(5) Have you or your spouse ever registered as a lobbyist or other legislative agent to influence federal or state legislation or administrative acts? Have you or your spouse ever received payment for acting as a lobbyist or legislative agent? If so, please supply details.

(6) If you or your spouse have performed any work for, received any payments from and/or made any payments to any foreign government, business, non-profit organization or individual, please describe the circumstances, and identify the source and amount. Also please specify if you or your spouse have ever been registered as an agent for a foreign principal.

(7) If you or your spouse have ever lived or worked abroad, please describe the circumstances.

(8) Briefly describe the most controversial matters you have been involved with during the course of your career.

(9) Please provide the names, addresses and telephone numbers of three professional references. If possible, please furnish names of individuals with whom you have worked as a peer, a subordinate and as a supervisor.

II. Publications, Writings and Speeches

(10) Writings: Please list and, if readily available, provide a copy of each book, article, column or publication (including but not limited to any posts or comments on blogs or other websites) you have authored, individually or with others. Please list all aliases or "handles" you have used to communicate on the Internet.

(11) Testimony: Please identify each instance in which you have testified before Congress or other legislative, administrative, investigative or regulatory body and specify the subject matter of the testimony. If available, please provide summaries or transcripts of your testimony.

(12) Speeches: Please identify all speeches you have given. If available please provide the test or recordings of each such speech or identify any recordings of speeches of which you are aware.

(13) Electronic communications: If you have ever sent an electronic communication, including but not limited to an email, text message or instant message, that could suggest a conflict of interest or be a possible source of embarrassment to you, your family, or the President-Elect if it were made public, please describe.

(14) Diaries: If you keep or have ever kept a diary that contains anything that could suggest a conflict of interest or be a possible source of embarrassment to you, your family, or the President-Elect if it were made public, please describe.

III. Relationships and Affiliations

(15) Please list all corporations, partnerships, trusts, or other business entities with which you or your spouse have ever been affiliated as an officer, director, trustee, partner, or holder of a significant equity or financial interest (i.e. any ownership interest of more than 5%), or whose decisions you or your spouse had the ability to influence. Please identify the entity, your relationship to the entity, and dates of service and/or affiliation.

(16) Please list each membership, including any board memberships, you or your spouse have or have had with any political, civic, social, charitable, educational, professional, fraternal, benevolent or religious organization, private club or other membership organization (including any type of tax-exempt organization) during the past ten years. Please include dates of membership and any positions you may have had with the organization.

(17) Have you or your spouse at any time belonged to any membership organization, including but not limited to those described in the preceding paragraph, that as a matter of policy or practice, denied or restricted membership or affiliation based on race, sex, disability, ethnic background, religion or sexual orientation or has been subject to a claim that it has done so? If so, please provide details.

(18) Please specifically describe any affiliation you, or your spouse or any member of your immediate family have, or have had, with any financial, banking, mortgage or insurance institution that is currently the subject of federal government intervention as part of the ongoing economic crisis. This question includes, but is not limited to, the following: Fannie Mae, Freddie Mac, AIG and Washington Mutual.

(19) If you currently serve or in the last ten years have served as an administrator, executor, trustee, receiver, or in any other similar fiduciary capacity, please describe for each: your exact position; the nature of your duties; the persons or entities for whom you act(ed) as a fiduciary; the dates during which you served in such a fiduciary capacity; and any supervising courts.

(20) Other than the entities identified in questions 15–19 above, please provide the names and details of any individuals and organizations with which you or your spouse have been associated with which might present a conflict of interest with your proposed federal office, or have the potential for embarrassment.

IV. Financial Information

(21) Please provide copies of all financial disclosure forms you or your spouse have been required to file within the past ten years, if applicable.

(22) Please furnish a copy of each net worth statement that you have prepared and submitted for any purpose (e.g., bank loans) during the past ten years.

(23) Please furnish a copy of all brokerage statements for investment accounts for the past year.

(24) Please list all loans in excess of $10,000 made to you or your spouse, or by you or your spouse, which existed at anytime during the past ten years. Please specify the creditor or debtor, interest rate, due date and any other key terms, and identify the purpose for which the liability was incurred. Please also specify the extent to which any such loans contained terms not generally available to the public, such as below-market rates.

(25) Please furnish a copy of each trust of which you, your spouse or any child under 21 is a grantor or beneficiary. Also please furnish a copy of any amendment, and any document indicating a change in trustee of any such trust.

(26) Please describe all real estate held in your name or in your spouse's name during the last ten years. Please include real estate held in combination with others, held in trust, held by a nominee, or held by or through any other third person or title-holding entity, and identify such other person or entity.

(27) Please describe the mortgage terms for any properties listed under Question 21 [26] including the rate, date, holder, service entity, and any special circumstances surrounding the acquisition of the mortgage(s).

(28) Have you or your spouse at any time held property (as a named owner of record individually or in combination with others) the title to which contained any restrictive covenant based on race, sex, ethnic background, religion or sexual orientation? If so, please provide all relevant information and records.

(29) Please describe any contractual or informal arrangement you may have made with any person or business enterprise in regard to future employment or termination payments or financial benefits that will be provided to you if you enter federal government employment or you leave your current employment.

(30) Do you, your spouse, or any member of your immediate family, or business in which you, your spouse, or immediate family member have a substantial interest, have any relationship with any government, whether federal, state, local, Indian or foreign, through contracts, consulting services, grants, loans or guarantees? If yes, please provide details.

(31) Are there any categories of personal financial records (e.g., individual, partnership or sole proprietorship tax returns, mortgage documents, loan agreements) that you (or your spouse) will not release publicly if necessary? If so, please identify these records and state the reasons for withholding them.

(32) Other than from relatives, or from close and longstanding personal friends on occasions such as birthdays or seasonal holidays, have you or your spouse ever received a gift exceeding $50.00 in value? Please identify the donor, the value of the gift, the date received and the circumstances in which the gift was made.

V. Tax Information

(33) Please furnish a copy of each federal and state (and, if applicable, municipal or foreign) tax return, including any amended return, for 2005 and all subsequent years. If filed separately, furnish the same documents for your spouse.

(34) Have you and your spouse filed all required federal, state, local and foreign income tax returns?

(35) Have you or your spouse ever filed a late tax return without a valid extension? If so describe the circumstances and resolution of the matter.

(36) Have you ever paid any tax penalties? If so, describe the circumstances and the resolution of the matter.

(37) Has a tax lien or other collection procedure ever been instituted against you or your spouse by federal, state or local authorities? If so, describe the circumstances and the resolution of the matter.

(38) Have you ever not paid U.S. and/or state income taxes because you were not resident in the United States, or for any other reason?

(39) Have you been or do you have any expectation that you will be the subject of any tax, financial, or other audit or inquiry? If so, please describe.

(40) Have you ever participated in an investment program or partnership which has been audited or investigated by federal, state or local authorities? If so, describe the circumstances and the resolution of the matter.

(41) Please answer each of the questions in this section for your spouse (for the past ten years) and for any business with which you have been affiliated as an officer, director, partner, trustee or significant owner (i.e., any ownership interest of more than 5%).

VI. Legal and Administrative Proceedings

(42) Please list any lawsuits you or your spouse have brought as a plaintiff or which were brought against you or your spouse as a defendant or third party, or in which you or your spouse have testified at trial or deposition. Include in this response any arbitrations, mediations, and contested divorce proceedings or other domestic relations matters.

(43) Please list and describe any administrative agency proceedings in which you or your spouse have been involved as a party or material witness, and describe the details of your involvement.

(44) Please list any insolvency or bankruptcy proceedings in which you or your spouse have been involved as a debtor, creditor, claimant, or defendant, and describe details of that involvement.

(45) If you have ever been investigated by any law enforcement agency (whether federal, state, military, local, Indian or foreign), arrested for, charged with, or convicted of violating any law, regulation or ordinance (whether federal, state, military, local, Indian or foreign), please identify each such instance and supply details, including: date; place; law enforcement agency; and court. Provide the same information for your spouse and for each child over 21, and for any business with which you have been affiliated (e.g., as a director, officer, partner, trustee, or holder of any significant ownership interest), and furnish all pertinent records. You may exclude traffic offenses for which the fine was less than $50.

(46) Have any members of your family or close social or business associates been arrested for, charged with and/or convicted of a crime, other than a minor traffic violation? If so, please identify and describe each such arrest, charge or conviction. Please provide the same information for anyone under your professional supervision, or anyone of your superiors.

(47) Have you or your spouse ever been accused, formally or informally, of any violation of government or agency procedure (specifically including security violations)?

(48) Please list any complaint ever made against you or your spouse by any administrative agency, regulatory body, professional association or organization, or federal, state, local, Indian or foreign ethics agency, committee, or official.

(49) Please list any malpractice claim made against you, formally or informally, and describe the resolution of the matter.

(50) Please list any claims of sexual harassment of other workplace misconduct, made against you or any employee directly supervised by you, including the resolution of the matter.

(51) Have any civil judgments or liens been rendered against you or your spouse? If so, please provide details.

(52) With regard to each obligation of child support and/or alimony owed by you or your spouse, please state the following: Have any payments been made late or have there been any lapses in payment? Have any motions or court actions for modification of child support or alimony been filed or instituted? Have any actions or motions to compel payment or initiate collection of late payments and/or past due amounts been filed or threatened? Have any writs of garnishment been issued? If yes, please provide details.

VII. Domestic Help

(53) Do you presently have or have you in the past had occasional (to be sure, a monthly housekeeper is covered) or regular domestic help? (e.g., a housekeeper, babysitter, nanny or gardener) If yes, please indicate the name and years of service for each individual and also provide a brief description of the services rendered.

(54) Were all individuals listed in Question 49 [53] legally eligible to work in the U.S. at the time that you employed them?

(55) Have you paid all taxes and social security obligations applicable to the employment of the individuals listed in Question 49 [53]? Do you use an outside service to pay such individuals? Have all payments related to the employment of these individuals been made in a timely fashion? If not, please identify the length and reason for the delay(s),

(56) Have you complied with all federal, state and local laws and regulations related to the employment of individuals listed in Question 49 [53]?

VIII. Miscellaneous

(57) If applicable, please list the names, addresses and phone number[s] of cohabitants within the last ten years. A cohabitant is a person with whom you share bonds of affection, obligation, or other commitment, as opposed to a person with whom you live for reasons of convenience (roommate).

(58) Please provide the URL address of any websites that feature you in either a personal or professional capacity (e.g., Facebook, My Space, etc.).

(59) Do you or any members of your immediate family own a gun? If so, provide complete ownership and registration information. Has the registration ever lapsed? Please also describe how and by whom it is used and whether it has been the cause of any personal injuries or property damage.

(60) Have you had a complete physical within the past year? Please describe your overall health and any medical treatment you are currently receiving.

(61) Have you had any association with any person, group or business venture that could be used—even unfairly—to impugn or attack your character and qualifications for government service?

(62) Do you know anyone or any organization, either in the private sector or government service, that might take steps, overtly or covertly, fairly or unfairly, to criticize your nomination, including any news organization? If so, please identify and explain the potential basis for criticism.

(63) Please provide any other information, including information about other members of your family, that could suggest a conflict of interest or be a possible source of embarrassment to you, your family, or the President-Elect.

Source: http://usgovinfo.about.com/od/thepresidentandcabinet/a/obama-questions.htm.

Appendix B: AFSA Guidelines for Successful Performance as a Chief of Mission

Executive Summary

The American Foreign Service Association, the professional association representing U.S. diplomats, offers this Guidelines paper as a resource to inform the executive and legislative processes of nominating and confirming U.S. chiefs of mission. Chiefs of mission are the president's envoys to foreign countries and multilateral institutions, usually carrying the title of ambassador. They lead our engagement with foreign governments and act as the CEOs of U.S. overseas missions and embassies. The Guidelines are drawn from the collective experience of a group of distinguished former chiefs of mission, both career and non-career, and from legislative and regulatory sources. The paper is non-partisan in nature. There are four broad guidelines, detailed at the end of the paper:

- Leadership, character and proven interpersonal skills;
- Understanding of high level policy and operations and of key U.S. interests in the country or organization of prospective assignment;
- Management; and
- Understanding of host country and international affairs.

Introduction

As a global power, the United States maintains bilateral relations with 180 countries and is represented at 14 missions to international organizations. These diplomatic missions are headed by a chief of mission (COM), who is nominated by the president, confirmed with the advice and consent of the U.S. Senate, and accredited to a specific country or organization.

We live in a complex, interconnected and rapidly changing world. The right actions of nations can promote understanding, appreciation, peace, and prosperity; the wrong actions can cause misunderstanding, predatory practices, or war. This is the domain of diplomacy. The role of chiefs of mission, who must manage these complexities, becomes even more critical—and challenging. Ambassadors are the primary representatives of one country to another—or from a country to an international organization—in effect, the face, voice, and ear of the sending nation. The actions and words of an ambassador have consequences for U.S. national security and interests far beyond the individual country or organization to which he or she is accredited.

It is essential, therefore, that ambassadors chosen to represent the president and lead our diplomatic missions possess the attributes, experience and skills to do so successfully.

This paper is the product of a group of former COMs, including both career and non-career appointees, who understand the challenges COMs face. They know firsthand what it is like to run an embassy, and the steep learning curve even the best-prepared of ambassadors face when they arrive in-country.

AFSA's goal is to contribute positively to the ongoing process of selection of COMs by successive administrations, to help ensure their success by "paying forward" what we have learned. We hope this will assist all involved in the process—from those involved in the selection process, to members of the Senate, to the American people who have a vested interest in having quality representatives abroad, to the prospective appointees themselves—and in so doing, help ensure the success of U.S. foreign policy and the effective and productive functioning of our embassies and missions abroad.

Role of the Chief of Mission

Constitutional and Legislative Authority

Chiefs of mission are the president's personal representatives abroad. Together with the Secretary of State, they assist in implementing the president's constitutional responsibilities for the conduct of U.S. foreign relations. The Foreign Service Act of 1980 (the "Act") calls for individuals appointed to possess knowledge and understanding of the history, culture, economic and political institutions, and interests of the country and its people, as well as language facility to the extent practicable. In accordance with the Act, most chiefs of mission come from the career Foreign Service, in recognition of the value of their professional training and experience. Non-career appointees can bring other highly valuable experience and attributes that can be instrumental in achieving the diplomatic mission.

Work of the COM

While COMs are the president's representatives, they report and offer recommendations to the president through the Secretary of State and, on occasion and in a coordinated manner, to members of the president's national security team and other members of the president's Cabinet. Chiefs of mission have the primary role in:

- Leading and coordinating U.S. representation abroad, conveying and advocating for U.S. foreign policy to foreign governments and international organizations through U.S. embassies and consulates in foreign countries and diplomatic missions to international organizations, directing the activities of other U.S. agencies and officials in the country or to the organization of accreditation (except those under a geographic command commander as determined by the president), advocating for and promoting American industry and conducting economic diplomacy, working with NGOs and civil society, and conducting public diplomacy in support of U.S. policy goals;
- Ensuring the security of mission staff, facilities and classified material, and protecting the interests of American citizens abroad;
- Communicating to Washington the nature and intentions of the host government or international organization, the range of prospective U.S. interests in play, and the resources needed to achieve those interests;
- Conducting and overseeing negotiations and concluding agreements and treaties on a vast and growing range of issues from trade to nuclear weapons;
- Leading the country team to ensure proper focus, priorities, high morale, and interagency coordination in the diplomatic mission's activities to develop and implement foreign policy; and
- Managing the mission's budget and other foreign affairs resources.

COMs must recognize that the international activities and programs of other executive branch agencies are growing. Overseas, it falls upon the shoulders of the COM to ensure that the U.S. government presents a coordinated and disciplined approach to policy and programs. The Department of State's lead role in the conduct of foreign affairs must be coordinated with other executive branch agencies. The COM engages in and manages the interagency process directly and through the country team to maintain focus on and pursue Administration policy and programs.

Challenges

U.S. missions, whether bilateral or multilateral, often consist of representatives of multiple U.S. government agencies, operating in an increasingly complex, interconnected and dynamic world. This presents the COM with delicate policy and leadership tightropes to walk while operating in a foreign culture. Mistakes can magnify quickly and risk becoming public, potentially damaging U.S. interests abroad and at home. U.S. governmental, political and economic policies and developments not directly related to a U.S. mission can have deep implications for the mission, and the COM as its head.

Reflecting upon some of these and other challenges for COMs and missions, and drawing lessons from both the qualities and weaknesses of COMs it observed during several years of inspections, the State Department Office of the Inspector General developed a set of suggested criteria in four areas: (1) Leadership of People and Programs; (2) Relations with Washington; (3) Relations with U.S. Stakeholders; and (4) Relations with the Host Country. In the inspector general's view, Leadership of People and Programs was the facet upon which the greatest emphasis should be placed, and its report advised against selecting anyone for a COM position who lacked a clear and positive record in this area.

In sum, a COM's role is at once outward-focused (policy and outreach in the host country) and inward-focused (leadership of the mission, liaison with Washington). It is probably obvious from the foregoing that a chief of mission's role is difficult to specifically define. Certain fundamental traits, however, are essential to successful performance in the environment in which COMs must work.

Recommended Guidelines for Successful Performance as a COM

We recommend the following guidelines be applied to *all* COM nominees, career (regardless of agency) and non-career, in a fair and impartial manner. It is important that these guidelines be transparent and easy to understand, as well as relatively simple to apply. We have, therefore, developed the four general guidelines described below to be used in the assessment of all future COM nominees.

- Leadership, Character and Proven Interpersonal Skills: The nominee has demonstrated the interpersonal skills necessary to represent the United States, including utmost integrity, honesty, moral courage, fairness, empathy, an appropriate measure of humility, awareness of personal strengths and weaknesses, overall judgment and decisiveness, and the ability to inspire, as well as a proven ability to be effective in taking on new challenges. A demonstrated understanding and mastery of working in a complex environment where the objectives of multiple and sometimes competing organizations must be balanced. A key skill is the ability to listen in order to better understand the host country's perspectives, as well as the mission staff's views and concerns. These skills can be demonstrated through leadership and management of government organizations, private sector companies, or non-governmental and private volunteer organizations.
- Understanding of High Level Policy and Operations and of Key U.S. Interests in the Country or Organization of Prospective Assignment: The nominee possesses the knowledge and capacity to lead the operations of a diplomatic mission effectively; participate constructively in the formulation of policy and implement policy in a creative manner that yields positive results where possible; the ability to communicate persuasively with government stakeholders (White House, State Department, other executive agencies and Congress), host nation officials, political leaders and civil society. He or she demonstrates the capacity to negotiate, and has the proven ability to take on various challenges, including working with U.S. and foreign business communities and other nongovernmental interests, and providing services to U.S. citizens.
- Management: The nominee has relevant management experience. He or she possesses a commitment to team building, the ability to innovate, problem-solving skills, experience in setting goals and visions, ability to manage change, strategic planning skills, experience in allocation of resources, and commitment to mentoring and career development. He or she has the capacity to work well with a deputy and other members of a team, and to delegate effectively.

- Understanding of Host Country and International Affairs, Ability to Promote/Advance U.S. Interests: The nominee has experience in or with the host country and/or other suitable international experience and capacity, has knowledge of the host country culture and language, and/or of other foreign cultures or languages. He or she has the ability to manage relations between the U.S. and the country/organization of assignment in order to advance U.S. interests, including the interests of U.S. commercial firms as well as individual U.S. citizens and nationals. The nominee skillfully interacts with different audiences—both public and private.

Working Group

Ambassador Charles A. Ray, Retired, and Chairman of the Working Group
Ambassador Ruth A. Davis, Retired
Ambassador Stuart E. Eizenstat, Retired
Ambassador Donald Gips, Retired
Ambassador Anthony S. Harrington, Retired
Ambassador James Franklin Jeffrey, Retired
Ambassador Laura E. Kennedy, Retired
Ambassador Alan Larson, Retired
Ambassador Gillian A. Milovanovic, Retired
Ambassador Michael M Wood, Retired
Janice G. Weiner, Executive Secretary of the Working Group
Robert J. Silverman, President of AFSA

Source: http://www.afsa.org/Portals/0/com_guidelines.pdf

Appendix C: Treaties Pending Before the Senate (as of May 7, 2014)

The following treaties have been submitted to the Senate; these treaties have not received Senate advice and consent to ratification:

- International Labor Organization Convention No. 87 Concerning Freedom of Association and Protection of the Right to Organize, adopted by the International Labor Conference at its 31st Session held at San Francisco, June 17–July 10, 1948 (Treaty Doc.: *Ex. S, 81st Cong., 1st Sess.*); submitted to Senate August 27, 1949.
- International Labor Organization Convention No. 116 Concerning the Partial Revision of the conventions adopted by the General Conference of the International Labor Organization at its first 32 sessions for the purpose of standardizing the provisions regarding the preparation of reports by the governing body of the International Labor Office on the Working of Conventions, adopted by the International Labor Conference at its 45th Session held at Geneva, June 26, 1961 (Treaty Doc.: *Ex. C, 87th Cong., 2nd Sess.*); submitted to Senate June 1, 1962.
- International Labor Organization Convention No. 122 Concerning Employment Policy, adopted by the International Labor Conference at its 48th Session held at Geneva July 9, 1964 (Treaty Doc.: *Ex. G, 89th Cong., 2nd Sess.*); submitted to Senate June 2, 1966.
- Vienna Convention on the Law of Treaties, done at Vienna May 23, 1969, and signed by the United States on April 24, 1970 (Treaty Doc.: *Ex. L, 92nd Cong., 1st Sess.*); submitted to Senate November 22, 1971.
- International Covenant on Economic, Social and Cultural Rights, done at New York December 16, 1966, and signed by the United States on October 5, 1977 (Treaty Doc.: *Ex. D, 95th Cong., 2nd Sess.*); submitted to Senate February 23, 1978.

- American Convention on Human Rights, done at San Jose November 22, 1969, and signed by the United States on June 1, 1977 (Treaty Doc.: *Ex. F, 95th Cong., 2nd Sess.*); submitted to Senate February 23, 1978.
- Maritime Boundary Agreement between the United States of America and the Republic of Cuba, signed at Washington December 16, 1977 (Treaty Doc.: *Ex. H, 96th Cong., 1st Sess.*); submitted to Senate January 19, 1979.
- Convention on the Elimination of All Forms of Discrimination Against Women, done at New York December 18, 1979, and signed by the United States on July 17, 1980 (Treaty Doc.: *Ex. R, 96th Cong., 2nd Sess.*); submitted to Senate November 12, 1980.
- Amendment to the 1973 Convention on International Trade in Endangered Species of Wild Fauna and Flora (CITES), done at Gaborone April 30, 1983 (Treaty Doc.: *98–10*); submitted to Senate October 4, 1983.
- Protocol II Additional to the Geneva Conventions of 12 August 1949, and relating to the Protection of Victims of Non-International Armed Conflicts, done at Geneva June 10, 1977, and signed by the United States December 12, 1977 (Treaty Doc.: *100–2*); submitted to Senate January 29, 1987.
- Convention on Biological Diversity, done at Rio de Janeiro June 5, 1992, and signed by the United States at New York on June 4, 1993 (Treaty Doc.: *103–20*); submitted to Senate November 20, 1993.
- United Nations Convention on the Law of the Sea, done at Montego Bay December 10, 1982 (the "Convention") and Agreement relating to Implementation of Part XI of the Convention, done at New York July 28, 1994 (the "Agreement"); Agreement signed by the United States on July 29, 1994 (Treaty Doc.: *103–39*); submitted to Senate October 7, 1994.
- Comprehensive Nuclear-Test-Ban Treaty, done at New York September 10, 1996, and signed by the United States on September 24, 1996 (Treaty Doc.: *105–28*); submitted to Senate September 23, 1997.
- International Labor Organization Convention No. 111 Concerning Discrimination in Respect of Employment and Occupation, adopted by the International Labor Conference at its 42nd Session held at Geneva June 25, 1958 (Treaty Doc.: *105–45*); submitted to Senate May 18, 1998.
- Inter-American Convention against the Illicit Manufacturing of and Trafficking in Firearms, Ammunition, Explosives, and other

Related Materials, done at Washington November 13, 1997, and signed by the United States on November 14, 1997 (Treaty Doc.: *105–49*); submitted to Senate June 9, 1998.

- Protocol for the Protection of Cultural Property in the event of Armed Conflict, done at The Hague May 14, 1954 (Treaty Doc.: *106–1*); submitted to Senate January 6, 1999.
- Rotterdam Convention on the Prior Informed Consent Procedure for Certain Hazardous Chemicals and Pesticides in International Trade, done at Rotterdam September 10, 1998, and signed by the United States on September 11, 1998 (Treaty Doc.: *106–21*); submitted to Senate February 9, 2000.
- Treaty between the United States of America and the Republic of Nicaragua Concerning the Encouragement and Reciprocal Protection of Investment, signed at Denver July 1, 1995 (Treaty Doc.: *106–33*); submitted to Senate June 26, 2000.
- Convention on the Safety of United Nations and Associated Personnel, done at New York December 9, 1994, and signed by the United States on December 19, 1994 (Treaty Doc.: *107–1*); submitted to Senate January 3, 2001.
- Stockholm Convention on Persistent Organic Pollutants, done at Stockholm May 22, 2001, and signed by the United States on May 23, 2001 (Treaty Doc.: *107–5*); submitted to Senate May 7, 2002.
- 1996 Protocol to the Convention on the Prevention of Marine Pollution by Dumping of Wastes and Other Matter, 1972, done at London November 7, 1996, and signed by the United States March 31, 1998 (Treaty Doc. *110–5*); submitted to Senate September 4, 2007.
- International Treaty on Plant Genetic Resources for Food and Agriculture, adopted by the Food and Agriculture Organization of the United Nations November 3, 2001, and signed by the United States November 1, 2002 (Treaty Doc. *110–19*); submitted to Senate July 7, 2008.
- Agreement on the Conservation of Albatrosses and Petrels, with annexes, done at Canberra June 19, 2001 (Treaty Doc. *110–22*); submitted to Senate September 26, 2008.
- Annex VI on Liability Arising From Environmental Emergencies to the Protocol on Environmental Protection to the Antarctic Treaty (Annex VI), adopted on June 14, 2005 (Treaty Doc. *111–2*); submitted to Senate April 2, 2009.
- Convention between the Government of the United States of America and the Government of the Republic of Hungary for the

Avoidance of Double Taxation and the Prevention of Fiscal Evasion with Respect to Taxes on Income, signed at Budapest February 4, 2010, with related exchange of notes (Treaty Doc.: *111–7*); submitted to Senate November 15, 2010.

- Protocol Amending the Convention between the Government of the United States of America and the Government of the Grand Duchy of Luxembourg for the Avoidance of Double Taxation and the Prevention of Fiscal Evasion with Respect to Taxes on Income and Capital, signed at Luxembourg May 20, 2009, with related exchange of notes (Treaty Doc.: *111–8*); submitted to Senate November 15, 2010.

- Protocol Amending the Convention between the United States of America and the Swiss Confederation for the Avoidance of Double Taxation with Respect to Taxes on Income, signed at Washington on October 2, 1996, signed at Washington September 23, 2009, with related exchanges of notes (Treaty Doc.: *112–1*); submitted to Senate January 26, 2011.

- Protocols 1, 2, and 3 to the South Pacific Nuclear Free Zone Treaty, done at Suva August 8, 1986, and signed on behalf of the United States on March 25, 1996 (Treaty Doc.: *112–2*); submitted to Senate May 2, 2011.

- Protocols I and II to the African Nuclear-Weapon-Free Zone Treaty, done at Cairo April 11, 1996 and signed that day on behalf of the United States (Treaty Doc.: *112–3*); submitted to Senate May 2, 2011.

- Protocol Amending the Convention on Mutual Administrative Assistance in Tax Matters, done at Paris May 27, 2010 and signed that day on behalf of the United States (Treaty Doc.: *112–5*); submitted to Senate May 17, 2012.

- Convention on the Law Applicable to Certain Rights in Respect of Securities held with an Intermediary, done at The Hague July 5, 2006 and signed that day on behalf of the United States (Treaty Doc.: *112–6*); submitted to Senate May 17, 2012.

- Convention on the Rights of Persons with Disabilities, adopted by the United Nations General Assembly on December 13, 2006 and signed on behalf of the United States on June 30, 2009 (Treaty Doc.: *112–7*); submitted to Senate May 17, 2012.

- Convention between the Government of the United States of America and the Government of the Republic of Chile for the Avoidance of Double Taxation and the Prevention of Fiscal Evasion with Respect to Taxes on Income and Capital, with Protocol, signed at Washington February 4, 2010, as corrected by exchanges of notes effected February 25, 2011 and February 10 and 21, 2012, with related agreement effected by exchange of notes on February 4, 2010 (Treaty Doc.: *112–8*); submitted to Senate May 17, 2012.

- Protocol Amending the Convention between the United States of America and the Kingdom of Spain for the Avoidance of Double Taxation and the Prevention of Fiscal Evasion with respect to Taxes on Income, and its Protocol signed at Madrid, on February 22, 1990, with memorandum of understanding, signed at Madrid January 14, 2013, as corrected by exchange of notes on July 23, 2013 and January 31, 2014 (Treaty Doc.: *113–4*); submitted to Senate May 7, 2014.

Source: http://www.state.gov/s/l/treaty/pending.

Appendix D: Provisions of the Foreign Service Act of 1980

SEC. 207. 15 CHIEF OF MISSION—

(a) Under the direction of the President, the chief of mission to a foreign country—

   (1) shall have full responsibility for the direction, coordination, and supervision of all Government executive branch[1] employees in that country (except for employees under the command of a United States area military commander); and

   (2) shall keep fully and currently informed with respect to all activities and operations of the Government within that country, and shall insure that all Government executive branch[1] employees in that country (except for employees under the command of a United States area military commander) comply fully with all applicable directives of the chief of mission.

[1]Sec. 136 of the Foreign Relations Authorization Act, Fiscal Years 1988 and 1989 (Public Law 100–204; 101 Stat. 1345), inserted "executive branch" in subsecs. (a)(1), (a)(2), and (b).

SEC. 304. APPOINTMENT OF CHIEFS OF MISSION—

(a) (1) An individual appointed or assigned to be a chief of mission should possess clearly demonstrated competence to perform the duties of a chief of mission, including, to the maximum extent practicable, a useful knowledge of the principal language or dialect of the country in which the individual is to serve, and knowledge and understanding of the history, the culture, the economic and political institutions, and the interests of that country and its people.

(2) Given the qualifications specified in paragraph (1), positions as chief of mission should normally be accorded to career members of the Service, though circumstances will warrant appointments from time to time of qualified individuals who are not career members of the Service.

(3) Contributions to political campaigns should not be a factor in the appointment of an individual as a chief of mission.

(4) The President shall provide the Committee on Foreign Relations of the Senate, with each nomination for an appointment as a chief of mission, a report on the demonstrated competence of that nominee to perform the duties of the position in which he or she is to serve.

Sec. 142(a) of the Foreign Relations Authorization Act, Fiscal Years 1992 and 1993 (Public Law 102–138; 105 Stat. 667), struck out text in the second sentence of subsec. (b) following "assignment," and inserted in lieu thereof text beginning with "may elect to continue * * *". The same sentence had been amended by sec. 177(b) of the Foreign Relations Authorization Act, Fiscal Years 1988 and 1989 (Public Law 100–204; 101 Stat. 1362).

(b) (1) In order to assist the President in selecting qualified candidates for appointment or assignment as chiefs of mission, the Secretary of State shall from time to time furnish the President with the names of career members of the Service who are qualified to serve as chiefs of mission, together with pertinent information about such members.

(2) Each individual nominated by the President to be a chief of mission, ambassador at large, or minister shall, at the time of nomination, file with the Committee on Foreign Relations of the Senate and the Speaker of the House of Representatives a report of contributions made by such individual and by members of his or her immediate family during the period beginning on the first day of the fourth calendar year preceding the calendar year of the nomination and ending on the date of the nomination. The report shall be verified by the oath of the nominee, taken before any individual authorized to administer oaths. The chairman of the Committee on Foreign Relations of the Senate shall have each such report printed in the Congressional Record. As used in this paragraph, the term "contribution" has the

same meaning given such term by section 301(8) of the Federal Election Campaign Act of 1971 (2 U.S.C. 431(8)), and the term "immediate family" means the spouse of the nominee, and any child, parent, grandparent, brother, or sister of the nominee and the spouses of any of them.

(c) Within 6 months after assuming the position, the chief of mission to a foreign country shall submit, to the Committee on Foreign Relations of the Senate and the Committee on International Relations of the House of Representatives, a report describing his or her own foreign language competence and the foreign language competence of the mission staff in the principal language or other dialect of that country.

Appendix E: President Obama's Letter of Instruction to Chiefs of Mission (which was sent as an unclassified telegram to all chiefs of mission in July 2009)

R 141634Z JUL 09
FM SECSTATE WASHDC
TO ALL DIPLOMATIC AND CONSULAR POSTS COLLECTIVE
UNCLAS STATE 072909
FOR CHIEFS OF MISSION FROM UNDER
SECRETARY KENNEDY
E.O. 12958: N/A
TAGS: AODE, AMGT, KMRS
SUBJECT: PRESIDENT'S LETTER OF INSTRUCTION TO CHIEFS OF MISSION

1. The President's Letter of Instruction to Chiefs of Mission (COM) is revised at the beginning of each new administration and sent to all newly appointed Ambassadors. It is the primary mechanism for communicating the President's foreign policy priorities and COM authority to U.S. missions overseas. The National Security Council (NSC) informed the Department of State on May 26, 2009 that President Obama has approved the language provided in paragraph two below as his Letter of Instruction to Chiefs of Mission. This letter will also serve as instructions for Ambassadors already in the field. Please share the full text of the

new letter with others in your mission, especially your country team.

2. (BEGIN TEXT)

Dear Mr./Madam Ambassador:

Thank you for your willingness to serve our country as my personal representative to [country/international organization].

Together we have a great task before us. We must renew America's security and standing in the world through a new era of American leadership. The United States will advance its interests through a core pragmatism rooted in America's enduring values. We must rebuild our traditional alliances and pursue new partnerships based on mutual interests and respect, so that together we can confront key common challenges of the 21st century, including weapons of mass destruction, terrorism, poverty, pandemic disease, dependence on fossil fuels and global climate change. America is strongest when we act alongside other nations and peoples. Our security also is enhanced through principled and sustained engagement with those who think differently. As my personal representative, you will be the front line of our efforts.

Our security and prosperity are inextricably linked with those of other countries and people around the world. To strengthen both our national and global economies, we must expand trade as well as financial and scientific cooperation, and we will advance mutual understanding through educational and cultural diplomacy. We must work in concert with others to prevent, resolve, and mitigate conflict, combat transnational threats, strengthen law enforcement cooperation, and promote democratic values and human rights.

I will need your support for our efforts to provide forward-thinking, sustained diplomacy in every part of the world. We will apply pressure where it may be needed, and look for opportunities to advance U.S. interests. As appropriate, you should reach out to other government agencies, nongovernmental organizations, the private sector, international organizations, and our military to leverage your own initiatives. I also urge you to pursue diplomacy and public outreach with 21st century tools and technology. As Chief of the U.S. Mission, one of your most important jobs will be to take care of our diplomatic personnel and to ensure that they have the tools they need to support your efforts. The Mission should be seen as a welcoming and supportive place for American citizens and American businesses abroad.

I have asked you to represent the United States in [country/international organization] because I am confident that you possess the skills, dedication, and experience necessary to meet the many challenges that we face in these extraordinary times.

This letter contains your detailed instructions as my personal representative and the U.S. Chief of Mission. These instructions have been shared with relevant departments and agencies, and I have directed that they give you their full cooperation. I expect you to carry out your mission to the best of your ability and in full conformance with the law and the highest ethical standards. I am counting on your advice and leadership as Chief of Mission to help protect America's interests and to promote America's values.

As Chief of Mission, you have full responsibility for the direction, coordination, and supervision of all U.S. Executive Branch employees in [country], regardless of their employment categories or location, except those under command of a U.S. area military commander or on the staff of an international organization. With these exceptions, you are in charge of all Executive Branch activities and operations in your Mission.

You will report to me through the Secretary of State. Under my direction, the Secretary of State is, to the fullest extent provided by the law, responsible for the overall coordination of all United States government activities and operations abroad. The only authorization channel for instruction to you is from the Secretary or me, unless the Secretary or I personally instruct you to use a different channel.

All Executive Branch agencies under your authority, and every element of your Mission, must keep you fully informed at all times of their current and planned activities. You have the right to see all communications to or from Mission elements, however transmitted, except those specifically exempted by law or Executive decision.

You have full responsibility for the direction, coordination, and supervision of all Department of Defense personnel on official duty in [country] except those under the command of a U.S. area military commander. You and the area military commander must keep each other currently and fully informed and cooperate on all matters of mutual interest. Any differences that cannot be resolved in the field will be reported to the Secretary of State and the Secretary of Defense.

I expect you to take direct and full responsibility for the security of your Mission and all the personnel for whom you are responsible, whether inside or outside the chancery gate. Unless an interagency agreement provides otherwise, the Secretary of State and you as Chief of Mission must provide for the security of all United States government personnel on official duty abroad other than those under the protection of a U.S. area military commander or on the staff of an international organization and their accompanying dependents. You and the U.S. area military commander should consult and coordinate responses to common threats.

I ask that you review programs, personnel, and funding levels regularly, and ensure that all agencies attached to your Mission do likewise. Rightsizing the United

States government presence abroad is a continuing requirement. To better meet our foreign policy goals, I will be expanding the Foreign Service and strengthening civilian capacity to work alongside the military. At the same time, we need to eliminate unnecessary duplication in our foreign operations. Functions that can be performed effectively and efficiently by personnel based in the United States or at regional offices overseas should not be performed at post. We should make greater use of the expertise of host country citizens, and outsource functions when it is effective and efficient to do so. In your reviews, should you find staffing to be either excessive or inadequate to the performance of priority Mission goals and objectives, I urge you to initiate staffing changes in accordance with established procedures.

Every Executive Branch agency under your authority must obtain your approval before changing the size, composition, or mandate of its staff. If a Department head disagrees with you on staffing matters, that individual may appeal your decision to the Secretary of State. In the event the Secretary is unable to resolve the dispute, the Secretary and the respective Department head will present their differing views to me for decision.

All United States government personnel other than those under the command of a U.S. area military commander or on the staff of an international organization must obtain country clearance before entering [country] on official business. You may refuse country clearance or may place conditions or restrictions on visiting personnel as you determine necessary.

I expect you to discharge your responsibilities with professional excellence and in full conformance with the law and the highest standards of ethical conduct. You should ensure that there is equal opportunity at your Mission and no discrimination or harassment of any kind. Remember as you conduct your duties that you are representing not only me, but also the American people and America's values.

Sincerely,
Barack H. Obama

(END TEXT)

3. A modified version containing the same basic text will go to chiefs of multilateral missions (certain international organizations and Geneva).

Appendix F: President George W. Bush's Letter of Instruction to Chiefs of Mission

The Honorable
NAME
American Ambassador
CITY

Dear Mr./Madam Ambassador:

Thank you for your willingness to serve the American people as our country's representative to [country/international organization].

The great struggles of the 20th century between liberty and totalitarianism ended with a decisive victory for the forces of freedom and a single sustainable model for national success: freedom, democracy, and free enterprise. Today, the United States enjoys a position of unparalleled strength and influence. In keeping with our heritage and principles, we do not use our position to press for unilateral advantage. We seek instead to create a balance of power that favors human freedom.

Our commitment to freedom is America's tradition. The advance of freedom is also the surest way to undermine terror and tyranny, and to promote peace and prosperity. Your task is to help in advancing this great cause by:

- waging a relentless global war against terrorism, to defeat those who seek to harm us and our friends;
- overcoming the faceless enemies of human dignity, including disease, starvation, and poverty; and
- assisting American citizens, institutions, and businesses as they pursue their charitable and commercial interests.

This letter contains your detailed instructions as my personal representative and the United States Chief of Mission. These instructions have been shared with relevant departments and agencies, and I have directed that they give you their full cooperation. I expect you to carry out your mission to the best of your ability and in full conformance with the law and the highest ethical standards. I am counting on your advice and leadership as Chief of Mission to help protect America's interests and to promote America's values.

Sincerely,
George W. Bush

Detailed Instructions

As Chief of Mission, you have full responsibility for the direction, coordination, and supervision of all United States Government executive branch employees in [country/at international organization], regardless of their employment categories or location, except those under command of a U.S. area military commander or on the staff of an international organization. Except for the activities of the personnel exempted above, you are in charge of all executive branch activities and operations in your [Mission/international organization].

You will report to me through the Secretary of State. Under my direction, the Secretary of State is, to the fullest extent provided by the law, responsible for the overall coordination and supervision of all United States Government activities and operations abroad. The only authorized channel for instruction to you is from the Secretary or me unless the Secretary or I personally instruct you to use a different channel.

All executive branch agencies under your authority, and every element of your Mission, must keep you fully informed at all times of their current and planned activities. You have the right to see all communications to or from Mission elements, however transmitted, except those specifically exempted by law or Executive decision.

You have full responsibility for the direction, coordination and supervision of all Department of Defense personnel on official duty in [country/at international organization] except those under the command of a U.S. area military commander. You and the area military commander must keep each other currently and fully informed and cooperate on all matters of mutual interest. Any differences that cannot be resolved in the field will be reported to the Secretary of State and Secretary of Defense.

I expect you to take direct and full responsibility for the security of your Mission and all the personnel for whom you are responsible, whether inside or outside the chancery gate. Unless an interagency agreement provides otherwise, the Secretary of State and you as Chief of Mission must protect all United States Government personnel on official duty abroad other than those under the protection of a U.S. area military commander or on the staff of an international organization and their accompanying dependents. You and the U.S. area military commander should consult and coordinate responses to common threats.

I ask that you review programs, personnel, and funding levels regularly, and ensure that all agencies attached to your Mission do likewise. Functions that can be performed by personnel based in the United States or at regional offices overseas should not be performed at post. In your reviews, should you find staffing to be either excessive or inadequate to the performance of priority Mission goals and objectives, I urge you to initiate staffing changes in accordance with established procedures.

Every executive branch agency under your authority must obtain your approval before changing the size, composition or mandate of its staff. If a Department head disagrees with you on staffing matters, that individual may appeal your decision to the Secretary of State. In the event the Secretary is unable to resolve the dispute, the Secretary and the respective Department head will present their differing views to me for decision.

All United States Government personnel other than those in [the] country under the command of a U.S. area military commander or on the staff of an international organization must obtain country clearance before entering [country/visiting international organization] on official business. You may refuse country clearance or may place conditions or restrictions on visiting personnel as you determine necessary.

I expect you to discharge your responsibilities with professional excellence and in full conformance with the law and the highest standards of ethical conduct. You should ensure that there is equal opportunity at your Mission and no discrimination or harassment of any kind. Remember as you conduct your duties that you are not only representing me, but also the American people and America's values.

Appendix G: President Clinton's Letter of Instruction to Chiefs of Mission

[To the author as ambassador to Peru]

Dear Mr. Ambassador:

Please accept my best wishes and appreciation for you efforts as my personal representative to the Republic of Peru.

We are at a moment of unique and historic opportunity for the United States and the world. With the end of the Cold War, we are entering an era so new that it has yet to acquire a name. Our task as a Nation, and yours a Chief of the United States Mission, is to ensure that this era is one conducive to American prosperity, to American security, and to the values America seeks to exemplify. To accomplish this task I need your full support for the three goals of my foreign policy that aim to keep our Nation strong at home and abroad: renewing and adapting America's security alliances and structures; rebuilding and revitalizing the American economy; and promoting democracy, human rights, and sustainable development.

You should give special attention in the security realm to halting arms proliferation, preventing, resolving, and containing conflict, and to countering terrorism and international crime; and in the economic arena, to opening and expanding markets for America's exports. No country can be exempt from upholding the basic principles in the Universal Declaration of Human Rights; all should understand that shared democratic values are the most reliable foundation for good relations with the United States. Finally, I will need your help as my Administration seeks to promote international cooperation to address global problems including the environment and population, narcotics production and trafficking, refugees, migration, and humanitarian assistance.

Achieving these goals will demand a dynamic diplomacy that harnesses change in the service of our national interests and values. It will require us to meet threats to our security and practice preventive diplomacy, and to anticipate threats to our interests and to peace in the world before they become crises and drain our human and material resources in wasteful ways. I have asked you to represent the United States in Peru because I am confident that you possess the skills, dedication, and experience necessary to meet the many challenges that this new and complex era presents. This letter outlines your principal authorities and responsibilities. I have informed all department and agency heads of these instructions, and I know you will receive their full support.

I charge you to exercise your authority with wisdom, justice, and imagination. Dramatic change abroad and austerity here at home have put a premium on leadership and teamwork. Careful stewardship of your Mission's resources stands in the forefront of your responsibilities. I urge you to see budgetary stringency not as a hardship to be endured but as an incentive to innovation.

As my representative, you, with the Secretary of State, assist me in the implementation of my constitutional responsibilities for the conduct of our relations with Peru. I charge you to exercise full responsibility for the direction, coordination, and supervision of all executive branch officers and personnel in Peru, except for personnel under the command of a U.S. area military commander, under another chief of mission in Peru, or on the staff of an international organization. This encompasses all American and foreign national personnel, in all employment categories, whether direct hire or contract, full- or part-time, permanent or temporary.

All executive branch personnel under your authority must keep you fully informed at all times of their current and planned activities, so that you can effectively carry out your responsibility for U.S. Government programs and operations. You have the right to see all communications to or from Mission elements, however transmitted, except those specifically exempted by law or Executive decision.

As Commander in Chief, I retain authority over U.S. Armed Forces. On my behalf you have responsibility for the direction, coordination, supervision and safety, including security from terrorism, of all Department of Defense personnel on official duty in Peru, except those under the command of a U.S. area military commander. You and such commanders must keep each other currently informed and cooperate on all matters of mutual interest. Any differences that cannot be resolved in the field should be reported by you to the Secretary of State; area military commanders should report to the Secretary of Defense.

Every executive branch agency under your authority, including the Department of State, must obtain your approval to change the size, composition, or mandate of its staff. Use this authority to reshape your Mission in ways that directly serve American interests and values. I ask that you review regularly programs, personnel, and funding levels, and ensure that all agencies attached to your Mission do likewise. Functions that can be performed by personnel based in the United States or at regional offices overseas should not be performed at post. In your review, seek guidance from the Secretary of State, who has the responsibility for establishing appropriate staffing levels. Given the restrictive resource environment in which we operate, I urge you to cooperate in every way you can with any downsizing efforts undertaken by other departments and agencies. If an agency head disagrees with you regarding staffing, he or she may inform the Secretary of State, to whom I have delegated responsibility for resolving such issues. In the event the Secretary is unable to resolve the dispute, the Secretary and the respective agency head will present their respective views to me, through my Assistant for National Security Affairs, for decision. In such instances, both the Secretary and I will uphold the party arguing for the best use of increasingly scarce resources.

The Secretary of State is my principal foreign policy adviser. Under my direction, he is, to the fullest extent provided by the law, responsible for the overall coordination and supervision of U.S. Government activities abroad. The only authorized channel for instructions to you is through him or from me. There are only two exceptions: (1) if I personally instruct you to use private channels, or (2) if the Secretary instructs you to use a non-State channel. The Secretary and I will look to you for your expert guidance and frank counsel. You should seek the same from your own staff. I urge you to foster a climate of openness, as debate and dissent serve a vital role in policy-making. Ultimately, there can be only one U.S. policy, which I expect you and all members of your Mission to follow and articulate. But by having a frank internal debate, we are better able to speak to others with one voice regarding U.S. foreign policy.

The Secretary of State and, by extension, chiefs of mission abroad must protect all U.S. Government personnel on official duty abroad (other than those personnel under the command of a U.S. military commander) and their accompanying dependents. I expect you to take direct responsibility for the security of your Mission. I also expect you to support strongly appropriate counterintelligence and counterterrorism activities that enhance security both locally and in the broader international context.

You should cooperate fully with personnel of the U.S. legislative and judicial branches in Peru so that U.S. foreign policy goals are advanced, security is maintained and executive, legislative and judicial responsibilities are carried out.

As Chief of Mission you are not only my representative in Peru but a servant of the people of our Nation. This is both a high honor and a great responsibility. I expect you to discharge this trust with professional excellence, the highest standards of ethical conduct, and diplomatic discretion. I ask you to ensure that your staff similarly adheres to the same strict standards and maintains our shared commitment to equal opportunity. I urge you in particular to see that discrimination or harassment of any kind find no acceptance at your Mission, just as they have no place in American society.

Always keep in mind that, for the Government and people of Peru, you and your Mission symbolize the United States of America and its values. Never forget the solemn duty that we, as public servants, owe to the citizens of America: the active protection and promotion of their well-being, safety, and ideals. There is no better definition of American national interest and no loftier object for your efforts.

Sincerely,

(signed William J. Clinton)

Appendix H: President George H. W. Bush's Letter of Instruction to Chiefs of Mission

MEMORANDUM FOR THE HEADS OF EXECUTIVE
DEPARTMENTS AND AGENCIES

SUBJECT: Authorities and Responsibilities of United States Chiefs of Mission

I am sending a letter of instruction to each of my Ambassadors and Chiefs of other U.S. Diplomatic Missions setting out their authorities and responsibilities. The text of the letter is attached.

I expect your support and cooperation in ensuring that the activities of your department or agency are conducted in accordance with the authorities and responsibilities of Chiefs of Mission, who serve as my personal representatives. Please circulate this memorandum and my letter to your staffs in the United States and abroad, and maintain it as part of the working files in all appropriate offices.

(Signed by President George H. W. Bush)

PRESIDENTIAL LETTER TO CHIEFS OF MISSION

Dear Mr./Madam Ambassador:

I send you my very best wishes and appreciation for your efforts as Chief of the United States Mission [in (full official name of country)/ at (international organization)]. We are entering a new, exciting time of change in international relations. The postwar era is drawing to a close. As leader of the democracies, our Nation faces an historic opportunity to help shape a freer, more secure, and more prosperous world, in which our ideals and our way of life can truly flourish. As President, I intend to advance these objectives and United States interests around the globe, and I look to you, as my personal representative [in (country)/at (international organization)], as my partner in this task.

As my representative, you, along with the Secretary of State, share with me my constitutional responsibility for the conduct of our relations with (country)/(international organization). I charge you to exercise full responsibility for the direction, coordination, and supervision of all Executive branch U.S. offices and personnel [in (country)/at (international organization)], except for personnel under the command of a United States area military commander, personnel under the authority of the Chief of another U.S. Mission (for example, one accredited to an international organization), or personnel detailed to duty on the staff of an international organization.

The Secretary of State is my principal foreign policy advisor. You will receive policy guidance and instructions from him or from me. Except in the most unusual circumstances, as I shall determine, messages on policy proposals and policy implementation will be sent to you through official Department of State channels. You will normally report through the Secretary. I want to emphasize that the Secretary of State has the responsibility not only for the activities of the Department of State and the Foreign Service, but also, to the fullest extent provided by law, for the overall coordination and supervision of United States Government activities abroad.

You are to provide strong program direction and leadership to all Executive branch agency activities to carry out United States foreign policy. It is also your responsibility to foster conditions in which our regional or worldwide activities can achieve success. I have notified all heads of departments and agencies accordingly and instructed them to inform their personnel in the United States and abroad.

You should cooperate fully with personnel of the U.S. Legislative and Judicial branches [in (country)/at (international organization)] so that United States foreign policy goals are advanced, security is maintained, and Executive, Legislative, and Judicial responsibilities are carried out.

You should instruct all Executive branch personnel under your authority of their responsibility to keep you fully informed at all times of their current and planned activities, so that you can effectively carry out your responsibility for United States Government programs and operations. You have the right to see all communications to or from Mission elements, except those specifically exempted by law or Executive decision.

As Commander in Chief, I retain authority over United States Armed Forces. On my behalf you have responsibility for the direction, coordination, supervision, and safety, including security from terrorism, of all Department of Defense personnel on official duty [in (country)/at (international organization)], except those personnel under the command of a U.S. area military commander. You and such commanders must keep each other currently informed and cooperate on all matters of mutual interest. Any differences that cannot be resolved in the field should be reported by you to the Secretary of State; unified commanders should report to the Secretary of Defense.

I expect you to report with directness and candor. If there are policies or programs with which you or personnel under your authority disagree, the Secretary of State and I will always welcome the opportunity to consider alternative courses of action. Nevertheless, there can be only one United States policy, which I expect you and all members of your Mission to follow and articulate. I am committed to a lean personnel profile overseas for reasons of foreign policy, security, and economy. Thus, it is my policy that overseas staffing be tied directly to the accomplishment of specific national goals, and reduced whenever and wherever possible. I therefore want you to assess regularly the staffing levels and overall costs of every element of your Mission to make certain they are consistent with our overall efforts to reduce the official U.S. presence abroad. You may initiate changes when you believe the staffing of any agency is either inadequate or excessive to the performance of essential functions. Every agency under your authority, including the Department of State, must obtain your approval for any change in the size, composition, or mandate of its staff. You must make the hard choices, and I expect you to relate Mission resources directly to priority policy and program activities, genuine need, and safety. However, you should be aware that overall staff reductions notwithstanding, some diplomatic missions may, as the need arises, be asked to accept augmentation to meet new and pressing national security demands.

If an Agency head disagrees with you regarding staffing, he may inform the Secretary of State, to whom I have delegated responsibility for resolving such issues. In the event the Secretary of State is unable to resolve a dispute, the Secretary of State and the Agency head will present their respective views to me, through my Assistant for National Security Affairs, for decision. In such instances, both the Secretary of State and I will uphold the party arguing for the best use of increasingly scarce resources.

The protection of all United States Government personnel on official duty abroad and their accompanying dependents is a crucial responsibility in this dangerous time. You must always keep security in the forefront of your concerns. The security of your Mission is your direct, personal responsibility. I also expect you to support strongly counterintelligence and counterterrorism activities that enhance security both locally and in the broader international context.

I know you share my total commitment to fair and equitable treatment for all, regardless of race, color, creed, sex, or national origin. It is your duty to demonstrate our shared commitment to equal employment opportunity. I expect you to run your Mission in an atmosphere free of discrimination. From my own personal experience as an Ambassador, I know that there are many ways you can foster a positive climate in this important regard by your own emphasis and example.

I also expect the highest standards of professional and personal conduct from all United States Government personnel. Public service is a trust requiring government personnel to place public duties above private interests. Accordingly, they must abide by the highest ethical standards. To ensure that the American people retain complete confidence in the integrity of their government, government personnel must abide not only by the letter of regulations but also by the spirit of public service. You have the authority and my full support to ensure that ethical conduct is a hallmark of our presence overseas, both on and off the job.

I am sure you will represent the United States with imagination, energy, and skill. You have my full personal confidence and best wishes.

Source: http://www.state.gov/documents/organization/28466.pdf.

Appendix I: Countries with Danger Pay Allowance

Table A.I Countries with Danger Pay Allowance

Country name	Rate (%)	Political appointee
Afghanistan	35	Yes—Retired General
Algeria	15	
Burundi	20	
Central African Republic	15	
Chad	15	
Colombia	15	
Côte d'Ivoire	15	
Haiti	5	
Iraq	35	
Israel	15	
Jordan	15	
Kosovo	15	
Lebanon	25	
Pakistan	35	
Saudi Arabia	15	Yes—Retired General
Somalia	25	
Sudan	25	
Yemen	30	

Danger Pay: The danger pay allowance provides additional compensation for employees serving at designated danger pay posts. It is paid as a percentage of basic compensation in 15, 20, 25, 30, and 35% increments.

Source: http://aoprals.state.gov/Web920/danger_pay_all.asp.

Appendix J: Countries with Hardship Differentials

The first column shows the percent of the hardship allowance, the second shows whether the ambassador was a political appointee, and the third shows the contributions in thousands of dollars of the political appointees.

Table A.J Countries with Hardship Differentials

Country	Rate (%)	Political appointee	Campaign contributions of the ambassador ($K)
Afghanistan	35	P	
Albania	20		
Algeria	20		
Angola	25		
Armenia	20		
Azerbaijan	20		
Bahrain	10		
Bangladesh	30		
Belarus	25		
Belize	20	P	100
Benin	20		
Bolivia	25		
Bosnia and Herzegovina	20		
Botswana	10	P	
Brazil	10		
Brunei	15		
Bulgaria	10		
Burkina Faso	20		
Burma	30		
Burundi	25		
Cambodia	25		
Cameroon	25		
Cape Verde	25		

Continued

Table A.J Continued

Country	Rate (%)	Political appointee	Campaign contributions of the ambassador ($K)
Central African Republic	30		
Chad	30		
China	15	P	
Colombia	5		
Côte d'Ivoire	20		
Cuba	30		
Democratic Republic of the Congo	30		
Djibouti	30		
Dominican Republic	15		
Ecuador	10		
Egypt	25		
El Salvador	15	P	
Equatorial Guinea	35		
Eritrea	30		
Estonia	10		
Ethiopia	25		
Fiji	20		
Gabon	15		
Georgia	25		
Ghana	20		
Greece	5		
Guatemala	15		
Guinea	30		
Guyana	25		
Haiti	30		
Honduras	15		
Iceland	10		
India	20	P	
Indonesia	25		
Iraq	35		
Jamaica	15		
Jordan	5		
Kazakhstan	25		
Kenya	30		
Kosovo	20		
Kuwait	10		
Kyrgyzstan	25		
Laos	30		
Latvia	10		
Lebanon	20		
Lesotho	20		
Liberia	30		
Libya	20		
Lithuania	5		

Continued

Table A.J Continued

Country	Rate (%)	Political appointee	Campaign contributions of the ambassador ($K)
Macedonia	15		
Madagascar	25		
Malawi	25		
Malaysia	10		
Mali	25		
Malta	5	P	
Marshall Islands	20		
Mauritania	25		
Mauritius	5		
Mexico	15	P	
Micronesia	20		
Moldova	20		
Mongolia	25		
Montenegro	15		
Mozambique	25		
Namibia	5		
Nepal	25		
Nicaragua	15		
Niger	25		
Nigeria	25		
Pakistan	25		
Palau	10		
Papua New Guinea	30		
Paraguay	5		
Peru	15		
Philippines	20		
Qatar	5		
Republic of the Congo	30		
Romania	5	P	129
Russia	15		
Rwanda	25		
Saudi Arabia	20	P	3
Senegal	15		
Serbia	15		
Sierra Leone	30		
Slovak Republic	10	P	52
South Africa	10	P	500
Sri Lanka	20		
Sudan	25		
Suriname	25		
Swaziland	15		
Syria	20		
Tajikistan	35		
Tanzania	25	P	

Continued

Table A.J Continued

Country	Rate (%)	Political appointee	Campaign contributions of the ambassador ($K)
Thailand	10		
The Gambia	20		
Timor Leste	35		
Togo	25		
Trinidad and Tobago	5	P	500
Tunisia	10		
Turkey	10		
Turkmenistan	25		
Uganda	25		
Ukraine	20		
Uzbekistan	30		
Venezuela	20		
Vietnam	25		
Yemen	20		
Zambia	20		
Zimbabwe	30		

Post Hardship Differential: Post hardship differential is meant to compensate employees for service at places in foreign areas where the conditions of environment differ substantially from the conditions of environment in the continental United States and warrant additional compensation as a recruitment and retention incentive. It is paid as a percentage of basic compensation in 5, 10, 15, 20, 25, 30, and 35% increments.

Source: http://aoprals.state.gov/Web920/hardship.asp; ambassador data comes from the AFSA website, as of February 1, 2011.

Appendix K: Inspector General's Personal Questionnaire for Inspections

PERSONAL QUESTIONNAIRE

(For American personnel of the Department of State and heads of other agencies at post.) The information you provide is privileged and confidential. The questionnaire is solely for the use of the Office of Inspector General. The questionnaire will not be shown to anyone at post outside of the inspection team and will be shredded immediately following the inspection.

Name: _____ Date Arrived at Post: _____

Section: _____ Agency: _____

Post: _____ Supervisor: _____

Position:

Rank/Grade (select one):

☐ SFS, SES, 07–010 ☐ FS 2–1, GS 13–15, O4/W4–06
☐ FS9–3, GS 5–12, E1-O3/W3

Number of overseas posts to which you have been assigned (select one):

☐ 1 ☐ 2 ☐ 3

Amount of time at post in months (select one):

☐ 0–3 ☐ 4–11 ☐ 12+

INSTRUCTIONS

The Office of Inspector General collects most Personal Questionnaires electronically. If you use this version of the questionnaire, your scores may not be included in the aggregated data available to the inspection team during the survey phase.

Do not complete this questionnaire if you have submitted a Personal Questionnaire electronically.

If you're completing this form, place it in a sealed envelope addressed to the OIG team and give it to the mission's inspection coordinator or to a member of the inspection team as early as possible during the inspection.

> *Our pledge: To the maximum extent permitted by law and regulation, we will not reveal your identity or share your information with anyone outside the Office of Inspector General. Any findings we share with officials of the Department of State will consist of aggregated data and summaries of anonymous comments. If we believe we cannot communicate the information you provide without revealing your identity, we will discuss the matter with you first. At the end of this inspection, an inspector will personally shred all paper surveys and delete all electronic questionnaires.*

All American direct-hire and eligible family member employees of the Department of State, and all heads of agency present at post under Chief of Mission authority, should complete Part A of this questionnaire. Department of State personnel should also complete Part B. Heads of agency should complete only Part A.

On a scale of 1 (poor) to 5 (excellent), please rate your Chief of Mission (including, but not limited to Ambassador or chargé d'affaires) and your deputy chief of mission on the leadership qualities listed below. If you are at a constituent post, please rate your principal officer. Principal officers include but are not limited to consuls general, consuls, and officers acting in these capacities during long-term vacancies.

Please score only current incumbents.

For clarity, please write the name of the person being rated in the box above each column. We encourage you to comment further on your scores in the box below the score card.

SCORING SCALE from 1 to 5 (Please select "N/A" if not applicable or unknown)

(Poor) 1 2 3 4 5 (Excellent)

	CHIEF OF MISSION	DEPUTY CHIEF OF MISSION	PRINCIPAL OFFICER

Last Name of Chief of Mission; Deputy Chief of Mission; and/or Principal Officer:

RATE THE DEGREE TO WHICH S/HE…

a. VISION/GOAL SETTING…establishes mission objectives and sets achievable targets; conveys a sense of mission and assigns resources appropriately.

b. COORDINATION … practices teambuilding, and fosters cooperation and unity of purpose among the various individuals, sections and agencies at post.

c. COMMUNICATION…keeps mission staff informed of policy, management and other significant issues; communicates in a manner aimed at gaining understanding and support.

d. DISSENT…permits and considers dissenting views on policy and management issues.

e. AWARENESS… keeps informed of mission activities, including the direction of sections and agencies and their relationship with others; understands the implications of resource/infrastructure constraints on accomplishments.

f. ENGAGEMENT/DRIVE…leads the mission and stays focused on the completion of goals and tasks.

g. JUDGMENT/DECISIVENESS…reaches sound decisions in a timely manner, and stands behind them; takes into account feasible alternatives; makes decisions that enable staff to prioritize their work.

h. PROBLEM SOLVING…identifies and manages organizational conflict and resolves differences; confronts performance or discipline problems; deals with them effectively.

i. FAIRNESS… deals in an open and evenhanded manner with all individuals and elements of the mission.

j. CLARITY…articulates and delegates operational requirements clearly and without ambiguity; sets clear timelines for the accomplishment of tasks.

k. FEEDBACK…keeps mission personnel informed of front office perceptions of individual and group performance; provides timely feedback.

l. ETHICS…maintains high standards of conduct; observes laws and regulations for the use of government funds, property and personnel; sets a positive example of behavior for the mission.

m. INTERPERSONAL … is approachable; listens; conveys information and feedback in a measured, professional manner.

Please use the space below to comment if you wish to expand or qualify your answers.

2. With which mission section(s) do you have the most contact?

How would you characterize your section's relationship with it/them (e.g., collaborative, professional, difficult)?

Using a scale of 1 (poor) to 5 (excellent), how would you rate the performance of the sections with which you have the most contact?

Section _____   Rate _____
Section _____   Rate _____
Section _____   Rate _____

Comments:

3. How would you describe the major strengths and weaknesses of the mission?

Strengths:

Weaknesses:

4. Using a scale of 1 (poor) to 5 (excellent), how would you rate overall mission morale and your own morale?

Overall mission morale: Rate _____
Personal morale: Rate _____

Comments:

5. Please describe the involvement of the Ambassador and Deputy Chief of Mission in supporting the security programs of the mission, including those that are designed to protect people, facilities and information.

6. Do you feel safe at your place of work? (Please indicate the building in which you work in the comments, e.g., chancery, GSO annex)

   ☐ Yes   ☐ No

   Do you feel safe at your place of residence?

   ☐ Yes   ☐ No

   Comments:

7. Are there examples of waste, fraud or mismanagement that the inspectors should look into? (If the answer is "yes," an inspector will discuss the matter with you.)

   ☐ Yes   ☐ No

   Please use the space below to comment if you wish to expand or qualify your answers.

8. Is there any other subject you wish to raise with the inspectors?

   ☐ Yes   ☐ No

   Please use the space below to comment if you wish to expand or qualify your answers.

PART B – FOR DEPARTMENT OF STATE EMPLOYEES *ONLY*

1. Name of your supervisor (rating officer)

2. Describe your supervisor's management style. How does s/he organize the work of the section, assign tasks, and relate to people?

3. Is your supervisor effective in dealing with post management and in representing your section's viewpoints and interests? How does s/he keep the section informed of guidance and information from post management?

4. Are there any aspects of your supervisor's performance you would like to change or improve?

5. Please comment on your relationship with your reviewing officer (second line supervisor).

6. What kind of feedback do you receive on your performance? Did your most recent employee evaluation report give a balanced view of your performance?

7. On average, how many hours in excess of 40 do you work per week? Is this time spent in the office and/or outside at official events?

8. Do you receive adequate mentoring in your current position, and have you been given the opportunity to attend the Department's leadership training courses that are required for your grade?

Workplace and Quality of Life Questionnaire

(For all US staff on overseas assignment to the mission)

Name: _____ Date Arrived at Post: _____

Section: _____ Agency: _____

Post: _____

Employment Category (select one):
  ☐ Foreign Service ☐ Eligible Family Member ☐ Civil Service ☐ Other

Rank/Grade (select one):
  ☐ SFS, SES, 07–010 ☐ FS 2–1, GS 13–15, O4/W4–06
  ☐ FS9–3, GS 5–12, E1-O3/W3

Number of overseas posts to which you have been assigned (select one):
  ☐ 1 ☐ 2 ☐ 3

Amount of time at post in months (select one):
  ☐ 0–3 ☐ 4–11 ☐ 12+

Name of current Ambassador (or Principal Officer):

_____

Name of current Deputy Chief of Mission (or Deputy Principal Officer):

_____

INSTRUCTIONS:

The Office of Inspector General collects most Workplace and Quality of Life questionnaires electronically. If you complete this version of the questionnaire, your scores may not be included in the aggregated data available to the inspection team during the survey phase.

Do not complete this questionnaire if you have submitted a Workplace and Quality of Life questionnaire electronically.

If you're completing this form, place it in a sealed envelope addressed to the OIG team and give it to the mission's inspection coordinator or to a member of the inspection team as early as possible during the inspection.

> *Our pledge:* To the maximum extent permitted by law and regulation, we will not reveal your identity or share your information with anyone outside the Office of Inspector General. Any findings we share with officials of the Department of State will consist of aggregated data and summaries of anonymous comments. If we believe we cannot communicate the information you provide without revealing your identity, we will discuss the matter with you first. At the end of this inspection, an inspector will personally shred all paper surveys and delete all electronic questionnaires.

We seek your assistance in evaluating the performance of your mission in general, with emphasis on mission workplace and quality of life issues. We will respect and protect the confidentiality of your responses and comments to the questions on the following pages, so please be candid. We will provide statistical summaries of the scores to post management in the expectation that, where warranted, good performance will be recognized and problem areas improved.

Employees at constituent posts are asked to rate the constituent post's leadership in the questionnaire's Executive section. Employees may comment on the Embassy's Ambassador and DCM at the end of this form. In rating management services, OIG assumes that services are provided at/by the constituent post rather than at the embassy. If services are provided at/by the embassy, please note so in the comments section at the end of this form.

A scoring scale follows. If you rate any item less than 3, we would appreciate your explanatory remarks in the comments section at the end of this form. Thank you for your assistance.

In the space below, please expand on problems identified in the above questions. Additionally, please describe the weaknesses of the mission.

SCORING SCALE from 1 to 5 (Please select "N/A" if not applicable or unknown)

(Poor)   1   2   3   4   5   (Excellent)

Executive	(Poor) 1 2 3 4 5 (Excellent)
Your assessment of overall senior management (COM/PO)	1 2 3 4 5 N/A
Your assessment of overall senior management (DCM/DPO)	1 2 3 4 5 N/A
Mission attentiveness to waste, fraud and mismanagement	1 2 3 4 5 N/A
Overall attentiveness of senior management (COM/PO) to morale issues	1 2 3 4 5 N/A
Overall attentiveness of senior management (DCM/DPO) to morale issues	1 2 3 4 5 N/A
EEO sensitivity at post	1 2 3 4 5 N/A

Regional Security Office	(Poor) 1 2 3 4 5 (Excellent)
Attention to security measures	1 2 3 4 5 N/A
Dissemination of personal security awareness information	1 2 3 4 5 N/A
Satisfaction with Marine Security Guard detachment	1 2 3 4 5 N/A
Safety and security of schools attended by children of mission employees	1 2 3 4 5 N/A
Adequacy of personal security information briefing provided by the RSO	1 2 3 4 5 N/A
Adequacy of emergency preparedness and security posture	1 2 3 4 5 N/A
Frequency of radio checks	1 2 3 4 5 N/A

Management Section	(Poor) 1 2 3 4 5 (Excellent)
Overall Running of Management Section	1 2 3 4 5 N/A
Customer service orientation of Management Section	1 2 3 4 5 N/A

General Services	(Poor) 1 2 3 4 5 (Excellent)
Overall management of General Services	1 2 3 4 5 N/A
Suitability of your housing	1 2 3 4 5 N/A
Suitability of Government-provided household furnishings	1 2 3 4 5 N/A
Efficacy of customs and shipping services	1 2 3 4 5 N/A
Quality and maintenance of office furniture and equipment at post	1 2 3 4 5 N/A
Adequacy of expendable office supplies	1 2 3 4 5 N/A
Responsiveness of motor pool	1 2 3 4 5 N/A
Maintenance/upkeep of motor pool vehicles	1 2 3 4 5 N/A
Efficacy of travel services	1 2 3 4 5 N/A
Responsiveness of procurement	1 2 3 4 5 N/A

Facilities	(Poor) 1 2 3 4 5 (Excellent)
Overall management of facilities	1 2 3 4 5 N/A
Adequacy of office space	1 2 3 4 5 N/A
Maintenance and upkeep of chancery	1 2 3 4 5 N/A
Quality of maintenance and repair on housing	1 2 3 4 5 N/A

Financial Services	(Poor) 1 2 3 4 5 (Excellent)
Overall management of financial services	1 2 3 4 5 N/A
Timeliness of travel voucher processing	1 2 3 4 5 N/A
Adequacy of cashier and miscellaneous payment services	1 2 3 4 5 N/A

Human Resources Services	(Poor) 1 2 3 4 5 (Excellent)
Overall management of human resource services	1 2 3 4 5 N/A
Equity of employee awards program for American staff	1 2 3 4 5 N/A
Opportunities for family member employment	1 2 3 4 5 N/A
Fairness of family member hiring	1 2 3 4 5 N/A

Information Management Services	(Poor) 1 2 3 4 5 (Excellent)
Overall management of information resources and services	1 2 3 4 5 N/A
Adequacy of internal telephone systems	1 2 3 4 5 N/A
Adequacy of radio program	1 2 3 4 5 N/A
Usefulness of embassy OpenNet (intranet) site	1 2 3 4 5 N/A
Usefulness of embassy Internet (public) site	1 2 3 4 5 N/A
Adequacy of mail services (incl. APO/FPO, DPO, pouch and Homeward Bound)	1 2 3 4 5 N/A
Adequacy of office Internet connectivity	1 2 3 4 5 N/A
Responsiveness of unclassified systems support	1 2 3 4 5 N/A
Responsiveness of classified systems support	1 2 3 4 5 N/A

Quality of Life Issues	(Poor) 1 2 3 4 5 (Excellent)
Equity and administration of post housing program	1 2 3 4 5 N/A
Overall management of Medical Unit	1 2 3 4 5 N/A
Adequacy of first aid training	1 2 3 4 5 N/A
Adequacy of medical supplies	1 2 3 4 5 N/A
Accessibility to recreation and fitness centers	1 2 3 4 5 N/A
Overall helpfulness of Community Liaison Office (CLO)	1 2 3 4 5 N/A
Appropriateness of CLO recreational activities	1 2 3 4 5 N/A
Adequacy of CLO sponsor program	1 2 3 4 5 N/A
Usefulness of orientation program	1 2 3 4 5 N/A
Usefulness of community newsletter	1 2 3 4 5 N/A
Overall community (i.e., family) morale	1 2 3 4 5 N/A
Quality of education for dependent children at post	1 2 3 4 5 N/A
Overall management of commissary and/or duty-free services	1 2 3 4 5 N/A
Quality of cafeteria/snack bar operation	1 2 3 4 5 N/A
Efficacy of post language program	1 2 3 4 5 N/A
Attention to fire and life safety issues	1 2 3 4 5 N/A
Adequacy of cellular telephone program	1 2 3 4 5 N/A
Adequacy of home Internet connectivity	1 2 3 4 5 N/A

Notes

Introduction

1. Roger Stone, "John Davis Lodge—A Man for All Seasons," December 19, 2012, http://stoneonstyle.com/archives/john-davis-lodge-a-man-for-all-seasons.
2. Lewis H. Diuguid, "Ambassador Lodge: Urgente," *Washington Post*, February 18, 1973.
3. Ibid.
4. Ibid.
5. Thomas DeLong, "John Davis Lodge—A Life in Three Acts: Actor, Politician, Diplomat," *Sacred Heart University Press*, 1999, 287.
6. Ibid., 310.
7. State Department, *Foreign Relations of the United States, 1969–1976*, vol. E-10, *Documents on American Republics, 1969–1972*, doc. 64.
8. State Department, *Foreign Relations of the United States, 1969–1976*, vol. E-10, *Documents on American Republics, 1969–1972*, doc. 73.
9. Ibid.

1 A Brief History of the Title

1. Jack Rakove, *Revolutionaries—A New History of the Invention of America*, New York: Houghton Mifflin, 2010, 243.
2. State Department, Office of the Historian, "Department History: Short History of the Department of State—Staffing and Administration."
3. State Department, Office of the Historian, "Department History: Short History of the Department of State—American Diplomatic Style."
4. George C. Herring, *From Colony to Superpower*, New York: Oxford University Press, 2008, 58.
5. Ibid., 96.
6. As the Senior Director for African Affairs at the time, I got to deal with such matters of state. When Sam Njoma, the president of Namibia, came to Washington as the first African head of state to visit the Clinton White House, he was treated to breakfast.
7. Herring, *From Colony to Superpower*, 96.

8. Ibid., 136.
9. Ibid., 139.
10. Warren Frederick Ilchman, *Professional Diplomacy in the United States*, Chicago: University of Chicago Press, 1961, 26.
11. Barbara Slavin, "Gingrich Takes Swipe at State Department," *USA Today*, April 22, 2003.
12. State Department, Office of the Historian, "Department History: Short History of the Department of State—American Diplomatic Style."
13. Herring, *From Colony to Superpower*, 179.
14. State Department, Office of the Historian, "Department History: Short History of the Department of State—A Foreign Policy of Inaction."
15. State Department, Office of the Historian, "FAQs," http://www.state.gov/r/pa/ho/faq.
16. http://www.democracyarsenal.org/2005/05/congress_abroad.html.
17. State Department, Office of the Historian, "Department History: Short History of the Department of State—Political Interference and Corruption," http://history.state.gov/departmenthistory/short-history/interference.
18. Ilchman, *Professional Diplomacy*, 20.
19. Evan Thomas, *The War Lovers*, New York: Little, Brown and Company, 2010, 58.
20. Ilchman, *Professional Diplomacy*, 1.
21. Ibid., 18.
22. Pendleton Act, http://www.ourdocuments.gov/doc.php?flash=true&doc=48.
23. "Life and Death in the White House," http://americanhistory.si.edu/presidency/3d1d.html.
24. Herring, *From Colony to Superpower*, 300.
25. State Department, Office of the Historian, "FAQs," http://www.state.gov/r/pa/ho/faq and http://www.state.gov/r/pa/ho/po/com.
26. State Department, Office of the Historian, "Department History: Short History of the Department of State—The Practice of Diplomacy," http://history.state.gov/departmenthistory/short-history/practice.
27. Ellis Briggs, *Farewell to Foggy Bottom*, New York: David McKay Company, 1961, 288.
28. William Howard Taft, Fourth State of the Union Address, December 3, 1912.
29. Ibid.
30. Press conference with President-Elect Barack Obama, January 9, 2009, Washington, DC.
31. Alex Spillius, "US Ambassador to London Louis Susman Won't Be a Lame Duck," *London Telegraph*, July 8, 2009, and Greg Burns, "Obama Ambassador Brings Chicago Deal-Making to Special Relationship," *Chicago Tribune*, April 8, 2010; and OpenSecrets.org, http://www.opensecrets.org/pres08/bundlers.php?id=n00009638
32. George Lardner, Jr., and Walter Pincus, "Nixon Set Minimum Contribution for Choice Diplomatic Posts," *Washington Post*, October 30, 1997,

http://www.washingtonpost.com/wpsrv/national/longterm/nixon/103097envoy.htm.

33. "Member States—Growth in the United Nations Membership, 1945–present," http://www.un.org/en/members/growth.shtml.

2 Who Gets to Be an Ambassador—The Traditional Route

1. It was originally at http://www.americanambassadors.org/index.cfm?fuseaction=FAQs.Frequently%5FAsked%5FQuestions, but the Frequently Asked Questions page was no longer on the website as of June 5, 2014.
2. James P. Pfiffner, "Presidential Appointments and Managing the Executive Branch," Political Appointee Project, http://www.politicalappointeeproject.org/commentary/appointments-and-managing-executive-branch.
3. All the data in this section is from an HR Fact Sheet put out by the Bureau of Human Resources of the State Department, and the information is current as of March 31, 2013.
4. This is my own personal list and does not exhaust the possibilities.
5. Susan Cornwell, "Danger and Separation from Families Changing Job of U.S. Diplomats," Reuters, May 19, 2013, http://www.reuters.com/article/2013/05/19/us-usa-diplomats-idUSBRE94I01G20130519.
6. Hannah Gurman, "The Other Plumbers Unit: The Dissent Channel of the U.S. State Department," Diplomatic History 35.2 (April 2011): 321–349.
7. Peter Van Buren, We Meant Well—How I Helped Lose the Battle for the Hearts and Minds of the Iraqi People, New York: Metropolitan Books, 2012.
8. http://careers.state.gov.
9. A fuller explanation can be found on the State Department website at http://careers.state.gov/officer/benefits#salary.
10. State Magazine, June 2013, http://www.state.gov/documents/organization/210235.pdf.
11. Data based on interviews with officers in the State Department's HR Bureau.
12. Foreign Affairs Manual, 3 FAM 2320, http://www.state.gov/documents/organization/84861.pdf.
13. Ibid., 3 FAM 2323.1–1.
14. The organization chart of the State Department can be found at http://careers.state.gov/learn/what-we-do/bureaus.
15. Susan Johnson, Ronald Neumann, and Thomas Pickering, "Presidents Are Breaking the U.S. Foreign Service," Washington Post, April 11, 2013.
16. State Department, Office of the Historian, "Under Secretaries of State for Public Diplomacy and Public Affairs," http://history.state.gov/departmenthistory/people/principalofficers/under-secretary-for-public-diplomacy.
17. Helle Dale, "The State Department's Revolving Door of Public Diplomacy," Heritage Foundation, May 8, 2013, http://blog.heritage.org/2013/05/08/the-state-departments-revolving-door-of-public-diplomacy/.

18. Public Diplomacy Council, "Ambassadors Call for a Public Diplomacy Professional at State Department," May 24, 2013, http://publicdiplomacy-council.org/commentaries/05-24-13/ambassadors-call-public-diplomacy-professional-state-department.
19. Paul Krugman, "Dow 36,000: How Silly Is It?" http://web.mit.edu/krugman/www/dow36K.html.
20. James K. Glassman, Sourcewatch.org, http://www.sourcewatch.org/index.php?title=James_K._Glassman.
21. Kerry Lauerman, "You Burn Out Fast When You Demagogue," Salon.com, September 14, 2003, http://www.salon.com/2003/09/14/carlson_4.
22. ADST Oral History Project, "Anthony Quainton," November 6, 1997, http://www.adst.org/OH%20TOCs/Quainton,%20Anthony.toc.pdf.

3 The Nontraditional Route

1. Dayton Mak and Charles Stuart Kennedy, *American Ambassadors in a Troubled World*, Westport, CT: Greenwood Press, 1992, 4.
2. Bradley Patterson and James Pfiffner, "The White House Office of Presidential Personnel," *Presidential Studies Quarterly* 31.3 (September 2001): 415–438.
3. Tevi Troy, "Measuring the Drapes," *National Affairs* (Spring 2013): 86–103, http://www.hudson.org/files/publications/NationalAffairs_Tevi Troy032513.pdf.
4. Ibid.
5. William J. Clinton, "Statement on Signing the Presidential Transition Act of 2000," The American Presidency Project, October 12, 2000, http://www.presidency.ucsb.edu/ws/?pid=1234.
6. Michael D. Shear, "Presidential Contenders to Get a Head Start on White House Transition," The Caucus, *The New York Times*, October 16, 2010, http://thecaucus.blogs.nytimes.com/2010/10/16/presidential-contenders-to-get-a-head-start-on-white-house-transition/?partner=rss&emc=rss&_r=0.
7. Patterson and Pfiffner, "The White House Office," 429.
8. Commission on Presidential Debates, "2012 Candidate Selection Criteria," http://www.debates.org/index.php?page=candidate-selection-process.
9. Troy, "Measuring the Drapes," 92.
10. The website can be found at https://apply.whitehouse.gov.
11. Miller Center, University of Virginia, "Interview with Chase Untermeyer," 2011 http://millercenter.org/president/bush/oralhistory/chase-untermeyer.
12. National Academy of Public Administration, "A Survivor's Guide for Presidential Nominees," 2013, http://www.napawash.org/wp-content/uploads/2013/05/SurvivorsGuide2013.pdf, 8.
13. Miller Center, University of Virginia, "Interview with E. Pendleton James," 2005, http://millercenter.org/scripps/archive/oralhistories/detail/3223.

14. Alison R. Holmes and J. Simon Rofe, *The Embassy in Grosvenor Square: American Ambassadors to the United Kingdom*, New York: Palgrave Macmillan, 2012, 220.
15. Oral history of Lange Schermerhorn, http://memory.loc.gov/cgi-bin/query/D?mfdip:1:./temp/~ammem_NOmD; oral history of Roger Harrison, http://memory.loc.gov/cgi-bin/query/D?mfdip:2:./temp/~ammem_tA2n.
16. Holmes and Rofe, *Embassy in Grosvenor Square*, and oral history of Richard Melton, http://memory.loc.gov/cgi-bin/query/D?mfdip:1:./temp/~ammem_FLNX.
17. "Obituaries: John J. Lewis," *The Independent*, February 20, 1995, http://www.independent.co.uk/news/people/obituaries--john-j-louis-jnr-1573987.html.
18. Holmes and Rofe, *Embassy in Grosvenor Square*, 223.
19. Exchange of letters between President Reagan and John J. Lewis, Jr., accepting his resignation as ambassador to the United Kingdom, September 19, 1983, http://www.reagan.utexas.edu/archives/speeches/1983/91983d.htm.
20. Zeke Miller, "Mitt Romney Inc.: The White House that Never Was," *TIME*, June 2, 2013, http://swampland.time.com/2013/06/02/mitt-romney-inc-the-white-house-that-never-was.
21. Romney Readiness Project, "Administration Design," Chapter 11, 128.
22. http://www.reagan.utexas.edu/archives/textual/smof/james.htm.
23. Miller Center, University of Virginia, "Interview with E. Pendleton James."
24. Miller Center, University of Virginia, Oral History Project, http://millercenter.org/president/reagan/oralhistory/lyn-nofziger.
25. David Johnson, "Nofziger Given 90 Days in Jail in Ethics Case," *The New York Times*, April 9, 1988.
26. Helene Von Damm, *At Reagan's Side—Twenty Years in the Political Mainstream*, New York: Doubleday, 1989, 212.
27. Miller Center, "Interview with E. Pendleton James."
28. George Herring, *From Colony to Superpower*, New York: Oxford University Press, 2008, 864–865.
29. State Department, Office of the Historian, "Department History: Short History of the Department of State—Department Appointments Politicized," http://history.state.gov/departmenthistory/short-history/politicized-appointees,
30. Von Damm, *At Reagan's Side*, 238–244.
31. Ibid., 225.
32. ADST Oral History Project, "Ronald Spiers," November 11, 1991, http://www.adst.org/OH%20TOCs/Spires,%20Ronald%20I.toc.pdf.
33. The State Department's bio on Tuttle can be found at http://www.state.gov/outofdate/bios/51341.htm.

34. Miller Center, University of Virginia, "Interview with Robert Tuttle and Maureen Molloy," 2005, http://millercenter.org/president/reagan/oralhistory/robert-tuttle.

35. Richard Severo, "Donald Regan, 84, Financier and Top Reagan Aide, Dies," *The New York Times*, June 11, 2003.

36. Kurt Campbell and James Steinberg, *Difficult Transitions*, Washington, DC: Brookings Institution, 2008.

37. http://www.fas.org/irp/offdocs/walsh/chap_30.htm.

38. ADST Oral History Project, "Frank Carlucci," December 30, 1996, http://www.adst.org/OH%20TOCs/Carlucci,%20Frank%20Charles%20III%20_April%201,%201997_.pdf.

39. Von Damm, *At Reagan's Side*, 299.

40. Ibid., 317.

41. Ibid., 322.

42. Tuttle continues to be a prolific donor to Republican campaigns. A search on the Federal Election Commission website shows dozens of recent contributions to candidates all over the country.

43. Holmes and Rofe, *Embassy in Grosvenor Square*, 343.

44. Miller Center, "Interview with Chase Untermeyer."

45. Patterson and Pfiffner, "The White House Office," 419.

46. George Lardner, Jr., and Walter Pincus, "Nixon Set Minimum Contribution for Choice Diplomatic Posts," *Washington Post*, October 30, 1997, http://www.washingtonpost.com/wp-srv/national/longterm/nixon/103097envoy.htm.

47. Ryan J. Reilly, "Richard Nixon: D.C. Socialite Wasn't Made Ambassador Just Because She Had 'Big Bosoms,'" *Talking Points Memo*, November 10, 2011.

48. Walter Pincus, "The Case of Peter Flanigan," *New Republic*, October 19, 1974.

49. One exchange took place between Wyman and Under Secretary of State Elliot Richardson on March 20, 1969. Wyman called to make a pitch for Farkas. Richardson had to explain that the State Department could not put Farkas's name forward and that Wyman had to deal with Flanigan to get the White House to do it. *Foreign Relations of the United States, 1969–1976*, vol. II, *Organization and Management of U.S. Foreign Policy, 1969–1972*, doc. 299.

50. Ibid.

51. Vera Glaser, "Brouhaha Brewing for the President?" *San Francisco Chronicle*, September 10, 1975.

52. Lawrence Van Gelder, "Ruth Farkas, 89, Nixon's Ambassador to Luxembourg, Dies," *The New York Times*, October 22, 1996, http://www.nytimes.com/1996/10/22/nyregion/ruth-farkas-89-nixon-s-ambassador-to-luxembourg-dies.html.

53. ADST Oral History Project, "James D. Phillips," May 5, 1998, 35–36.

54. Dennis C. Jett and Johannes Fedderke, "What Price the Court of St. James? Political Influences on Ambassadorial Postings," Economic

Research Southern Africa Working Paper, no. 234, September 2012, http://www.econrsa.org/system/files/publications/working_papers/working_paper_234.pdf.

55. ADST Oral History Project, "Ruth Lewis Farkas," October 24, 1985, 38.

56. Karl A. Lamb, *Reasonable Disagreement: Two U.S. Senators and the Choices They Make*, New York: Routledge, 142.

57. http://www.presidency.ucsb.edu/ws/?pid=17227.

58. Elaine Sciolino, "Senator Moves to Block Approval of Fund-Raiser Chosen as Envoy," *The New York Times*, November 10, 1989.

59. Miller Center, "Interview with Chase Untermeyer."

60. There are links to both acts at http://www.senate.gov/general/Features/WatergateHearings.htm.

61. http://www.businessinsider.com/election-cost-2-billion-2012-12.

62. Editorial Board, "Sabotage at the Election Commission," *The New York Times*, July 5, 2013.

63. http://www.fec.gov/pages/brochures/contriblimits.shtml.

64. Adam Liptak, "Supreme Court Strikes Down Overall Political Donation Cap," *The New York Times*, April 2, 2014.

65. http://www.propublica.org/article/how-much-did-sheldon-adelson-really-spend-on-campaign-2012.

66. http://www.huffingtonpost.com/2012/09/24/sheldon-adelson-donations_n_1910094.html.

67. Seth Hanlon, "Sheldon Adelson's Return on Investment," Center for American Progress Action Fund, August 2012, http://images.politico.com/global/2012/09/hanlon_adelsonc4brief.html.

68. Obama for America and Obama Victory Fund 2012 Volunteer Fundraisers, http://www.barackobama.com/pages/volunteer-fundraisers-q2.

69. Miller Center, "Interview with Robert Tuttle and Maureen Molloy."

70. Miller Center, "Interview with Chase Untermeyer."

71. Manhattan College, "Manhattan College to Award Charles Gargano '79 with Honorary Degree," Manhattan College News and Events, September 23, 2011, http://manhattan.edu/news/manhattan-college-award-charles-gargano-79-honorary-degree.

72. Noel Brinkerhoff, "Who Is Vinai Thummalapaly?" *AllGov*, August 10, 2009, http://www.allgov.com/news/appointments-and-resignations/ambassador-to-belize-who-is-vinai-thummalapally?news=839351.

73. Michael Powell and Jodi Kantor, "After Attacks, Michelle Obama Looks for a New Introduction," *The New York Times*, June 18, 2008.

74. "Obama's Top Fund-Raisers," *The New York Times*, September 13, 2012, http://www.nytimes.com/interactive/2012/09/13/us/politics/obamas-top-fund-raisers.html?_r=0.

75. "PSU Sociology Professor to Be Named Ambassador," *The Daily Collegian*, September 7, 2001, http://www.collegian.psu.edu/archives/article_9e3c3f28-5889-55b1-8ba6-89fa34a805d3.html.

76. "Skull and Bones," *Undernews*, May 2006, http://prorev.com/skull.htm.

77. Angela Pidduck, "Ambassador Roy Austin," http://sputnick.com/angela/ambassador_roy_austin.htm.
78. White House Press Office, "Remarks by the President in Nomination of Governor Jon Huntsman as Ambassador to the People's Republic of China," May 16, 2009, http://www.whitehouse.gov/the_press_office/Remarks-by-the-President-in-nominating-Governor-Jon-Huntsman-as-Ambassador-to-the-Peoples-Republic-of-China.
79. Neil King, Jr., "U.S. Ambassador to China Plans Exit," *The Wall Street Journal*, February 1, 2011.
80. Juliet Eilperin and Sean Sullivan, "Three Reasons Why the White House Is Sending Max Baucus to China," *Washington Post*, December 18, 2013.
81. Dennis Hevesi, "Adm. William Crowe Dies at 82, Led Joint Chiefs," *The New York Times*, October 19, 2007, http://www.nytimes.com/2007/10/19/washington/19crowe1.html?_r=0.
82. Eric Schmitt, "Ambassador Eikenberry's Cables on U.S. Strategy in Afghanistan," *The New York Times*, http://documents.nytimes.com/eikenberry-s-memos-on-the-strategy-in-afghanistan.
83. L.A. Times Opinion Staff, "John Bolton: The Squawking of a Chickenhawk," *Los Angeles Times*, April 27, 2011, http://opinion.latimes.com/opinionla/2011/04/to-paraphrase-ronald-reagan-there-he-goes-again-in-tuesdays-opinion-pages-former-un-ambassador-john-r-bolton-weighs-in.html.
84. Caroline Kennedy, "A President like My Father," *The New York Times*, January 27, 2008, http://www.nytimes.com/2008/01/27/opinion/27kennedy.html.
85. Miller Center, University of Virginia, "Interview with Jimmy Carter," http://millercenter.org/president/carter/oralhistory/jimmy-carter.
86. Miller Center, "Interview with Chase Untermeyer."
87. Nicholas Confessore and Sheryl Gay Stolberg, "Well-Trod Path: Political Donor to Ambassador," *The New York Times*, January 18, 2013.

4 The Last Steps—Clearance and Confirmation

1. "Obama-Biden Administration Job Questionnaire," as of November 16, 2008, http://usgovinfo.about.com/od/thepresidentandcabinet/a/obama-questions.htm.
2. "The Lesson of Zoe Baird," *The New York Times*, January 23, 1993, http://www.nytimes.com/1993/01/23/opinion/the-lesson-of-zoe-baird.html.
3. Center for Responsive Politics, "Barack Obama's Bundlers," http://www.opensecrets.org/pres12/bundlers.php.
4. Philip Sherwell, "Poker Costs Barack Obama His Next Ambassador to Paris," *The Telegraph*, April 26, 2013.
5. Maggie Haberman, "Terry McAuliffe Quips about Hillary Clinton 2016 Run," *Politico*, March 14, 2013.

6. US Attorney's Office, Southern District of New York, "Two More Defendants Plead Guilty in Manhattan Federal Court in Connection with Russian-American Organized Crime Gambling Enterprise," US Attorney's Office press release, November 15, 2014, http://www.fbi.gov/newyork/press-releases/2013/two-more-defendants-plead-guilty-in-manhattan-federal-court-in-connection-with-russian-american-organized-crime-gambling-enterprise.

7. Sherwell, "Poker Costs Barack Obama."

8. William Alden, "Lasry out of the Running for Ambassador to France," *The New York Times*, April 23, 2013.

9. "Obama's Top Fund-Raisers," *The New York Times*, September 13, 2012, http://www.nytimes.com/interactive/2012/09/13/us/politics/obamas-top-fund-raisers.html.

10. Gerri Peev, Tim Shipman, and Meghan Keneally, "US Ambassador Anna? Vogue's Editor-in-Chief to Get British Embassy as Thank You from Obama," *MailOnline*, December 3, 2012, http://www.dailymail.co.uk/news/article-2242660/Anna-Wintour-US-Vogues-editor-British-embassy-thank-Obama.html.

11. Linda Das, "Think the Boss in The Devil Wears Prada Was a Total Monster? Well She Was Even Scarier in Real Life," August 20, 2010, *MailOnline*, http://www.dailymail.co.uk/femail/article-1304528/Lauren-Weisberger-The-Devil-Wears-Prada-boss-scarier-real-life.html, and "Anna Wintour," *Bio*, 2014, http://www.biography.com/people/anna-wintour-214147.

12. Nicholas Confessore and Sheryl Gay Stolberg, "Well-Trod Path: Political Donor to Ambassador," *The New York Times*, January 13, 2013.

13. Al Kamen, "Anna Wintour: The Ambassador Wears Prada?" *Washington Post*, May 1, 2013.

14. "Anna Wintour," *Bio*.

15. Christopher Hastings, "Anna Wintour Awarded OBE," *The Telegraph*, June 14, 2008, http://fashion.telegraph.co.uk/news-features/TMG3364968/Anna-Wintour-awarded-OBE.html.

16. Peev et al., "US Ambassador Anna?"

17. "Anna Wintour," *Bio*.

18. Cara Kelly, "Anna Wintour Backs Hillary Clinton at Oscar de la Renta Exhibit Opening," *Washington Post*, July 9, 2013.

19. "Mayor Bloomberg the Surprise Guest at Conde Nast Cocktail Party," *Women's Wear Daily*, April 24, 2013, http://www.wwd.com/media-news/fashion-memopad/toast-of-the-town-6906687?module=media-news.

20. http://www.state.gov/m/ds/clearances/c10978.htm.

21. The form can be found at http://www.opm.gov/Forms/pdf_fill/SF86.pdf.

22. It is 15 years for presidential appointments and 10 years for others.

23. Vienna Convention on Diplomatic Relations, Article 4, paragraph 1.

24. Michael Gordon, "Former Envoy to Syria Said to Be Choice for Cairo Post," *The New York Times*, August 4, 2013.

25. Yochi Dreazen, "The Cable," *Foreign Policy*, December 23, 2013.
26. Michael Gordon, "U.S. Representative to Syrian Opposition Is Retiring," *The New York Times*, February 4, 2014.
27. Congressional Research Service, "The Senate Role in Foreign Affairs Appointments," Congressional Research Service committee print, July 1982.
28. *Committee on Foreign Relations, United States Senate, Millennium Edition 1816–2000*, US Government Printing Office, Washington, October 2000.
29. Ibid.
30. Congressional Research Service, "The Senate Role in Foreign Affairs Appointments."
31. Richard Berke and Steven Lee Myers, "In Washington, Few Trifle with Jesse Helms," *The New York Times*, August 2, 1997.
32. ADST Oral History Project, "Melissa Wells," March 27, 1984, http://www.adst.org/OH%20TOCs/Wells,%20Melissa%20Foelsch.toc.pdf.
33. Berke and Myers, "In Washington, Few Trifle."
34. Adam Liptak, "Supreme Court Rebukes Obama on Right of Appointment," *The New York Times*, June 26, 2014.
35. Benjamin Weiser and Michael Luo, "Fund-Raiser Is Accused of $74 Million Fraud," *The New York Times*, August 26, 2009.
36. Author interview with former State Department official, March 15, 2014.
37. Colin Moynihan, "Donor to Democrats Pleads Guilty to $292 Million Fraud," *The New York Times*, March 18, 2010.
38. Fred Schulte, "White House Pulls Ambassador-Nominee Accused of Drunk Driving," The Center for Public Integrity, June 29, 2012, http://www.publicintegrity.org/2012/06/29/9248/white-house-pulls-ambassador-nominee-accused-drunk-driving.
39. Julian Pecquet, "Senate Panel Clears 24 Ambassadors and Other Diplomatic Nominees," *The Hill*, October 31, 2013, http://thehill.com/blogs/global-affairs/untreaties/188814-senate-panel-clears-24-ambassadors-and-other-diplomatic.
40. "New US Ambassador Meets Dutch Press, Indirectly Criticizes Wilders," DutchNews.nl, March 27, 2014, http://www.dutchnews.nl/news/archives/2014/03/new_us_ambassador_meets_dutch.php.
41. Agence France-Press, "Dutch Politician Geert Wilders Takes Aim at Moroccans and Sparks Outrage," *The Guardian*, March 20, 2014, http://www.theguardian.com/world/2014/mar/20/dutch-politician-geert-wilders-moroccans-outrage-pvv-party-anti-islam.
42. "New US Ambassador Meets Dutch Press."
43. Fred Kaplan, "Our Man in Baghdad," *Slate*, June 20, 2012, http://www.slate.com/articles/news_and_politics/war_stories/2012/06/brett_mcgurk_nomination_to_be_u_s_ambassador_to_iraq_Ended_because_of_a_scandal_revealed_through_leaked_Email_messages_.html.

44. Joe Coscarelli, "Sexy E-mails with Wall Street Journal Reporter Threaten Iraq Ambassador's Nomination," *New York Magazine*, June 8, 2012, http://nymag.com/daily/intelligencer/2012/06/brett-mcgurk-sexy-emails-iraq-ambassador-nomination.html.

45. Andre Tartar, "Obama Sticking with Embattled Ambassadorial Nominee, Won't Commit to Leaks Investigation Testimony," *New York Magazine*, June 17, 2012, http://nymag.com/daily/intelligencer/2012/06/obama-sticking-with-embattled-ambassador-nominee.html.

46. A videotape of the hearing can be found on the Senate Foreign Relations Committee website here: http://www.foreign.senate.gov/hearings/nomination-01–16-2014

47. The video tape of the hearing can be found on the SFRC website here: http://www.foreign.senate.gov/hearings/nominations-7-15-14

48. James O'Shea, "US Senate finally confirms US Ambassador to Ireland Kevin O'Malley," irishcentral.com, September 19, 2014.

49. *The Daily Show with Jon Stewart*, "Diplomat Buyers Club," February 12, 2014, http://www.thedailyshow.com/watch/wed-february-12-2014/diplomat-buyers-club, and Andrew Johnson, "Jon Stewart Mocks Obama for Ambassador Picks," *National Review Online*, February 13, 2014, http://www.nationalreview.com/corner/371066/jon-stewart-mocks-obama-ambassador-picks-andrew-johnson.

50. CNN, "Anderson Cooper Mocks Obama's Poorly Prepared Ambassador," June 29, 2014, http://www.youtube.com/watch?v=7eNniomuL3w, which carries part of Tsunis's hearing.

51. Abby D. Phillip, "5 Most Cringe-Worthy Blunders from Obama's Ambassador Nominees," ABC News, February 7, 2014, http://abcnews.go.com/blogs/politics/2014/02/5-most-cringe-worthy-blunders-from-obamas-ambassador-nominees.

52. Devin Henry, "Minnesota Delegation to Obama: Don't Send Tsunis to Norway," *Minnesota Post*, June 23, 2014, http://www.minnpost.com/dc-dispatches/2014/06/minnesota-delegation-obama-dont-send-tsunis-norway.

53. There is some dispute as to whether Woody Allen coined the phrase and whether he used 80 percent of another figure. See for instance this blog post: http://www.atthehelmblog.com/2013/03/03/woody-allens-success-secrets/. For the sake of making the point in this particular case, it will be assumed he did and that 80 percent is the figure to use.

54. The access records can be found on the White House website at http://www.whitehouse.gov/briefing-room/disclosures/visitor-records. Such transparency stands in contrast to the early days of the Bush 43 administration, when there was an energy policy task force headed by Vice President Cheney. That group made policy recommendations to Congress, but the White House refused to reveal the names of the energy company executives that participated. Organizations seeking that information sued

to get it released, but the Supreme Court sided with the administration, and it was not released. See for instance, Kate Sheppard, "Dick Cheney's Last Laugh," *Mother Jones*, June 10, 2010, http://www.motherjones.com/politics/2010/06/dick-cheney-bp-spill.

55. Reflecting his declining interest in Mozambique as the Cold War came to an end, Helms had only a couple dozen QFRs when the successor to Wells was nominated in 1990 and none when I came up for confirmation for the post in 1993.

56. Liz Harper, "Venezuela's Formal Rejection of Ambassador-Designate Larry Palmer," *Americas Quarterly*, December 21, 2010, http://www.americas-quarterly.org/node/2058, and "Ambassador to Barbados: Who Is Larry Palmer," Matt Bewig, January 16, 2012, http://www.allgov.com/news/appointments-and-resignations/ambassador-to-barbados-and-the-eastern-caribbean-who-is-larry-leon-palmer?news=843889.

57. https://diplomaticrooms.state.gov/Pages/rooms.aspx?rm=8.

58. Anne Gearan and Ed O'Keefe, "Senate Turf Fight Hurts Approval of Obama's Diplomatic Nominees," *Washington Post*, March 6, 2014.

59. Ibid.

60. Committee on Governmental Affairs, US Senate, "The Presidential Appointment Process—Reports of Commissions that Studied the Staffing of Presidential Administrations: A Summary of Their Conclusions and Recommendations for Reform," 2001.

5 What an Ambassador Does

1. Juliet Eilperin, "Gaffes Prompt Diplomatic Debate," *Washington Post*, February 15, 2014.

2. ADST, "Moments in Diplomatic History—Shirley Temple Black, Diplomat," January 10, 2010, http://adst.org/2014/02/shirley-temple-black-diplomat.

3. Aljean Harmetz, "Shirley Temple Black, Hollywood's Biggest Little Star, Dies at 85," *The New York Times*, February 11, 2014.

4. ADST Oral History Project, "William Bradford," March 9, 1989.

5. The ADST oral histories have a convenient search function.

6. ADST Oral History Project, "John Linehan," April 6, 1993; "L. Dean Brown," May 17, 1989; and "John Evans," October 19, 2099.

7. ADST Oral History Project, "John Evans."

8. Ibid.

9. Author interview with former State Department official, March 14, 2014.

10. Department of State, daily press briefing, February 7, 2014, http://www.state.gov/r/pa/prs/dpb/2014/02/221458.htm.

11. AFSA, Governing Board resolution, March 5, 2014, http://www.afsa.org/AboutAFSA/AFSAStatementonAmbassadors/March5th2014AFSA-

GoverningBoardResolution.aspx?utm_source=AFSA+Members&utm_campaign=25f198c6d2-GB_Resolution3_12_14&utm_medium=email&utm_term=0_b122e92e7f-25f198c6d2-215002045.

12. "Minimal Demonstrated Qualifications for Their Posts," *American Diplomacy*, March 10, 2014, http://www.unc.edu/depts/diplomat/item/2014/0105/an_AFSAnominees.html.

13. AFSA, "Chiefs of Mission Guidelines," https://www.afsa.org/chiefsofmission.aspx.

14. AFSA, "Guidelines for Successful Performance as a Chief of Mission," http://www.afsa.org/Portals/0/com_guidelines.pdf.

15. Department of State, daily press briefing, March 7, 2014, http://www.state.gov/r/pa/prs/dpb/2014/03/223150.htm#DEPARTMENT.

16. AFSA, "AFSA Works with White House and State Department to Increase Transparency of Ambassador Nominations," AFSA press release, April 4, 2014, https://www.afsa.org/OutreachPrograms/MediaandPressReleases/AFSAWorkstoIncreaseTransparencyofNominations.aspx.

17. Only the certificates of nominees who have been announced since April 2014 have been posted.

18. Matt Bewig, "Ambassador to Norway: Who Is George Tsunis?" *AllGov*, December 7, 2013, http://www.allgov.com/news/appointments-and-resignations/ambassador-to-norway-who-is-george-tsunis-131207?news=851850.

19. "Obama's Pick for Norway Post Has 'None of the Skills,'" *MPR News*, May 6, 2014, http://www.mprnews.org/story/2014/05/06/dail-circuit-norway-ambassador.

20. Associated Press, "Franken, Klobuchar Oppose Obama's Nominee for Norway Ambassador," *Minnesota Post,*, June 3, 2014.

21. This is based on a number of inspectors and former inspectors the author has interviewed.

22. Shankar Vedantam, "Minority Aspirants to Federal Bench Are Hindered by Underrating," *NPR News*, February 26, 2014, http://www.npr.org/2014/02/26/283066703/minority-aspirants-to-federal-bench-are-hindered-by-underrating.

23. ADST Oral History Project, "Charles Schmitz," July 29, 1993.

24. Shawn Zeller, "Who's in Charge Here?" *Foreign Service Journal*, December 2007.

25. Thom Shanker and Scott Shane, "Elite Troops Get Expanded Role on Intelligence," *The New York Times*, March 8, 2006, http://www.nytimes.com/2006/03/08/international/americas/08forces.html?pagewanted=print&_r=0.

26. David Ignatius, "The Blurring of CIA and Military," *Washington Post*, June 1, 2011, http://www.washingtonpost.com/opinions/the-blurring-of-cia-and-military/2011/05/31/AGsLhkGH_story.html.

27. State Department, OIG inspection report of Embassy London, report no. ISP-I-09–37A, July 2009, http://oig.state.gov/documents/organization /130931.pdf.

28. "US Embassy Nassau: Where Absence Makes the Heart Not/Not Grow Fonder," *DiploPunidit*, March 1, 2012, http://diplopundit.net/2012/03/01/ us-embassy-nassau-where-absence-makes-the-heart-notnot-grow-fonder, and State Department, OIG inspection report, no. ISP-I-12–08A, January 2012, http://oig.state.gov/documents/organization/184725.pdf.

29. White House, "President Obama Announces Intent to Nominate Key Administration Posts," White House press release, June 4, 2009, http:// www.whitehouse.gov/the_press_office/President-Obama-Announces- Intent-to-Nominate-Key-Administration-Posts-6-4-09.

30. Michelle Malkin, "A Failed Celebr-Ambassador Returns to Washington," May 5, 2014, and "US Embassy Nassau," *DiploPundit*.

31. Center for Responsive Politics, "Barack Obama's Bundlers," http://www. opensecrets.org/pres12/bundlers.php?id=N00009638.

32. Center for Responsive Politics, "Contributions from Celebrities," http:// www.opensecrets.org/pres12/celebs.php?cycle=2012.

33. State Department, OIG inspection report, no. ISP-I-12–8A, January 2012, http://oig.state.gov/documents/organization/184725.pdf

34. White House Press Office, Remarks by President Obama at a DNC event, April 22, 2011, http://www.whitehouse.gov/the-press-office/2011/04/22/ remarks-president-dnc-event.

35. State Department, OIG inspection report, no. ISP-I-09–40A, July 2009, http://oig.state.gov/documents/organization/129778.pdf.

36. State Department, OIG inspection report, no. ISP-I-11–17A, January 2011, http://oig.state.gov/documents/organization/156129.pdf.

37. Frank James, "U.S. Ambassador Exits Europe Post before Scathing Report about Her," National Public Radio, February 4, 2011, http://www.npr.org/ blogs/itsallpolitics/2011/02/04/133506783/u-s-ambassador-exits-europe- post-before-scathing-report-on-her-style.

38. Al Kamen, "Embassy Openings for Open Wallets," *Washington Post*, January 11, 2011.

39. E. J. Dionne, Jr., "For an Obamacon, Communion Denied," *Washington Post*, June 3, 2008.

40. State Department, OIG inspection report, no. ISP-I-11–16A, Febuary 2011, http://oig.state.gov/documents/organization/160374.pdf.

41. Ewen MacAskill, "US Ambassador to Malta Resigns after Critical State Department Report," *The Guardian*, April 18, 2011.

42. Ted Kopan, "Ex-Ambassador Eyes Hillary Clinton VP Spot," *Politico*, January 17, 2014, http://www.politico.com/story/2014/01/douglas-kmiec- hillary-clinton-vice-president-102321.html.

43. State Department, OIG inspection report, no. ISP-I-11–19A, March 2011, http://oig.state.gov/documents/organization/161345.pdf.

44. State Department, OIG inspection report, no. ISP-C-12–20, March 20, http://oig.state.gov/documents/organization/187831.pdf.
45. Matt Bewig, "Ambassador to Denmark: Who Is Laurie Fulton?" July 9, 2009, *AllGov*, http://www.allgov.com/news/appointments-and-resignations/ambassador-to-denmark-who-is-laurie-fulton?news=839163.
46. State Department, OIG inspection report, no. ISP-I-12–38A, August 2012, http://oig.state.gov/documents/organization/196460.pdf.
47. Jason Straziuso, "US Ambassador to Kenya Resigns over 'Differences,'" Associated Press, June 29, 2012, http://news.yahoo.com/us-ambassador-kenya-resigns-over-differences-093557493.html.
48. State Department, OIG inspection report, no. ISP-I-14–07A, March 2014, http://oig.state.gov/documents/organization/224205.pdf.
49. Marie Harf, Deputy Spokesperson, daily press briefing, March 28, 2014.
50. State Department, Office of the Historian, "Chiefs of Mission for Bahrain," http://history.state.gov/departmenthistory/people/chiefsofmission/bahrain.

6 Where Ambassadors Go

1. Max Fisher, "This Very Telling Map Shows Which U.S. Ambassadors Were Campaign Bundlers," *Washington Post*, February 10, 2014, http://www.washingtonpost.com/blogs/worldviews/wp/2014/02/10/this-very-telling-map-shows-which-u-s-ambassadors-were-campaign-bundlers.
2. The paper is currently being revised, but here is an earlier version: Dennis C. Jett and Johannes Fedderke, "What Price the Court of St. James? Political Influences on Ambassadorial Postings," Economic Research Southern Africa Working Paper no. 234, September 2012, http://www.econrsa.org/system/files/publications/working_papers/working_paper_234.pdf.
3. As of February 2011.
4. The posts and their hardship differentials were Afghanistan (35%), Belize (20%), Botswana (10%), China (15%), El Salvador (15%), India (20%), Malta (5%), Mexico (15%), Romania (5%), Saudi Arabia (20%), Slovak Republic (10%), South Africa (10%), and Trinidad and Tobago (5%).
5. A Short History of the Department of State—The Department addresses Inequality, https://history.state.gov/departmenthistory/short-history/inequality
6. Margot Carrington, "How Are FS Women at State Faring?" *Foreign Service Journal* (May 2013): 39–43.
7. Alanna Vagianos, "There Are Still Few Women at the Top of Fortune 500 Companies, Says Report," *The Huffington Post*, December 11, 2013, http://www.huffingtonpost.com/2013/12/11/women-in-leadership-roles_n_4418725.html.
8. Jack Stripling, "Survey Finds a Drop in Minority Presidents Leading Colleges," *Chronicle of Higher Education*, March 12, 2012, http://chronicle.com/article/Who-Are-College-Presidents-/131138.

9. AFSA, "Female U.S. Ambassadors," http://www.afsa.org/femaleambs.aspx.

10. Much of this information came from State Department, Office of the Historian, "African Americans in the Foreign Service," http://history.state.gov/about/faq/african-americans-in-the-foreign-service.

11. "Clifton R. Wharton," *BlackHistoryNow*, April 11, 2011, http://blackhistorynow.com/clifton-r-wharton-sr.

12. Elaine Sciolino, "With Foreign Policies under Fire, Top State Dept. Deputy Is Ousted," *The New York Times*, November 9, 1993; A. M. Rosenthal, "Op-Ed: On My Mind, The Wharton Case," *The New York Times*, December 3, 1993; Editorial Board, "Mr. Wharton as Scapegoat" *Albany Times Union*, November 5, 1993; Carla Anne Robbins, "State Department's Clifton Wharton Resigns as the Agency's No. 2 Official," *Wall Street Journal*, November 9, 1993; "Christopher's Top Deputy Announces Resignation, Wharton Blames Leaks for Move," *The Baltimore Sun*, November 9, 1993; Carl Rowan, "Clinton Fiddled While Black Diplomat Burned," *The Newark Star Ledger*, November 19, 1993; Chuck Stone, "Clinton Executes Second Political Lynching," *Kalamazoo Gazette*, November 15, 1993.

13. Michael L. Krenn, "'Outstanding Negros' and 'Appropriate Countries': Some Facts, Figures, and Thoughts on Black U.S. Ambassadors 1949–1988," *Diplomatic History* 14.1 (January 1990): 131–142.

14. Ibid.

15. Table 690. Money Income of Households—Percent Distribution by Income Level, Race, and Hispanic Origin, in Constant (2009) Dollars: 1990 to 2009, http://www.census.gov/compendia/statab/2012/tables/12s0690.pdf

16. Paul Tough, "Who Gets to Graduate?" *The New York Times*, May 15, 2014.

17. Dennis Jett, "Why Have There Been So Few Openly Gay Ambassadors?" *Washington Post*, July 26, 2013.

18. Michael Guest, "Don't Judge Chuck Hagel by 1998 Comment," *Politico*, January 6, 2013, http://www.politico.com/story/2013/01/dont-judge-chuck-hagel-by-1998-comment-85806.html.

19. ADST Oral History Project, "Robert J. Ryan, Sr.," November 7, 1991.

20. "Ugandan President Yoweri Museveni Signs Anti-Gay Bill," BBC, February 24, 2014, http://www.bbc.com/news/world-africa-26320102, and Max Fisher, "A Map of Where Homosexuality Is Criminalized," *Washington Post*, December 11, 2013.

21. Abby Ohlheiser, "Ugandan lawmakers promise to revive their anti-gay law, just days after the country's constitutional court stuck it down," *Washington Post*, August 5, 2014.

22. US Embassy Santo Domingo website, http://santodomingo.usembassy.gov/ambassador.html.

23. Remington Gregg, "Ted Osius Becomes 7th Openly LGBT Person Nominated to Serve as Ambassador by Obama Administration," HRC

Blog, May 19, 2014, http://www.hrc.org/blog/entry/ted-osius-becomes-seventh-openly-lgbt-ambassador, and "Presidential Nominations Sent to the Senate," May 15, 2014, http://www.whitehouse.gov/the-press-office/2014/05/15/presidential-nominations-sent-senate, and David Mann, "Leading the Way: Vietnam's Push for Gay Rights," *The Diplomat*, April 18, 2014, http://thediplomat.com/2014/04/leading-the-way-vietnams-push-for-gay-rights.

24. "Obama Nominates Sixth Openly Gay Diplomat as the Next Ambassador to Vietnam," *LGBT Weekly*, May 19, 2014, http://lgbtweekly.com/2014/05/19/obama-nominates-sixth-openly-gay-diplomat-as-the-next-ambassador-to-vietnam.

25. Jett, "Why Have There Been So Few Openly Gay Ambassadors?"

26. Marc Lacey, "Gay Activist Named Envoy over Objections," *Los Angeles Times*, June 5, 1999.

27. James Hormel and Erin Martin, *Fit to Serve*, New York: Skyhorse Publishing, 2011.

28. "U.S. Relations with the Holy See," fact sheet, October 31, 2013, http://www.state.gov/r/pa/ei/bgn/3819.htm.

29. George Armstrong, "Vatican and US to Establish Full Diplomatic Relations," *The Guardian*, January 11, 1984, http://www.theguardian.com/theguardian/2013/jan/11/vatican-usa-diplomatic-relations-1984-archive.

30. Kevin Diaz, "Abortion Debate Dogs Envoy to Vatican," *Minneapolis Star Tribune*, November 8, 2009, http://www.startribune.com/politics/statelocal/69532947.html.

31. John Thavis, "Vatican Dismisses Report That It Rejected US Ambassador Picks," *Catholic News Service*, April 9, 2009, http://www.catholicnews.com/data/stories/cns/0901631.htm.

32. Joseph Berger, "William A. Wilson, Reagan's Envoy to Vatican, Dies at 95," *The New York Times*, December 6, 2009.

33. William Safire, "Loose-Cannon Crony," *The New York Times*, June 16, 1986.

34. George Shultz, *Turmoil and Triumph*, New York: Macmillan, 1993, 678–679.

35. Roberto Suro, "The White House Crisis; Italians Say White House Agreed to Secret U.S. Overtures to Libya," *The New York Times*, December 19, 1986; and Bernard Gwertzman, "3 Ex-Reagan Aides Say Envoy to Vatican Visited Libya on His Own," *The New York Times*, December 20, 1986.

36. Alfonso Chardy, "Reagan Aides and the Secret Government," *Miami Herald*, July 5, 1987.

37. Gwertzman, "3 Ex-Reagan Aides."

38. Loren Jenkins, "Envoy to Vatican Denies Wrongdoing," *Washington Post*, May 21, 1986.

39. Author interview with former State Department official, May 20, 2014.

40. State Department, Office of the Historian, "Chiefs of Mission for Ireland," http://history.state.gov/departmenthistory/people/chiefsofmission/ireland

41. John Fay, "Obama's Very Own 'Ghost Estate' with No US Ambassador to Ireland," *IrishCentral*, May 4, 2014, http://www.irishcentral.com/news/ Obamas-very-own-ghost-estate-with-no-US-Ambassador-to-Ireland.html, and Niall O'Dowd, "Mary Lang Sollinger, Top Fund Raiser, Said to Be Choice for US Ambassador," *IrishCentral*, May 19, 2014, http://www.irish-central.com/opinion/niallodowd/Mary-Lang-Sollinger-top-fundraiser-said-to-be-lead-choice-for-US-Ambassador.html.

42. John Stanton, "Key House Democrat Questions Obama's Failure to Pick an Ambassador to Ireland," *BuzzFeed*, May 22, 2014, http://www.buzz-feed.com/johnstanton/key-house-democrat-questions-obamas-failure-to-pick-an-ambas.

43. James O'Shea, "US Senate finally confirms US Ambassador to Ireland Kevin O'Malley," irishcentral.com, September 19, 2014.

44. Jason Seher, "White House Avoids Bundlers in Recent Round of Ambassador Nominations," CNN, June 5, 2014, http://politicalticker. blogs.cnn.com/2014/06/05/white-house-avoids-bundlers-in-recent-round-of-ambassador-nominations; Justin Sink, "Another Obama Bundler Named Ambassador," *The Hill*, June 6, 2014, http://thehill.com/policy/ international/208517-another-obama-bundler-named-ambassador; and Michael Gordon, "Obama Nominates Ambassadors to France and Ireland," *The New York Times*, June 6, 2014, http://www.nytimes.com/2014/06/07/ world/europe/obama-nominates-ambassadors-to-france-and-ireland-jane-hartley-kevin-omalley.html?_r=1.

45. Vera Blinken and Donald Blinken, *Vera and the Ambassador*, Albany, NY: State University of New York Press, 2009, 133–134.

46. Senate, "Congressional Record," Senate Executive Reports of Committee, March 11, 2014, http://beta.congress.gov/congressional-record/2014/3/11/ senate-section/article/S1517-2.

47. Elise Gould, Economic Policy Institute, "U.S. Lags behind Peer Countries in Mobility," October 10, 2012, http://www.epi.org/publication/usa-lags-peer-countries-mobility.

48. Miller Center, University of Virginia, "Interview with Chase Untermeyer," http://millercenter.org/president/bush/oralhistory/chase-untermeyer.

49. Kirk Spitzer, "Japan Says Kennedy Dolphin Tweet Improper," *USA Today*, January 21, 2014.

7 Why It Matters and How It Might Be Changed

1. Kate Sheppard, "Dick Cheney's Last Laugh," Mother Jones, June 10, 2010, http://www.motherjones.com/politics/2010/06/dick-cheney-bp-spill

2. Tevi Troy, "Measuring the Drapes," *National Affairs* no. 15 (Spring 2013): 86–103, http://www.tevitroy.org/13096/measuring-the-drapes.

3. Eric Schmitt, "U.S. Envoy's Cables Show Worries on Afghan Plans," *The New York Times*, January 25, 2010, and Thomas E. Ricks, "Lose a General, Win a War," *The New York Times*, June 23 2010.

4. "Are Modern U.S. Embassies Becoming Too Costly to Build?" *CBS News*, June 4, 2014, http://www.cbsnews.com/news/increased-cost-of-building-design-excellence-u-s-embassies.

5. 2012 Republican Party Platform, "American Exceptionalism," http://www.gop.com/2012-republican-platform_Exceptionalism/#Item1.

6. Seema Mehta, "Romney, Obama and God: Who Sees America as More Divine?" *Los Angeles Times*, April 13, 2012, http://articles.latimes.com/2012/apr/13/news/la-pn-obama-romney-america-exceptional-20120413.

7. Ibid.

8. Igor Volsky, "Fox News Has Proof that Obama 'Wants out of America,'" *ThinkProgress*, June 4, 2014.

9. President Obama, speech at West Point, May 28, 2014, http://www.whitehouse.gov/the-press-office/2014/05/28/remarks-president-west-point-academy-commencement-ceremony.

10. President Obama, address to the United Nations General Assembly, September 24, 2013, http://www.whitehouse.gov/the-press-office/2013/09/24/remarks-president-obama-address-united-nations-general-assembly.

11. Juliet Eilperin, "Obama Tells Other World Leaders: 'I Believe America is Exceptional,'" *Washington Post*, September 24, 2013.

12. Mehta, "Romney, Obama and God."

13. The recordings of the confirmation hearings of Tsunis and Bell can be found on the Senate Foreign Relations Committee website at http://www.foreign.senate.gov/hearings/nomination-01-16-2014.

14. US Senate, "The Senate's Role in Treaties," http://www.senate.gov/artandhistory/history/common/briefing/Treaties.htm.

15. State Department, "Treaties Pending in the Senate," as of May 7, 2014, http://www.state.gov/s/l/treaty/pending. The list of these treaties is also included in appendix C.

16. W. Stull Holt, *Treaties Defeated by the Senate*, Baltimore, MD: Johns Hopkins Press, 1933.

17. Patrick Temple-West, "U.S. Treasury Official Urges Senate Action on Tax Treaties," Reuters, December 12, 2013.

18. John McKinnon, "Rand Paul Fights Tax Treaties Citing Privacy Concerns," *Wall Street Journal*, May 7, 2014, http://blogs.wsj.com/washwire/2014/05/07/rand-paul-fights-tax-treaties-citing-privacy-concerns. This article contains a link to the letter from Paul to Reid at http://online.wsj.com/public/resources/documents/PaulLetter050714.pdf.

19. Rachael Bade, "Rand Paul in Cross Hairs of Tax Evasion War," *Politico*, March 2, 2014, and Jacques Leslie, "The True Cost of Hidden Money," *The New York Times*, June 15, 2014.

20. Matthew Mosk, "Romney Parks Millions in Cayman Islands," *ABC News*, http://abcnews.go.com/Blotter/romney-parks-millions-offshore-tax-haven/story?id=15378566.

21. Pew Charitable Trust, "Law of the Sea," http://www.pewtrusts.org/our_work_detail.aspx?id=328754.

22. Editorial Board, "Roaring on the Seas—China's Power Grab Is Alarming," *The New York Times*, June 18, 2014.

23. Mark Landler, "Law of the Sea Treaty Is Found on Capitol Hill, Again," *The New York Times*, May 23, 2012, and Orrin Hatch, "The Law of the Sea Treaty Will Sink America's Economy," *Fox News*, May 23, 2012, http://www.foxnews.com/opinion/2012/05/23/law-sea-treaty-will-sink-america-economy.

24. Jennifer Steinhauer, "Dole Appears, but G.O.P. Rejects a Disabilities Treaty," *The New York Times*, December 4, 2012, http://www.nytimes.com/2012/12/05/us/despite-doles-wish-gop-rejects-disabilities-treaty.html, and Albert R. Hunt, "On Disabilities Treaty, the Right Fights with the Right," *The New York Times*, February 23, 2014, http://www.nytimes.com/2014/02/24/us/politics/on-disabilities-treaty-the-right-fights-with-the-right.html.

25. T. Jeremy Gunn, "The Religious Right and the Opposition to U.S. Ratification of the Convention of the Rights of the Child," Emory International Law Review, 20.1 (2006): 111–128, http://www.law.emory.edu/fileadmin/journals/eilr/20/20.1/Gunn.pdf. The apocalyptic effects of the treaty can be found at http://www.parentalrights.org/index.asp?Type=B_BASIC&SEC=%7B55EE90CC-F282-48CF-A7BD-C326F6524FCC%7D.

26. Amnesty International, "Convention on the Rights of the Child," http://www.amnestyusa.org/our-work/issues/children-s-rights/convention-on-the-rights-of-the-child-0.

27. Dick Morris and Eileen McGann, *Here Come the Black Helicopters!—UN Global Governance and the Loss of Freedom*, New York: Broadside Books, 2012.

28. Steven A Holmes, "Dick Morris's Behavior, and Why It's Tolerated," *The New York Times*, September 8, 1996.

29. As of June 15, 2014, http://www.amazon.com/Here-Come-Black-Helicopters-Governance/dp/0062240595/ref=cm_cr_pr_product_top.

30. Pew Research Center for the People and the Press, "Political Polarization in the American Public," June 12, 2014, http://www.people-press.org/2014/06/12/political-polarization-in-the-american-public.

31. Yale Project on Climate Change Communication, "Politics and Global Warming—Democrats, Republicans, Independents, and the Tea Party," http://environment.yale.edu/climate-communication/files/Politics-GlobalWarming2011.pdf.

32. Emma Roller, "The House Science Committee Has Held More Hearings on Aliens than on Climate Change," *National Journal*, May 21, 2014,

http://www.nationaljournal.com/energy/the-house-science-committee-has-held-more-hearings-on-aliens-than-on-climate-change-20140521.

33. "When Election Regulators Are Mocked," *The New York Times*, April 13, 2013.

34. Tom Hamburger and Matea Gold, "Crossroads GPS Probably Broke Election Law, FEC Lawyers Concluded," *Washington Post*, January 15, 2014.

35. Joe Nocera, "Rethinking Campaign Finance," *The New York Times*, May 16, 2014.

36. Brian Stelter, "With Political Ad Profits, Swing-State TV Stations Are Hot Properties," *The New York Times*, July 7, 2013.

37. Lawrence Lessig, "Big Campaign Spending: Government by the 1%," *The Atlantic*, July 10, 2012, http://www.theatlantic.com/politics/archive/2012/07/big-campaign-spending-government-by-the-1/259599.

38. Tom Brune, "George Tsunis of Cold Spring Harbor Nominated to Be Ambassador to Norway," *Newsday*, September 10, 2013, http://www.newsday.com/news/nation/george-tsunis-of-cold-spring-harbor-nominated-to-be-ambassador-to-norway-1.6049381.

39. Ramsey Cox, "Dems Blast GOP for Blocking Ambassadorships," *The Hill*, June 17, 2014, http://thehill.com/blogs/floor-action/senate/209679-dems-blast-gop-to-blocking-ambassadorships.

40. Amy Harder, "Senior U.S. Energy-Policy Advisor Carlos Pascual Steps Down," *Wall Street Journal*, June 14, 2014, and Elaine Ayala, "Coalition of Latino Group Urging Confirmations of Castro, 13 Other Latino Officials," *MySanAntonio*, June 18, 2014.

41. "Why Hasn't the U.S. Gone Metric?" *Slate*, October 6, 1999, http://www.slate.com/articles/news_and_politics/explainer/1999/10/why_hasnt_the_us_gone_metric.html, and "How Did the Meter Get Its Length?" *NPR Morning Edition*, June 23, 2014.

Index